KT-216-294

South East Essex College
of Arts & Technology

Camarvon Road Southend-on-Sea Essex SS2 6LS
Tel: (01702) 220400 Fax: (01702) 432320 Minicom: (01702) 220642

TELEVISION FORM
AND
PUBLIC ADDRESS

TELEVISION FORM
AND
PUBLIC ADDRESS

John Corner
School of Politics
and Communication Studies,
University of Liverpool

Edward Arnold
A member of the Hodder Headline Group
LONDON   NEW YORK   MELBOURNE   AUCKLAND

First published in Great Britain 1995 by
Edward Arnold, a division of Hodder Headline PLC,
338 Euston Road, London NW1 3BH

Distributed exclusively in the USA by St Martin's Press Inc.,
175 Fifth Avenue, New York, NY 10010, USA

British Library Cataloguing in Publication Data
A catalogue record for this book is available from the British Library

ISBN 0 340 56753 8 (Pb)
ISBN 0 340 62538 4 (Hb)

1 2 3 4 5 95 96 97 98 99

Composition by Scribe Design, Gillingham, Kent, UK
Printed and bound in United Kingdom by J.W. Arrowsmith, Bristol

For Denise,
William and Ruth

ACKNOWLEDGEMENTS

Although I have touched on some of the themes and arguments of this book in previous writing, all its chapters are new work and I would like to thank those colleagues and friends who took the trouble to read first drafts and to make what were often extremely helpful comments and suggestions. Julia Hallam, Sylvia Harvey, Karen Lury, Adrian Mellor, Kay Richardson and Maggie Scammell all contributed here. Paddy Scannell read the whole manuscript and suggested structural revisions as well as points for further development; more broadly, his own work on public broadcasting and on media language was very much in my mind at several stages. Jay Blumler offered some useful pointers on political history and on recent policy debates. I would also like to thank Peter Dahlgren and Kjell Nowak of Stockholm University and the Bonnier Foundation in Stockholm for inviting me to spend a short period as Bonnier Visiting Professor in the Department of Journalism, Media and Communication. This allowed me to do some intensive work for a few weeks just when it was most helpful. Lastly, I owe a debt to Lesley Riddle, my editor at Edward Arnold, who has encouraged me greatly on this project and offered guidance at each stage of its development.

For permission to reproduce images from televised material, I would like to thank the generous cooperation of the *999* production team at BBC Bristol and the BBC Picture Library, BBC News, Elida–Gibbs Ltd, Levi Strauss (UK) Ltd and Trade Films Ltd.

INTRODUCTION

This book explores the relationship between the communicative forms of television and their social agency. The focus for this exploration is provided by those types of programme which employ the most direct forms of 'public address' and by those issues concerning the consequences of television which regularly re-emerge as topics of public debate. In that sense, the notion of 'public address' in my title carries two, related, meanings; both an idea of television as a kind of public address system and an idea of it as routinely addressing itself to matters of public concern and public value. Such a focus involves a considerable degree of selection. Even within the terms of my broad criteria, there are programmes and issues which might have been tackled here but have not been. I hope that what is discussed passes the test of being relevant and interesting. However, another selection principle at work has been my own personal teaching and research interest in certain types of programme and in certain ways in which television has become a public issue. My ambition has been to achieve some harmony between what counts as important and what is of interest to me, often a difficult feat in academic life.

In this brief introduction I want to sketch out some of the questions and problems which seem to me to lie at 'both ends' of the range of issues which I shall address. That is to say, both at the 'formal' end of the range, where what is most immediately under consideration is how television is put together as images and sounds, and at the 'social' end too, where the interpenetration of screened output with broader cultural structures and action is the (multiple) object of investigation. I will move on to outline some of the ideas which I have used in my own study, and then introduce the organisation of the chapters, indicating the kind of coherence which I hope they have, both internally and as parts of the whole.

The Analysis of Television Form

Television has received extensive analytic attention over the last decade or so as 'media studies' has become a more prominent field within teaching and research. In Britain, the shift has been more noticeable than in the United States, where a strong tradition of 'communications' inquiry had been established earlier as an outgrowth of the social sciences, but an increase in the volume and range of studies has occurred there too. One aspect of this growth has been a new and more sensitive attention to media form, drawing on the critical theories and analytic procedures of the humanities. This is not to say that earlier discussion of television had failed to register the character of the linguistic, symbolic processes at work (though some of it had) but that, in a decisive shift, television output became widely regarded as 'text' rather than 'message' (with the additional consequence that audiences became 'readers'). Trivial and contestable though both terms may be when taken on their own, the move to text-related studies was a move towards paying more attention to the complexities of communicative organisation and process out of which even the most apparently routine and unexceptional piece of television was constructed. In a way which had strong parallels with literary criticism and what was then the emerging field of cinema studies, television became 'interesting' in terms of its formal processes, its particular ways of combining images and sounds and its possibilities for using a distinctive technology to explore both the more objective and the more subjective dimensions of the social world and of social experience.

A very important factor in the development of formal analysis was an analytic language which was adequate to the business of describing how television worked communicatively. Here, literary criticism was only partly helpful (and sometimes, with its emphasis on established literary forms, a handicap). 'Film studies' had attempted to give detailed attention to the organisation of the moving image and to the distinctive characteristics of cinematic 'realism' and cinematic story telling, so influence from this quarter was bound to be quite strong. The television industry itself had, of course, its own 'language' for talking about the kinds of 'look' and sound it wanted and about the 'rules' and the 'recipes' by which programmes were to be constructed. However, this language was often strongly implicit rather than formalized or codified and, since it was designed to inform the making of television within particular institutional assumptions, it was not always up to the task of analysis and questioning.

There is no doubt that derivations from linguistics have become, since the late 1970s, the greatest shaper of academic television analysis. Of these, versions of 'semiotics' – the analysis of sign systems within the broad terms of structuralist linguistic and social theory – have been most influential. By its ability to engage both with the visual and the aural aspects of television and by the confidence with which its vocabulary of terms can be used to break down communication into its constituent parts, semiotic analysis has often seemed to get beyond literary impressionism and offer a truly 'scientific' grip on the forms and content of the mass media.[1] I say 'often seemed' because there is now widespread recognition that the semiotic project, at least in the form in which it came to dominance in 1980s' media research, is unsatisfactory. This unsatisfactoriness is partly due to the vulnerability of structuralist tenets (about the social formation of meaning; about the 'system' of language; about the nature of sign relationships; about how the meaning-making process relates to readers and viewers) in the light of more recent thinking on these matters.[2] It is also partly due to the perception that, to use the old phrase, semiotics has continually 'promised more than it has delivered', in that it has not, as a research tool, been able to produce fresh insights into television-society relations on anything like the grand scale frequently suggested. Moreover, there is a feeling that it has frequently become over-elaborate in its terminology, falling victim to excessive categorisation and schematisation whilst failing to 'catch' the subtleties of what it is addressing.

I shall say more about this issue in later chapters, but throughout this book I have generally kept my discussion free of semiotic analysis. This is not because I think the perspective is now entirely without use, since I believe that much valuable work continues to be done from it. But, as I have suggested, the semiotic vocabulary now carries with it a number of assumptions about meaning making and meaning power which I do not want to import into my explorations here. My own terms clearly carry assumptions too, but, where I have failed to be aware of these and to render them explicit, then at least they have the merit of opening up a little more the push and play of argument.

At the cost of sounding banal, my view throughout the book has been that television is a *fascinating* form of communication as well as an important one. My discussion is often grounded in rather basic descriptive accounts, upon which I am sure there could be considerable improvement (including that from a revised semiotics). But the main aim has been to engage with the primary features of sound and image, and to attempt to connect these features with the social business of watching and responding to television. Clearly, this often means looking closely at examples of 'content' as well as of 'form' and seeing the interplay between the different kinds of thing which television shows and the different ways in which it can show things.

The Analysis of Television as a Social Agency

Although 'formal' analysis has been perhaps the most notable growth area in media studies over the last decade, there has been a huge growth, too, in studies looking at how television impacts upon different areas of social life. Some of these studies have shown an interest in television form, others have not. Of the ones that have, a major linking concept between form and social agency has been that of 'ideology'. Around this term there has developed a large and often theoretically difficult literature, one which I shall discuss later in the book. But if we understand this awkward concept essentially to indicate the ways in which the social production of meanings serves to support power relationships (including covert support), then it is clear that television, as a major source of social imagery and public information, is very much implicated.[3] Questions are raised, for instance, about the selection and organisation of its imaging of the world, about the 'realism' of its accounts and about the social relationships which its various representatives on screen strike up with viewers. Questions are also raised about the way in which viewers watch and interpret television and use it as a resource within their private lives and in the making of decisions and the carrying out of actions of a more public kind. Of course, we need not suppose that the way they consciously 'use it' exhausts its consequences for them or its bearing upon what they do. In subsequent chapters, this play-off between 'uses' and 'effects' will be seen to occur in a number of ways; differently in relation to news than in relation to advertising, for example.

On the whole, 'ideological' analysis was stronger in asking the first set of questions outlined above (about form and content) than the second set (about reception and use). As the ideological model has come to be more deeply questioned over the last few years, there has been a general shift away from ideas linking television form to social structure and process *directly* and an increasing emphasis on contexts and processes of reception. Once again, I shall discuss this shift in more detail later.

Another, related, factor is what has recently been seen as the tendency for media studies to adopt a 'media-centric' view of society.[4] In such a view, the media are firmly placed as central and attributed with a high degree of political, social and cultural power. They are regarded as 'causal' across many aspects of contemporary social structure, action and belief. It is very hard when committed to the study of something *not* to let its importance get out of proportion and this has undoubtedly occurred in media research. It has been aided by wider political and public attitudes towards television, which often do tend to regard it as both central and causal.

Recognition of the very wide range of factors *other* than television which contribute to the constitution of private and public life is important. The articulation of these factors with television, in varying contexts, is also a necessary object of investigation, making arguments about 'the social consequences of television' immediately less neat and clear-cut. Although my book is much more a study of television form than a work of sociology, I hope that I have recognised the existence and importance of other factors, together with the implications which they carry for my main topic of interest. Having acknowledged the risks of media centrism (or, here, of tele-centrism), it is nevertheless worth registering just how deep the permeation of television into public and everyday life now is.[5] Moreover, the separation out of the 'non-televisual' aspects of political, social and private affairs is a good deal less easy than it might appear to be. With what certainty, for instance, is it possible to determine the origin of our ideas about family life, about other kinds of occupation than our own, about what would constitute the 'good life', never mind the origin of our immediate knowledge of national and world affairs? Whilst media-centricity can result in a disabling overestimation of media influence, it would be prudent not to push television too far into the wings of modern social analysis since it is, on any estimate, one of the defining institutions of modern society.

Television's 'Public Address'

The coherence of this book is based on bringing together certain ideas about television form with ideas about its social character. Though the combination is not by itself new, I hope to have opened up a few fresh lines of inquiry as well as given a fresh edge to some old ones. My main aim has been to steer as clear an analytic route as I can through certain major instances where the links between depictive form and social process are at issue. In doing so, a number of ideas or, perhaps better, 'figures of thought' about the nature of television recur, being developed in different ways according to the matter under scrutiny. By way of introducing the organisation of the chapters which follow, I might mention three of these – the centripetal/centrifugal interplay; the idea of contigency; the distinction between the referential and the poetic. I very much hope that the reader finds more ideas in the book than these, since they are both highly general and unoriginal, but taken together they usefully indicate something of the broader intellectual design.

The sense of television having both a 'centripetal' and a 'centrifugal' relationship to culture and society seemed to arise at several points where I was considering a particular programme form or an aspect of concern about television. The terms have a figurative aptness for describing the double movement of mediation (see Fiske, 1987). At the most general level, one part of this is the powerful capacity of television to draw towards itself and incorporate (in the process, transforming) broader aspects of the culture. This occurs differently in the situation comedy than in the commercial, differently in the chat show than in the drama documentary, but few cultures prior to the emergence of television have had such an extraordinary comprehensive 'staging' area upon which (and through which) selective instances and modes of public and private living are displayed. This is part of what Raymond Williams was getting at when, talking about television, he memorably commented on the character of 'Drama in a Dramatized Society' (Williams, 1974b). But the point I am making is not primarily about the dramatic mode itself but about the sheer capacity of television for *cultural ingestion* and the way in which so much in the culture necessarily bears some relationship to what is 'on' television, perhaps routing its relationship to other cultural factors via television, whether consciously or not. The complementary action is the 'centrifugal' moment, television seeming to *project* its images, character types, catch-phrases and latest creations to the widest edges of the culture, permeating if not dominating the conduct of other cultural affairs. This double movement, ingestion and projection, is of great importance not only for the study of television but for any adequate anthropology of modern culture, and it is not suprising that many recent commentators on the medium have, in different ways and using different terminology, attempted to address it. In doing so, getting that sense precisely of the double movement, and taking this through into both formal and socially substantive analysis, is both difficult and necessary.

'Contingency' has recently become a helpful notion in thinking about television – 'Of uncertain occurrence; conditional. . .incidental' (*Concise Oxford Dictionary*). As television studies have become more intensive and detailed, factors of contingency have shown themselves with more frequency in research findings. The shift away from grand, general theories about 'influence' in both social scientific and critical/ideological studies has meant that researchers have been more sensitive to the occurrence of variables and to those things whose cause cannot be directly explained or whose consequence cannot be predicted within the analysis. An increased interest in the precise nature of television viewing and of television use has radically extended the sphere of the 'contingent' in British, American and European research.

As a register of complexity and of non-explicability, as a guard against the foreclosure of over-confident theories proclaiming neat causal relationships, 'contingency' is valuable. Certainly, it is hard for the researcher bent on close, case-study analysis not to be regularly confronted by it. The danger is that it can be used as an excuse for not proceeding further with the search for determinants, explanations and 'patterns' and simply become part of the 'celebration of chance' which has been a tendency in recent academic studies across several disciplines. Contingency points to complexities of interrelationship which may finally evade analysis, but to install it *too* firmly as an idea risks giving up on television studies as social investigation, just as not admitting it at all risks theoretical self-delusion and analytic insensitivity.

The distinction between the 'poetic' and the 'referential' is taken from the linguist Roman Jakobson (1960), though it has since been widely influential in literary and media studies. By these terms Jakobson indicated the way in which a particular communication may both refer to things in the world and at the same time have its own character as an artefact – an object of significant form, attracting appreciation and perhaps producing pleasure. Television raises the distinction in a special way because its mode of being referential involves such a detailed reproduction of the likenesses and sounds of the real world. At times, this referentiality appears to attain to the level of 'transparency' – what you see on the screen *is* real. Equally, however, as I shall illustrate later, television's 'poetics' are of a wide-ranging and powerful kind, able to 'move' the viewer in a variety of ways. Perhaps it seems awkward to talk of a television 'poetics', given the literary origins of the term and its association with deliberately elaborate forms of communication. The term 'aesthetics' (relating more generally to the forms of art and to the nature of the beautiful and the pleasing) might be used instead. But to think of how television operates like a special kind (like several special kinds) of poetry can be highly instructive.

The interrelationships, in any piece of television, between referential and poetic/aesthetic elements, often become extremely difficult to determine, not only because of their complexity but also because they *shift*. Yet debate about, for instance, the effects of depictions of violence, about the kinds of knowledge got from news broadcasts and about the sorts of appeal which adverts exert, often turns on just what the relationship is between viewers' engagement with the 'aesthetics' and the ways in which depictions *refer* them to the real world of circumstances, actions and beliefs.

All the analysis and discussion contained in the following chapters bears on ideas about television's relationship to the 'public' and to its own 'public' status. There are two questions which could be raised against the use of this term as an organising principle for a book and, although I engage with these matters at various points throughout my discussion, it is perhaps worth tackling these two questions in a preliminary way here. First of all, it might be asked what my working definition of 'public' is, since the word can be used in a number of ways and with different kinds of political resonance (in the context of a Britain which, at the time of writing, is undergoing increased 'privatisation' under a Conservative government, the term has a strongly polemical ring to it). My response is that I am mainly concerned with those forms of television, and those debates about it, which foreground its 'civic' (and often national) dimension as an agency of knowledge and discussion, both a provider of information and a common cultural resource, the nature of which is a matter for public scrutiny and public concern. 'Public' is different from 'social' of course. In one way or another, all television must be regarded as 'social' but 'public' points to particular ways of being social and it is these ways which I am particularly interested in examining.[6]

That the modern public might, in many important respects, be *constituted* by television services seems to me to be self-evident. George Gerbner has remarked that 'publics are created and maintained through publication' (Gerbner, 1976), and in many countries television is the primary means of publication. This should not be taken to mean that 'public consciousness' is therefore simply a projection of the television system – this would indeed be media-centricity with a vengeance! But to see how network television constructs a community of address which frequently becomes 'public' in scale and in mode (what is talked about and how it is talked about) and then proceeds to do certain things within the framework thus established seems to me to be of considerable interest. This might be contrasted to television's more 'private' modes, where programme form and viewing relationship operate within a different register and according to a different system of priorities and expectations, one more organised in terms of individualised consumption. Distinguishing between the two can prove difficult, of course, and this difficulty is likely to increase given changes in form currently under way in many areas of international programme production and distribution. Moreover, although my interests are predominantly in non-fiction and this has influenced my selection of topics, there has been in Britain a strong tradition of entertainment with a marked 'public' character to it, including the now disappearing genre of variety programmes screened live from a theatre and certain kinds of situation comedy which have achieved a national prominence by catching with precision at certain patterns and shifts in national cultural life. In Britain, at least, there is also room for more attention to the public character of television drama, which has often had a considerable consequence nationally and has frequently been written and produced to achieve this.[7] In my chapters on documentarism and on ideas of 'quality' I am able at least to touch on this topic.

A second query might be to raise the question as to just how far television has now become 'private' rather than 'public'. Any answer to this is plagued by the fact that there are often quite radical national differences and yet there is a need, in the kind of discussion I am attempting, to avoid advancing arguments which are too parochial. Although shifts *are* occurring (again, attention is given to them at various points in the book), my judgement is that an inquiry into television's modes of public address can still find a great deal to concern itself with, and that the study of imminent and longer term shifts will be aided by such concern.

The movement of the book is from an overall emphasis on formal questions to an emphasis on consequences. This is reflected in the balance of each chapter. So the early chapters spend some considerable time establishing specific aspects of television form as well as connecting with wider questions. The move to advertising in Chapter 5 gives a discussion equally weighted in its address to communicative mode and social implications. The two final chapters, on influence/interpretation and on 'quality', give primacy to broader, contextual assessments.

In Chapter 1, I examine some of the principal features of television as a public medium, discuss other critical accounts of it and look in detail at an example of what is in Britain a recently developed programme format – the 'true life drama' series – noting its continuity with, and its difference from, earlier forms. This is a foundational chapter, providing a context of commentary and analysis for what is to follow and opening up certain themes which will be pursued throughout the book.

Chapter 2 considers the question of how television relates to political order. An early example of research, grounded in formal analysis, is drawn on critically to advance those arguments about television's negative and positive political consequences which have been such a recurrent feature of academic and public debate.

Chapters 3 and 4 look at two main non-fictional forms of television, news and documentary. These are examined in relation both to their formal organisation as information genres and to the socially grounded principles which guide the construction of their accounts. Again, a detailed example is drawn on to aid the discussion of 'impartiality' and 'bias' in the news, whilst in exploring television documentary I have taken selected examples from both Britain and America as well as providing a brief historical account of its formation.

In Chapter 5, I engage with some of the questions surrounding television advertising, a 'public' form of an internationally pervasive kind (though one often regarded as emphatically anti-civic in orientation). This brings up yet another instance of 'influence' anxieties at the same time as it raises quite specific questions about image, speech and mode of address. The role of fantasy in programme–viewer interaction is discussed here, an issue which I think could be more widely raised in relation to television's appeals and effects than it has been to date.

Chapter 6 develops an account of how theories of media influence relate to recent studies of viewer interpretation. Influence and interpretation research still seem frequently to be facing in opposite directions. By looking at an area which has received perhaps the most extensive treatment – depictions of violence – I try to make some connections and raise questions of a kind not so often found on the agenda of debate. Here once again, the play of fantasy and imagination becomes a matter of interest.

In Chapter 7, the discussion is at its broadest. I look at the positioning of television in relation to high culture and to other popular forms. As well as considering the general character of television aesthetics and of the medium as a mediator of the arts, the recent debate in Britain about television 'quality' is examined and set briefly in historical context. The emergence of new aesthetics (and new viewing expectations) for television, grounded in changing production conventions and technologies of distribution is explored, drawing together points made earlier.

Although each of my chapters focuses on a specific genre or area of debate, I have attempted to bring out the continuity in the forms and the issues discussed. Questions of visualisation, of the character of image/sound combination, of address to the viewer, of social use and influence occur throughout and are frequently cross-referenced.

I have tried to move as directly as possible towards and through what I consider to be the principal matters. Frequently other writers have addressed the same topic, and references to their work and to other sources are contained in the notes. I have generally been light in my citation, preferring to develop my own arguments and to acknowledge those of others without seeing it as my duty to offer either an exposition or a critique of them. There are exceptions to this, where it seemed to me that a particular stretch of discussion by someone else, in a book or article, contributed strongly to the theme or case I wanted to develop.

This book is not a student textbook in the conventional sense of a secondary exposition of the field. However, I hope it will be found accessible and useful on various kinds of course, since part of the stimulus for writing it comes from teaching, as part of it comes from the wish to address current concerns of research and debate.

Throughout, I have been aware (sometimes nervously so) of the way in which a whole range of factors bear on my account whilst being, in many cases, excluded from explicit treatment within it. Such factors include the national variations in television system and in programme conventions; the great changes in technology now affecting the medium; the very way in which matters of form are interconnected with production practices and with the manner in which television is institutionalised. I have hoped, nevertheless, to engage with forms and processes which are so often implicated in discussion of television and in television research, even when they are not the primary topic or even acknowledged.

1

TELEVISION AS PUBLIC COMMUNICATION

To talk of television as 'public communication' in the mid-1990s might seem questionable not only because of a suggested narrowness of perspective but perhaps because the very choice of terms is thought to betray a misconception about the practices and processes under study. However, in this opening chapter I want to explore the character of television as a complex message system which, although it is usually received 'in private', has a strong 'public' character unlikely to disappear in the foreseeable future, even though shifts in the organisation of production and distribution may modify it substantially. I want to follow a line of discussion with this as my focus, well aware that there are other ways of coming at the same world-wide phenomena, indeed of emphasising their communicative and public nature, and that my way necessarily involves a certain order of priorities and even exclusions.

Having tried to open up some questions about the specificity of television, I shall then look at how this specificity has been addressed in the work of two theorists and critics who have taken a broad view of the medium and whose accounts have been widely influential. Finally, by examining an example of current television in depth, I hope to close in on themes relevant to the discussion of subsequent chapters.

I think a useful route into a sense of television's distinctiveness, both aesthetic and social, can be got from reflecting on its capacities as a medium which is electronic, visual and still widely institutionalised as 'mass', despite the largely domestic settings of its reception. Of course, there is absolutely no originality simply in identifying television under these headings. But, in combination, the three categories work to differentiate television from other forms (with which it is often unhelpfully lumped as 'the media') and point towards those more subtle and elusive factors which have provided a focus for recent criticism and research. It is worth considering each of the categories in turn.

Electronic

Television's sounds and images are produced electronically, regardless of whether they are live or recorded and then transmitted later. The method of electronic image depiction (like photography in this respect) often means that the physical reality depicted in the image is involved in the *production* of the image. Light rays returning from the objects/people at which the camera is pointed provide the basis upon which the 'likeness' is technologically achieved. This aspect has been called the 'indexical' quality of the television image, linking it with photography and distinguishing it from modes of representation, like painting, where no such direct linkage between depicted and depiction occurs.[1] Whilst allowing for the scope of trickery, including the increasingly sophisticated possibilities for electronic image editing and image building (as we know from photography, 'the camera cannot lie' is an increasingly suspect adage), this provides the television image with a strongly *evidential* character (as we also know from photography, the 'truth' of pictures is still widely credited). In addition to providing this directness of depiction, the electronic technology of television gives the possibility of transmitting 'live' pictures over vast distances to be viewed by a large number of people simultaneously. 'Live' transmissions are mostly a small percentage of the scheduled output of television stations, certain cable and speciality channels being the exception. However, as a number of critics and writers have observed, the idea of 'liveness' has always been a key component of television's own professional ideology, of its representational conventions (specifically, of its non-fiction aesthetics) and of its modes of address.[2] To these ideas of 'indexicality' and of 'liveness' is closely linked the notion of 'immediacy' (widely referred to across the years by critics on both sides of the Atlantic as *the* televisual quality). The photographic technology upon which cinema depends, although it, too, can allow the creation of the illusion of immediacy, is simply not able to produce anything like a 'live' image to its audiences and so is not able to develop a public profile grounded in the possibility of instantaneous seeing. Radio, of course, was able to develop electronically produced 'live sound' transmission at a much earlier date, but 'live sound' (excepting the case of music) mostly turns around the hearing of 'live' speech, since the idea of 'live action' on radio is, communicatively, a severely limited one, usually requiring for its realisation considerable descriptive work by a presenter. It is precisely the relative *independence* enjoyed by the television audience in respect of its comprehension and interpretation of the depicted image which allows the 'immediacy' factor to function so effectively as both a principle of audience engagement with television and a continuing marker of television's uniqueness. The Gulf War of 1992 provides the most recent major reaffirmation and further development of this principle.

The simultaneity and range of the electronic message form means that this immediacy can be given, via various transmission technologies, an unprecedented geographical reach, with implications for audience size. These 'electronic communities' which are broadcast television's audiences (and which are sometimes entirely called into being through its services) may be tightly localised or highly segmented in character but they may also be national or indeed international. However, in nearly all cases, they experience social relations with the medium of a kind distinct from those experienced by press and magazine readerships and cinema audiences. This is, not surprisingly, a kind of experience developed from that of broadcast radio, but it is one with broadened scope both for the exercising of implicit sociability (of the 'taken for granted') and the generation of feelings of co-presence.[3] Television's 'social manners' are partly a product of its capacities for running underneath its speech a wide range of visualisations, including depictions of personal demeanour and gesture.

So the electronic basis of television systems serves to shape, though certainly not by itself to determine, key aspects both of their aesthetic and social character.

Visual

Television's ability to produce moving images, live or recorded, is clearly the single most important defining feature of it as a medium ('radio with pictures' in some early, rather dismissive descriptions). One of the consequences of this, as I noted above, is to give to viewers a sense of independent surveillance and evidence ('see for yourself') which is both a mode of communicative engagement and a primary point of (relative) trust between the television industry and its audiences. In respect of the former, the television 'message' brings with it, among other things, an expanded sensory/informational field (as educators all over the world have been quick to notice) as well as distinctive kinds of satisfaction and pleasure.

One way of regarding television's many forms of picturing activity is to see them as giving the medium a 'dramatic' aspect quite unlike anything the press, radio and or even cinema can produce.[4] Because of its capacity to show 'real' action, and often to show real human action within a tight and powerful grammar of shots depicting bodies, faces and events-in-process, television's overall dramatic character has developed in relation *both* to fictional portrayals and to its wide and expanding range of non-fictional representations too. This has not happened in the cinema because, for a long time now, cinema has been predominantly if not exclusively a medium for narrative fiction. The development of a dramatic, non-fictional aesthetic in television has been to a very large extent dependent on a technology of lightweight camera and sound recording equipment which can allow the 'direct' represention of realities (often with minimal directorial intervention). In noting this technological capacity, however, it is important not to understate those social purposes concerning the *use* of the medium, and the appropriateness of forms and styles, which have shaped the emergence of the televisual 'look' (both the way things look on television and the way in which we are encouraged to look at them). The terms 'realism' and 'naturalism' have often been used to describe the degree of verisimilitude (again a duality; of likeness to 'real things' and also to 'seeing things in reality') which has resulted. However, conceptual imprecision in the borrowing of these terms from literary criticism has made them notoriously tricky to use, as I shall discuss in a following chapter.[5] Such 'realistic' representations may well possess an exciting quality which, paradoxically, has strong links with dramatic fiction, both in the way it is generated textually and the way it is realised in the minds of viewers. Although it has a considerable history, redevelopment of the 'dramatic' character of television is at the heart of much recent innovation in news, current affairs and feature programming and therefore it is of importance to the whole future of television as public communication. Later in this chapter, I will take an extract from a new type of programme on British television in order to explore the nature of these visually led formats a little further.

So an analysis of television will not get very far if it fails to keep alert to television's visualisations. This may seem an unnecessary point to make, but the history of television research suggests that it is not. However, television is also very much a medium of speech as well as of images, and it is in the combination of the two, sometimes rather subtle and even slippery, that its public communicative power and its openness to what is often heated public controversy and debate lie.

Mass/Domestic

Regarding television as a 'mass medium' involves a way of classifying its production, distribution and reception. Two objections to this might be raised. First of all, the objection that it involves an unacceptable categorisation of the audience as a 'mass', a term at once both culturally condescending and sociologically dubious. Raymond Williams remarked that 'there are in fact no masses, but only ways of seeing people as masses' (Williams, 1958, p. 11), and he argued against the use of the term, regarding it as a block to any clear perception of the individuated level of public communication processes. He also thought it perpetuated a view of popular audiences and readerships as homogeneous hordes inhabiting a cultural and social realm different from and inferior to that occupied by the researcher or critic. It would be my argument that the scale of production, distribution and reception of most broadcast television, as well as the form of its economic organisation, still justifies the descriptive use of the term 'mass' and that this usage can stop well short of slipping into unflattering and distortive ideas about '*the* masses'. For some critics of television, it is precisely the asymmetrical character of its 'mass' distribution (a small number of outlets to a large number of recipients) and the power relations this can imply which are the substantive points at issue in the politics of the medium. This situation is set against more *interactive* alternatives (mostly premised on the use of fibre-optic cable), though these have not yet been industrially explored to the point where their real feasibility as technologies of dispersed production as well as consumption can properly be assessed.

A second objection to the use of the term might be that, in the mid-1990s, an increase in smaller scale, localised and more segmented ways of providing 'broadcast' television to viewers has given 'mass' an outdated ring, harking back to earlier days of limited-choice national television systems. The development of a whole range of newer, 'narrowcast' provision (and even more recently the steady increase in home camcorder use) is undoubtedly changing the nature of television as a social institution.[6] However, against this has to be set the continuing dominance of major production houses and network distribution as well as the shift towards a new level of international operations based on satellite systems.

So the 'mass' nature of broadcast television still seems to me to be widely evident as a feature of its economy and institutional structure. Like many of the other features, it also has implications for the nature of television aesthetics, for the characteristic ways in which television thinks about its different kinds of viewer, addresses them, organises its imaging of realities and fictions and both draws from and feeds into the public culture. This is particularly so when the 'mass' character of production and distribution is combined with the 'domestic' mode of reception.

As I shall discuss further below, the fact that television is typically received in the 'privacy' of the home, within a certain range of typical social relations and concurrent activities, is one that has been given much closer attention by recent research than it received in earlier studies.[7] Many of the distinctive speech forms, visual conventions and generic 'rules' of the medium are only comprehensible, let alone analysable, when considered as part of this electronic bridging between the home and the various realms which television is able to access and/or construct. Not for nothing has the idea of magical conveyance (television as bringing the world into your living room or, conversely, transporting you out 'there') been so frequently used from the 1950s onwards as a selling point, first of all in the retailing of television sets and then in the marketing of particular programmes. The imaginatively potent alignments and interfusions of this 'world/home' couplet have been judged by many researchers to be a central feature of television as a political agency, taking the analysis far beyond *explicitly* political communication and raising much broader questions about the kinds of sentiment and the knowledge of world events which it encourages. Again, the Gulf War provides a momentous and widely discussed instance of global/domestic linkage, if also an extraordinary one.

In getting an initial sense of television, then, the categories 'electronic', 'visual' and 'mass/domestic' work as useful pointers, however definitionally loose they may be. They give us some hold on the idea of television as an important (perhaps *the* most important) element of *electronic modernity*, of those features of the political, social and personal, and of those parameters of space and time, established internationally as 'modern life'. For these features precisely involve, among other things, a reconfiguration of the relations between what is seen as public and what is seen as private, a reconfiguration grounded in the immediacies of publicly circulated imagery.[8]

Seeing it Whole: 'Television' in Critical Perspective

Television has been theorised from a great many different perspectives in the humanities and social sciences, and the aspect with which I am most concerned here – its communicational character, or its 'messaging' properties – has been the subject of extensive and close scrutiny. In other chapters, I shall routinely refer to ideas about the medium which have helped understanding of it. These ideas include, for instance, Raymond Williams's concern with television 'flow' (developed in Williams, 1974a). This term indicates the underlying continuity of representational form, of mode of address and appeal, 'through' the different programmes in a schedule, and even across different channel choices. For Williams, this creates for television an intertextual identity which is finally as consequential for the viewing experience as the programmes considered as separate communicative entities. There is also John Fiske and John Hartley's (1978) suggestive notion of television as 'bardic' – operating to engage and to integrate people within its affirming, celebratory and often boundary-defining discourse in a way which has a resemblance to the traditional function of community poets and storytellers.

Such ideas, focusing variously on the visual and verbal processes of television, have been developed in the context of commentaries on specific aspects of the medium. However, what I want to look at now are two attempts at addressing the communicative nature of television not only comprehensively but in a concentrated way. The first is by Stuart Hall and the second is by John Ellis. Both of these writers spend some time working to develop a basic account of what is going on at the level of the 'taken for granted' in television, before moving on to more theoretically ambitious commentary. Both accounts have, in some respects, been overtaken by cultural and industrial shifts affecting television since the time of writing. But both have a clarity and suggestiveness which I believe continues to give them a working life.

Hall's 'Television as a Medium and its Relation to Culture' (Hall, 1975) was written as Part 4 of a report to UNESCO on culture and British television, submitted in 1971. Its aim is to explore 'the nature of the TV discourse, the "elementary forms" and the types of transformation which the TV medium effects on its materials'. Hall wishes to pay attention to the technological factors which shape the aesthetic forms and the social relations of television (a focus which became the central area of inquiry for Williams' celebrated pioneer study *Television: Technology and Cultural Form* three years later). What he very much wants to avoid, however, is a kind of technological determinism which fails to recognise the way in which the technology itself is shaped by existing social relations ('the corpus of traditional practices and uses') and by communications' policy decisions (again, this is an argument which Williams was later to mount at greater length).

Using a suggestive phrase, Hall talks of the 'technics' of the medium ('those qualities of the television medium which, though not belonging to the technical sphere *as such*, seem to be intrinsic to its nature, its use and to its characteristic mode of communication' p. 89). The 'technics' of television include its hybridity, its routine use of the content of another medium as its own raw material. In respect of arts coverage, Hall notes how this leads to a situation in which television 'uses up – indeed, exhausts – the contents of other media and of everyday life; but it does not, characteristically, decisively *impose* its forms upon that material' (p. 91). His observations here predate important generic shifts in television which undoubtedly have had the effect of increasing its aesthetic imposition upon 'raw material' and of having that imposition critically recognised (in Britain, a whole range of visually 'busy' and stylistically flamboyant arts programmes would be examples here, as well as an upsurge of innovation around 'youth' programming from the mid-1980s onwards).

These changes in generic forms allowed for, Hall's comments serve to bring out what he calls the 'channel' function of television with a nice clarity. This function – the relaying of something via television with little by way of *substantial* changes to its nature as an event or performance (as, for instance, in certain musical or sporting occasions) – is initially contrasted with television's 'medium' function, displayed in programming where television's own aesthetic practice is, as it were, 'on the surface', to be recognised, appreciated and criticised. Hall finally wants to complicate any neat division here, however, and to see the articulation between 'event', recording technology, production convention and tranmission method as allowing more permutations than might at first appear to be the case. For instance, he notes that in some plays in the BBC's *Wednesday Play* series of the 1960s, certain parts were recorded beforehand and played back so as to mix with live performance elements at the time of transmission. Moreover, what might appear to be pure examples of relay television (certain kinds of live outside broadcast for example) will involve a degree of transformative activity simply as a result of the *process* of 'televisation', even if it is one of the conventions of 'good television' not to call attention to (indeed, to suppress) this level of professional, symbolic work.

Further exploring 'technics', Hall looks at how sports programmes like the pioneering BBC *Grandstand* showed the distinctive possibilities of television as hybridised 'assembly' to unique effect. Moving across different recorded and live material and situating it within a live studio presentation, such programmes achieve an over-arching coherence and unity which gives them the character, says Hall, of a 'television original'. His concluding argument – a good deal more familiar today than in the early 1970s – is that television, despite its appeal to 'transparency', is inevitably a 'throughly manipulated medium' and that this manipulation-in-production needs to be admitted and openly worked with if television is to achieve optimum use and value as an agency of democratic politics and cultural development. As I noted, given the changes in programming form and viewing relations which have occurred since, the nature of the play-off between 'medium' and 'channel' functions in television is no longer quite as Hall saw it. Nevertheless, the new conventions of 'good television' which have emerged – across fiction, entertainment and journalism – are still more often than not based on a veiled social practice which passes itself off as either technologically necessary or as simply professional 'common sense'.

The broad intellectual scheme of Hall's investigation involves a search for the different, interrelating levels at which television's aesthetic and social identity is determined. This quest had its roots in a kind of structuralist sociology of the media which has subsequently failed to develop or to consolidate itself. It was always at risk from a tendency towards over-refined, under-evidenced typologies. Yet Hall's paper, despite showing some signs of this affliction, is a model of suggestive, critical lucidity on just those points which a study of television can so easily and debilitatingly take for granted.

The second general account of television which I want to examine is the one given by John Ellis in his book *Visible Fictions* (Ellis, 1982). Ellis uses the relatively developed and critically self-conscious aesthetics of cinema as a way of locating television by comparison and contrast. The degree of reliance on cinema practice and cinema criticism is not altogether satisfactory since it has the effect, whatever the intention, of putting television rather swiftly into the position of poor relation and of perhaps reducing the interest in pursuing inquiry into those things which are *not* thrown up by the comparison. The fact that half of Ellis's book is actually about cinema anyway, and that he does tend to find it more interesting, adds further to this sense of a kind of cultural slighting. Television is doubly diminished – being found symbolically less rich and therefore offering less scope for interpretative pleasure than cinema, and also being regarded as a good deal more politically suspect because of its routine involvement in public information and the culture of the 'everyday'. This judgement goes along with a rather careless approach to television's non-fictional output in which a focus upon narrative form tends to push other aspects of television discourse, including its speech forms, into either a simplistic rendering or into the margins.

Such reservations admitted, the real strength of Ellis's analysis, as in Hall's, lies in its direct address to the question of how television *works* communicatively. With a nice concern for fundamentals, Ellis starts with the question of the size of the television screen, the quality of television sound and the contexts (social and spatial) within which television is routinely watched. At this early point, the comparison with cinema is instructive, although already inclined to be too hasty and categoric in its distinctions. By pointing to the field of visual and aural signification which television has (or then had) at its disposal, Ellis makes some useful headway into a discussion both of television form and the characteristic psychosocial character of television viewing. So, for instance, he notes that in much television the combination of image and sound tends to be one in which sound predominates, or, at any rate, one in which the overall construction is 'sound-led'. The use of emphatic, marked title music to annnounce the start of a programme is one example of this; grounded here in the need to re-engage viewers or perhaps bring them back into the room.

Elsewhere, Ellis sees sound as being partly compensatory for the reduced visual intensities of television when compared with cinema. Much television drama is script based in a way which cinema, with its more powerful repertoire of the image, need not be. And non-fiction television is able to use sound (and vision) in a uniquely effective way in the form of 'direct address', whereby viewers find themselves spoken to directly from the screen and perhaps have simulated eye contact with the speaker. In a further comparison of communicative features and viewing contexts, Ellis notes how television's routine, frequent uses of the close-up shot (for instance, in series drama as well as in news commentary) carry a different symbolic inflection from the use of close-up in cinema, where a relatively sparing employment combined with the large screen size allows the device to mark intensity and heightened significance.

Although television sound has improved considerably since the time Ellis was writing, his comments here still have analytic value. So do his observations about the relationship between the size of figures on the screen and in life – close-ups on television become approximately life size, in cinema they become considerably larger, with consequences for relations of viewing. Through his adoption of a more polemical and assertive style than Hall, Ellis runs a higher risk of 'essentialism' – collapsing diverse aspects of the medium together to the point where the unified and general 'television' which results lifts away entirely from the specific documented practices under scrutiny. This is made worse by an asymmetry in the comparative approach, since film can be generalised about more easily than television – it is 'generally' narrative fiction seen in a cinema as commercial entertainment (though essentialism is still a risk here too). The problem becomes apparent in the making of a comparative point which has subsequently received extensive (and mostly approving) citation. Ellis sugggests that whereas cinema attracts the viewers' 'gaze', the typical mode of attention to television is the 'glance'. Whilst it may well be the case that the general viewing relations of cinema audiences to a screened film have a good degree of constancy (given by the darkened auditorium, large screen, high sound levels and a disposition consequent on having decided to pay for out-of-home entertainment), the viewing relations of television are nothing like as predictable. They can vary from the most casual and interrupted levels of attention through to intensive, absorbed viewing without any concurrent activity going on and perhaps with room lights off. The effect of classifying television as a 'glance-based' medium, with whatever qualification, is radically to understate its capacities for viewer engagement and to ignore the range of viewing behaviours adopted by audiences.

The disabling consequences of ignoring the activity of viewers emerge in another context, when Ellis speculates on the way in which the setting up of implicit relationships in the language of news programmes works to regulate social identity. In this account, the 'bonding' relationship offered by broadcasters to viewers ('you' at home looking at us and listening and 'we' here in the studio or on location looking at you and talking), successfully mobilises the viewer's self-identity *against* the various third parties, 'theys', negatively identified in the news stories. Ellis's qualities as an alert critic of the medium here fall victim to a familiar problem, that of extrapolating too freely from an analysis of a text's form to predictions about its social effects. I shall say more about this in the next chapter.

Despite my reservations, Ellis's account remains a fine piece of commentary. By starting with the primary experience of television as 'sound and vision', he establishes his arguments at the level where culture and technology interact in the physical fact of the 'box in the corner'. His view is that television needs describing clearly as well as explaining, and that you cannot do the latter without the former – a view which will find echoes throughout this book. Ellis also offers a clear, general account of the production process in television, noting how it results in different conventions of visual story-telling from those of cinema. His observation that it produces a tendency towards a different and longer basic unit – the *segment*, giving strong spatial and temporal continuity, sometimes over several minutes, rather than the more mobile, brief and dynamic 'single shot' grammar of film – has been picked up widely in subsequent writing on television and I shall have occasion to draw on it later too.

The New Dynamics of Public Communication: A Case Study

Hall and Ellis are by no means the most recent examples of television analysis, but I have selected them for discussion because of the clarity with which certain 'basics' are addressed. Television has continued to change, but these basics remain in need of attention. I now want to bring together some of the points I have made by reference to a contemporary (1993) example taken from BBC network television. The descent to a particular instance is a risky one for a discussion which has previously kept to quite a high level of generality. Examples are nearly always 'illuminating' but the relationship between preceding discussion and specific instance can be awkward. Certainly, the example cannot reasonably be expected to 'prove' what has gone before – the misfit in levels is too radical for that.

My own example is intended to be illustrative, and although it certainly cannot be thought to illustrate 'television' generally, it does seem to me to bring out a good number of themes in my earlier discussion. It also has the merit of being from a new programme format, at the moment one much more developed in the U.S.A. than in Britain and Europe. This is a reworked approach to 'real-life' programming, gaining its novelty from a more rapidly paced mix of entertaining drama and documentary/current affairs exposition than was possible within earlier recipes for making non–fictional television. In Britain, the mix currently includes a strong 'public service' element, giving it a particular relevance to the main themes of this book.

999 started as a series on BBC1 in 1992, with extensive publicity in press and magazines as well as trailers on BBC channels. In each 50 minute episode of the programme – now into its second series as a confirmed ratings' success – the journalist and newsreader Michael Buerk introduces a small number of items or stories (usually three or four) concerning the work of the emergency services. The 1993 series includes recorded 'as-it-happens' reports, with presenters ('video reporters') accompanying various emergency teams on their duties. Undoubtedly, however, the principal feature has been the mini-dramas, in which past emergency stories are re-enacted within a novel mix of reportage, interview and dramatisation involving the actual people concerned. In Britain, an understanding of the development of this kind of programme would need to have reference to long–running, successful and often controversial programmes like *Crimewatch UK* (BBC, 1984–).[9] This is a crime-reconstruction series derived from American models, playing off a 'dramatic entertainment' function (sometimes rather dubiously) against its strongly foregrounded role of helping the public/audience to assist the police with their investigations. Such an analysis would also need to consider the distinctively British achievement of dramas like the hospital series *Casualty* (BBC, 1986–) or the fire brigade series *London's Burning* (LWT, 1988–) which combine popular fiction with a strongly documentary interest in the realities of public insti-tutional work (see the more general discussion of documentarism in Chapter 4).

I want to look at some aspects of a mini-drama which appeared in the opening episode of the second series of *999* (broadcast on 13 April 1993).[10] First of all, since the material is not generally available, I need to offer a description of the content and its organisation. I will do this in three parts: a narrative description of the incident portrayed, a commentary on the modes of depiction employed and a basic outline of this depiction as it works as a visual and sound sequence.

A narrative description

The story concerns a 5-year-old child involved in an accident with a container lorry whilst in a car at night with her father. The accident occurs as lorry and car pass one another on a country road. It leads to a container toppling from the lorry on to the car, crushing it and trapping those inside. A motorist arrives on the scene a few minutes later and helps to remove one of the two adults. The fire brigade and ambulance services arrive, under the direction of the Chief Fire Officer of the County. The precarious positioning of the container (the car is pinned underneath it) makes rescue of the two people remaining inside, including the young girl, difficult and dangerous. It involves the use of hydraulic jacks and air bags. At some personal risk, the Chief Fire Officer comforts the girl by holding her hand through the trapped car's window (the hand is all of her that can be seen) and talking to her. The girl's father is finally removed using cutting equipment. A nursing sister takes over from the Chief Fire Officer for a while in order that he can direct operations. The situation becomes even more dangerous as the rescue team attempt to jack up the container, risking the possibility of it slipping and toppling further down on to the car. Fireman work to free the girl using mechan-ical cutters on the seating but the noise distresses her and so the slower method of hand cutting has to be used. After two hours, the girl is finally removed and proves to be without serious injury. She is taken away to hospital by ambulance. Following the incident, two of those involved in the rescue received awards for bravery.

I have thought fit to render the basic storyline (itself a selective organi-sation of the available data) in this detail because it will make more comprehensible those points about its further transformation into television upon which I want to comment. The sequence of events is the baseline from which the television account is constructed as a documentary project. The movement and emotional shape of that account as narrative drama and as an exploration of subjective experience is also grounded in this sequence.

Modes of depiction

The basic mode of depiction is *dramatic reconstruction*, in which the incident is enacted, with appropriate sounds and dialogue, and through a visualisation which, using a mix of positions, angles and shot types, depicts the scene, the people and the action. This is supported at a number of points by the use of brief *actuality sequences*, material taken from the fire brigade's own video of the rescue and captioned accordingly. Inserted into this vizualised narrative are several sequences of *personal testimony*, in which the real people centrally involved comment 'now' on their actions and feelings 'then' in tight facial close-up (three-quarter profile) accompanied by *captions* identifying them. These comments are usually integrated into the main depictive flow by being placed as voice-over across the narrative for a few moments (often with the speaker's 'acted self' in shot) before the shift to the speaker's face.

The depiction as a whole is anchored in the *voice-over commentary* of the presenter. After he has introduced the story from a position outside it but related to it – in front of a fire engine – his commentary, regularly overlaying the action, provides a necessary element of exposition. Finally, there is *music*. This is used in the earlier sequences, most obviously in the build-up to the accident itself. Its rhythm and tones suggest both intensity and threat.

On this analysis, there are six basic communicational components at work in the representation of the story on the screen. Some indication of how they are combined can be got from a selective look at the structure of the item.

An outline of structure

The item's overall running time is approximately 14 minutes. Below I indicate the more salient features of structure and organisation. I have broken the item up into sequences and sub-sequences in the development of the story. Speech which marks a significant move in the story's mood or direction I have indicated but only by *selected and extracted* phrases. Since my concern with the event is not a substantive one, it seemed appropriate in this analysis to remove from the transcript the real names of the people involved.

(a) **Introduction**. Michael Buerk (medium shot presentation to camera in front of parked fire engines).

> *Narration*: 'The main job of the Fire Service is, as it has always been, to fight fires. But in recent years it has increasingly become a much more general rescue service, particularly using its practical skills and speed of response at road accidents to free the victims. The Staffordshire Fire Service had to deal with a particularly distressing accident involving a young child. Nobody knows exactly how it happened, but a lorry load weighing several tons crushed the car, trapping two men, who were freed relatively quickly, and a 5-year-

old girl, who wasn't. The fireman, the ambulance crews and the medical teams had to work in constant danger for hours, not knowing if they would get the little girl out alive.'

(b) **Build-up to accident.** Rapid sequence of intercut shots (20 in total) and sounds showing (i) lorry driver (face unseen) climbing into lorry and lorry driving off and (ii) car drawing up outside house, little girl coming out of house, greeting father and waving goodbye to mother as car drives off with her as passenger. The (i) strand of the sequence is presented in tint throughout and with acute angle shots of parts of the driver's body, cab and trailer. The (ii) strand is shot in natural colours and conventional camera angles.

(c) **Accident.**
(i) Car and lorry individually seen on road (it is now dark and raining). Headlights. Music on soundtrack. 'Reconstruction' logo on bottom left of screen.
> *Narration*: '...it was only a short distance to her father's home in Uttoxeter. But on the way there was an accident no one has been able to explain'.

(ii) Car passes lorry on road. Brake sounds. Lorry container load tumbles off trailer on to car. Headlights, noise, stillness. Car headlights still on, spinning wheels. Smoke. General shot of scene, enveloped in bluish haze, held for six seconds.

(d) **Arrival of help.**
(i) Car arrives. Man runs to wreckage. Removes one person from car. Dialogue. Screams.
Over this and intercut with it:
> *Narration*: '[a motorist] came round the corner a moment later and found the road blocked by twisted metal...'
> *Testimony* (tight close up of speaker – motorist): 'When I first saw the car under there I thought it was crumpled really badly. I wouldn't have thought anyone would be alive at all...' (further description of feelings and actions).
> *Narration*: 'Despite the evident danger, [he] stayed...'

(ii) Fire brigade arrives. Begins rescue attempt (see Fig. 1.1). Officer issues orders.
> *Narration*: 'The container weighed seven tons. It was unstable and could have fallen at any time. It was a major incident. The Chief Fire Officer for Stafford [......] felt he had to be there.'
> *Testimony*: (tight close up of speaker – Chief Fire Officer): 'I was struck, overawed by the size of the container, the effect it had had on the car...it was almost unbelievable that anyone could survive in it.'

(e) **The rescue effort**
(i) Chief Fire Officer crawls underneath container and takes little girl's hand. Fire brigade video of general scene (with caption identification) intercut with dramatisation.

Fig. 1.1. 999: Emergency Services 'on scene'

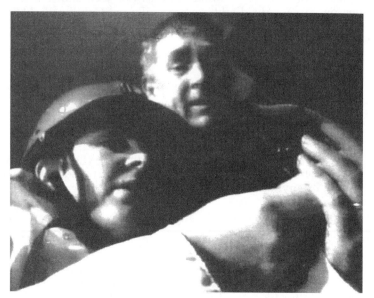

Fig. 1.2. 999: Under the Container: Hands and Faces

Testimony: (Chief Fire Officer about feelings on making contact with girl): '. . .It was the first time in 29 years where I've actually attended an incident where I could only see a casualty's hand. And a 5-year-old's hand is a very small hand.'

Narration: 'Before they could help, they had to get the father out of the driver's seat. . .'

Fig. 1.3. 999: The Voice of Testimony

(ii) Driver removed (cries of pain). Nursing Sister takes over from Chief Fire Officer as girl's companion under container (see Fig. 1.2).

Narration: Despite the obvious danger, Sister [. . . .] was taken under the lorry's container. It still could have fallen at any time.'

Testimony: (sister about feelings on taking over; see Fig. 1.3): . . .'All we'd got was this tiny little hand actually coming out and we couldn't see anything else. . .'

(iii) Container lifted by jacks. Cutting out of girl from wreck, first by mechanical saws, then manually. Snatches of Cinderella story heard being told by Sister amidst noise and rescuers' voices.

Narration: 'Then came the most critical time, as the fire brigade tried to lift the load, never knowing if the movement would bring seven tons of metal crashing down'.

(iv) Sister removed from underneath container due to risk. Chief Fire Officer returns to hold girl's hand.

Narration: 'To get to [the girl], they had to cut away the driver's seat. . .

Testimony: (Chief Fire Officer): 'Moving the seat was more difficult than we had hoped. . .the noise was horrendous.'

(v) Final cutting out and removal of girl (intercut with fire brigade video) after further scenes of her being talked to by Chief Fire Officer.

Testimonies: (on final stages of the rescue). (Sister) '. . .we only had a little hand'; (Chief Fire Officer) '. . .We felt the seat moving . . . she almost hurled herself towards us and she came out into my arms.'

Narration: 'It had taken more than two hours to cut [her] free.'

(vi) Placing of girl in ambulance; departure of ambulance. Flashing lights. Sirens.

> *Testimonies*: (Chief Fire Officer –) 'total elation. . .satisfaction on faces of men' (Sister –): '. . .to see a smiling face when she came out was lovely.'

(f) **Postscript.**

> *Introductory narration*: '[the girl] is now 9 years old but still has vivid memories of the night.'
>
> *Testimony 1*: (girl with large teddy bear). 'When I got in the car it was all muddy on one side, so I moved over on to the other side and a fireman said that if I hadn't moved right over to the other side I would have been dead. . .[describes incident and feelings both in shot and also as voice-over across scenes of rescue intercut with fire brigade video]. . .and the ambulance, the fireman and the policeman all had a collection and they gave me a teddy and I named it after [. . .] the one who rescued me.'
>
> *Testimony 2*: (Chief Fire Officer [with visible emotion]): 'All emergency services. . .would agree that there is a particular poignancy in the death of a child. . . unfortunately we see it all too frequently. . .and it was nice on this particular occasion to beat the reaper.'
>
> *Narration*: (spoken over crash scene in freeze-frame and with super-imposed close-ups of the two awardees): 'Six people were nominated for bravery that night. [The motorist and the sister] received the Queen's Award for Gallantry.'

This example of contemporary television certainly employs a 'hybrid' format, to refer back again to Hall's 'technics' of the medium. It is a format by which, at the levels of aims, forms and viewing experiences, the programme attempts to integrate what have until recently been conventionally distinct communicative devices and communicative intentions in British television.

At the core of the mix is the duality produced by grafting together a public information project (a report) and a popular entertainment project (a story). But an examination of the item reveals an 'assembly', an organisation, which is a good deal more complex, and more interesting for what it reveals about the distinctive symbolic capacities of broadcast television, than this couplet of story and report on its own suggests. I want to explore those aspects of the 'assembly' which seem to me to connect with the ideas put forward earlier in this chapter. I will do so under four headings.

1. Story Form and Narrative Immediacy

The story of the accident is 'well shaped' in that the main events are organised into a comprehensible, coherent and also dramatically satisfying unity. At either end, the story is strongly framed by non-narrative segments – Buerk's to-camera introduction and his concluding comments about the awards for bravery. These form part of the programme's report strand discussed below. The story itself is organised as a sequence of dramatised episodes linked by commentary. This allows for time compression and the achievement of optimum dramatic shape within the available running time. Sequence (b) in the outline above, the first dramatised episode, uses a terse editing style to establish the mininum circumstantial context and details necessary for the comprehension of what is to follow both as a report on an accident and a human drama. Moreover, it does so by employing a strategy of visualisation which provides the account with some of the excitement of television and cinematic fiction. This is achieved by a combination of three factors:

(i) the presentation within a form of dramatised immediacy of events (the moving off of the lorry, the picking up of the little girl from her house) which the viewer *already knows* will end in an accident. This produces an interpretative framework of foreknowledge in which the depictions necessarily take on a deeper, more emotively marked, meaning. Each event becomes 'overprinted' with its calamitous destiny.
(ii) Reinforcement of this effect of fatefulness by rapid intercutting between shots of the lorry's departure and journey and shots of the girl and the car. In order to make clear the spatial separation but co-temporality of these scenes, the lorry shots are in tint.
(iii) Further connotational suggestions of menace in the lorry shots by use of angular camerawork (the lorry is never seen whole) and by loud engine and brake noises on the soundtrack. [In fact it is very likely that aspects of this sequence were derived from scenes in an early Spielberg film, *Duel* (1971), which is precisely about the threat posed to a motorist by a heavy goods vehicle. Such intertextual borrowing (not, a *reference*) is a common practice in television of all kinds, adding, in ways not usually made explicit, to the symbolic density and the social meaning of images.] The presence of a music track works to confirm the exciting/sinister imagery and to guide its interpretation by the viewer.

2. Reference and Report

Direct address by the presenter (in shot for the introductory sequence) serves to secure the 'drama' within the context of 'true life'. It is this mode, interfused with but also regulating the dramatic mode, in which the 'public' purposes of the programme are projected, addressing viewers as members of a public in the quite direct sense that they pay for, are routinely dependent upon, and might find it of interest (and maybe of duty) to find out more about, the services featured in the story. In the terms of the presenter's opening address, what follows is to be read as illustrating a general public informational point about the work of emergency services, specifically in this case the work of the fire brigade outside their primary role. As a documentary project, the reconstruction therefore has its justification not so much in terms of the immediate circumstances dramatised but in terms of the general skills, commitment and fortitude for which it provides evidence. The public informational strand of the item is sustained by regular reference to the working practices used and the risks incurred on the particular occasion reconstructed. This strand is also contributed to by

the sequences of captioned testimony from those involved, regularly refer-
encing the dramatisation back to the real event and both confirming its
status as a real event at the same time as amplifying aspects of the
emergency service's procedures. This does not by any means exhaust the
communicative function of the testimony sequences however. They also
play a key part in organising the emotional structure of the item, routing
viewers' perceptions of the external, objective event through the subjective
realm of experience in a manner I discuss below.

3. Times: Then and Now

Earlier I noted how the dramatic immediacies of the reconstruction are
integrated with the reportorial immediacies of direct address presentation.
One is a representation of 'then' – the time of the accident – whereas the
other is marked as 'now' talking about 'then', as are the sections of testimony. Although the reconstruction itself works imaginatively in the tense
of a dramatic present (i.e. one *witnesses* things happening within a frame
of co-present action), the narration and the sections of testimony regularly
mark this dramatic present as 'then' by the use of past tense speech. It is
important for the drama that its affective power is not too reduced by the
pastness of what it depicts. But it is important for the item as a report and
as a collection of *memories* that the ongoing drama is regularly referred back
to the original event which it reconstructs. The tacking between our experience of witnessing events 'happening' and being told about 'what
happened' generates a distinctively televisual mode of representation, able
both to generate narrative excitement and directly to install knowledge and
evaluation upon the actions narrativised.

4. Emotion and Knowledge

I have shown how data about the accident are organised by the item within
two different communicative modes: the dramatisation, with its conventional liberty to reconstruct with some licence as to 'non-significant' partic-
ulars, and the report, anchored in the referentiality of the accounts of
leading participants. I have also shown how these two modes have discrete
– if here interwoven – kinds of visualisation and speech.

   The human, emotional pull of the item, as distinct from its exciting qualities, is primarily generated through what I have referred to as the testimony sequences; 'testimony' because there is no sense in which these
scenes work within the conventional format of the interview. There is little
indication, if any, of the speech being in response to *questions*, and the mode
of visual depiction departs from the range of conventional interview shots.
It employs an extreme close-up in which the face fills the screen from top
to bottom with either the left or right side of the frame providing the space
required to balance the close-up and thereby, I think, providing what is
said with an extra resonance. These sequences, then, appear more as self-
authored accounts rather than as responses to reportorial investigation. The
mode of visual depiction confirms the experiential and profound character
of what is being said. It is the imaging of an intensive subjectivity (the

feeling of being in the event) which complements the more objectified versions against which it is placed. Certain phrases in the speakers' accounts document not only their own feelings but also specific features of the event which served to focus these feelings – the 'little hand' which was all rescuers saw of the girl until the end; the manner of final exit from the car, the girl 'coming out' into the arms of her rescuers in a way which, in context, has the force of a 'rebirth' into the world; the crystallising significance of the 'smiling face'. All these features receive a complementary visualisation in the narrative.

In such a context as this, it may seem wide of the mark to talk of the item as also being an exciting one. Yet as I showed in my discussion of its opening dramatisations, the generation of excitement is one of its communicative functions – and arguably an important one in successfully engaging audiences of the size which the programme has enjoyed. As well as being provided with knowledge about emergency services and about how it feels to be involved in such work, we are also cued into a drama presented in such a way as to excite. This is not only apparent in the early stages, where the editing style and use of music clearly seek that response, but is continued by the regular introduction into the narration of references to danger and risk, building up towards a crisis point when the team attempt to jack up the container ('then came the most critical time. . .'). In directly informational terms, the frequency of these references is *excessive*, but their role in the overall symbolic economy of the item is to sustain *intensity*; they are part of the programme's aesthetics of *attraction*. Although, in context, to talk of this as 'entertainment' appears to contradict the item's own emphatic seriousness, let alone the gravity of the event itself, it is to an expanded notion of the 'entertaining' that we need to turn if we are to explain the communicative complexity of such forms. Of course, a treatment of this kind could not be sustained so easily, if at all, had the outcome not finally been a 'happy' one. The selective nature of television in this regard may become an important issue if, as seems likely, the newer kinds of 'reality television' become widely established. It is relevant to note here that, no doubt for personal, professional or legal reasons, reference to the lorry driver and representation of him are completely missing from the dramatisation after the opening sequences. The shift from real to reconstruction involves transformations and adjustments occasioned by more than the availability of information and dramatic suitability.

Seeing and Knowing: A Concluding Note

I have given an extended critical account of this *999* story because I believe that there is still a great deal more to be discovered about the microprocesses of television communication. Much of what I say in later chapters will be more general than this, but it is only by analysing television at a primary level than we can ground generalities about the medium and confidently address the larger questions about its public character. The multiple immediacies of the *999* story, its movement between tenses, between objective and subjective viewpoints, between instruction and dramatic entertainment and between particular incident and general truth, are illuminating well beyond the relatively new and still uncertain genre from which it comes.

This chapter has been about the character of television communicative form and I want to conclude it by examining in more detail a general feature of television which is probably at the root of more debate about the medium than any other single factor. This is the capacity which television has to let people 'see for themselves'. Some commentators would reject this formulation out of hand, regarding it as being either forgetful of, or ignorant of, the processes of production by which television comes to the screen. As we have just seen, these processes typically involve selection of what to show, directorial decisions as to *how* to shoot it and subsequent editing decisions about how to organise it which, from one kind of critical perspective, utterly compromise the 'seeing' function. Far from having any of the 'transparency' which those who work within it are so fond of celebrating, the argument goes, television is a 'construct'. In this sense, it has an *opaque* character, being an artefact whose true referentiality is to the practices of its own production rather than to anything that might be perceived 'through' it. This position has considerable analytic force and is useful as a polemical counter to affirmations of 'transparency' which fail to engage with the medium as a symbolic practice having social and institutional motivations. I noted how, in the early 1970s, Stuart Hall developed a particularly cogent and influential critique of this kind.

Yet the power of television continues to inhere in the sorts of experience of 'second-hand seeing' which it provides for viewers; vicarious perceptions which, whilst they are *being* experienced as television immediacies, are routinely not regarded as 'authored'. One has to be careful here. There is a great deal more work needed on the precise ways in which audiences view television and this is likely to show a psychology of viewing more complex than many researchers have assumed. Within this pyschology, the interaction between direct engagement with screened material and an awareness of television as *style* and as selective, motivated communication will be critical. Such an interaction regulates the relationship between television form and content and the viewer's knowledge and pleasure. That said, 'second-hand seeing' which seems like 'first-hand' is, and is likely to remain, central to the television experience. It involves a particular force of knowing which is denied to the communicative repertoire of print and radio.

The seeing–knowing connection in television is grounded in the imaginative power of viewed particularity. Here, once again, television's electronic and visual immediacy is the basis of communicative practice. Even the most 'graphic' piece of print journalism cannot help but retain a distance between the events described and the reader's experience of them. If a present-tense account is used, the gap cannot be closed, only imaginatively bridged. Similarly, in radio, the reporter's own physical presence as a voice intercedes between what has happened or is happening and the listener. The immediacies of live radio cannot escape from this. And the transformation of events into words – written or spoken – involves a *dissection* of particularity, a breaking down of the particular into phrases and sentences, a transformation of it into linear units of meaning from which it might be assembled as a 'whole' again in the mind of the reader or listener. In earlier comments, I suggested that this should not be thought of exclusively as a communicative *limitation*; it is also the source of distinctive capacities. But television's difference in this respect is vital to its character. For television does not constitute particularity through *description*, but seeks to *image* it for our direct response. This partly explains television's enormous power to shock viewers who *already* knew about the conditions and actions depicted, but knew non-visually and non-particularly. The 'memorable' nature of images as sensory information is an important factor here, but so is the way in which confronting the viewer with imaged particularity can engage not just their perceptions but their personal and social identity as 'witnesses'. (Voyeurism and its related modes of *dis*engagment are a possibility here too, however, and I shall return to this point in a later chapter.)

A final, complicating factor is the way in which the apprehension of particularity on television occurs within a general mode of attention attuned not to the incidental or to the random but to the *significant*, to that which holds and proffers some kind of general meaning. The capacity of television to combine shown particular with implied general is the source both of its discursive power and its controversiality.

So television 'seeing' can have a resonance which elicits from its viewers certain kinds of *investment of self* which other media cannot so easily generate, if at all. This capacity is an important aspect of its 'public' character – to call viewers into empathy and understanding; to create a 'virtual community' of the commonly concerned,[11] of vicarious witness; to cut through accomodating abstraction with the force and suprise of 'things themselves'. Yet it is also a capacity which can begin to erode a public requirement for *explanation* in addition to *instances*, for ideas as well as images. Both sides of this depictive division will be explored further.

2

MEDIUM AND POLITICAL ORDER

A major question about television, underlying much recent analysis when not explicitly raised within it, concerns the ways in which it has transformed the character of political activity and in the process changed the nature of political institutions too. A dominant tradition in media research within the United States and western Europe has regarded this transformation *pathologically* – seeing it as undercutting the always vulnerable base of democratic politics, corrupting the activities of government by further empowering official and commercial elites in the management of public information and the projection of 'opinion' and thereby working effectively to disenfranchise the electorate. The extent to which television services might serve as 'agencies of distraction', keeping populations not only under-informed and (perhaps) misinformed but also happily unconcerned about this, has also been widely discussed.

This negative perspective on the new order of public communication may be contrasted with the views of those who have seen the primary effect of television to be positive. Here, the interpretation is one which registers a greater democratisation of public life, consequent upon higher levels of public accountability and a greatly increased popular understanding of, and attention to, government policies and activities. Although too crude to carry discussion very far on its own, the basic question 'television and democracy; constraint or tool?' is an important one to keep in mind in the different and changing contexts of international and national politics. Whatever way it is treated in media research, it is one which will certainly not go away as a focus for political and public debate. Indeed, recent events in eastern Europe look likely to raise it in fresh and urgent ways.

Many anxieties and arguments about the negative political consequences of television are, of course, primarily concerned with other things than television's character as a form of public communication. They may be to do with the funding and organisation of the television industry, with the degree of regulation exerted by state or commercial forces, or with the producing institutions and the systems of distribution. Even ones which focus on media 'messages' may well put the stress on *content*. To paraphrase a famous formulation of the pioneer U.S. researcher, Harold Lasswell (Lasswell, 1971), this is to ask 'who gets to say *what* to whom'. Such inquiries may be linked directly to ideas about influence ('and with what *effect*?' is the finishing phrase of Lasswell's classic research question). My main aim in this book, however, is to raise questions about the *how* of television, but in doing this I would want to claim that 'how' questions are implicated, often deeply, in *all* arguments about the media. The fact that these kinds of question are most frequently taken for granted in the political (and sociological) literature as well as in wider debate makes it that much more necessary to demonstrate their centrality and reconnect them to those aspects of television which have received the most attention.

A pioneering study by the Chicago-based sociologists Kurt and Gladys Lang, 'The Unique Perspective of Television and its Effect' (Lang and Lang, 1953) is brilliantly suggestive about a number of questions which are still on the agenda of research into television and politics. Despite its focus on one specific kind of television coverage – the public event relayed live – a critical examination of the Langs' research, and an evaluation of how its findings and conclusions look some forty years later, will act as a good basis for my own discussion and arguments. The Langs' case study comes from a period in the social history of the medium before it was taken for granted in the way it is today. By giving us a sense both of the social character of the medium and of an approach to its study in the very earliest phase of popular television, its provides a useful context for ideas about current research.

The 'Unique Perspective' Analysed

The Langs' study concerns the television coverage given to a major civic event in Chicago which formed one part of a national political event in the United States. In 1951, in the middle of the Korean War, President Truman recalled General Douglas MacArthur from his military command in the Far East, following the opening up of an unbridgeable gap between presidential foreign policy at the time and MacArthur's own forcefully stated, hawkish attitudes towards the 'communist threat' and the military strategy that should be adopted to face it and defeat it. The recall prompted declarations of popular support for MacArthur, who was signalled as a 'hero', sometimes by explicit contrast with the President himself. On his return, MacArthur went on an invited tour to major cities, ostensibly as part of a 'civic' obligation (following the practice established by returning commanders at the end of World War II) and to dedicate memorials to those who had died in the Korean War. However, his visits had strong political connotations too. Working from their Chicago base, it was the much-anticipated visit of MacArthur to that city, its 'MacArthur Day', which the Langs made the focus of their research.

The study was initially designed as a 'participant-observer' exploration of crowd behaviour at a major public event (including the possibility of 'mass hysteria'), with close attention to the television coverage providing comparative materials. In the analysis however, the organisation and character of this coverage, and the nature of its *contrast* with accounts both of crowd behaviour and crowd experiences, provided the research with its principal area of findings. These led to pessimistic conclusions about the political consequences of the new medium's 'unique perspective'. Such consequences were chiefly identified in what the authors' term 'the landslide effect' (p. 11) – a cumulative process by which television's version of events came to be installed uncritically as the official version of 'what happened'. In researching the processes which led to this situation, the authors highlight the way in which the preview commentary offered by the media (including television) in the days before the event, had served to create a framework of expectations as to the scale, popular intensity and political significance of what was *about* to happen. This framework was then used to organise the coverage of the event as it *did* happen, despite a considerable mismatch between anticipation and reality in respect of crowd turn-out and crowd behaviour. Media-fuelled expectations, and then television's interest in fulfilling these in its depictions, were combining with television's techniques of mediation to produce a new and suspect kind of reality for TV viewers, so the Langs feared. Moreover, they were doing so in ways which were likely to exert a considerable sway on public sentiment and public opinion (in this case, in favour of the General and the political values which he represented). Finally, it was 'T.V. reality', validated in the experience of viewers, reproduced in further media comment and appropriated within party political strategies, which was likely to become the 'reality' of official record, the reality of public datum.

Given the importance of such an argument to the business of this book, I want to examine in more detail some of the analytic points upon which it is built. As I have noted, these points not only stand as perceptive early indicators of topics which subsequent television research would often address (though not always with the same clarity), they also provide categories for organising my own discussion.

Anticipation and Inference

The degree of 'distortion' which a reportorial framework based on anticipation introduced into the television account was not regarded by the researchers as the result of a conspiracy to distort. It was essentially seen as a function of television's *institutional* character – in particular, its need to encourage a large viewing audience with the promise of an event of magnitude and intensity. Following the success of this strategy, there was either a *reluctance* on the part of producers and reporters to recognise that the reality did not live up to this promise or (rather different) a *failure* to recognise that it wasn't doing so. In the former case, the cause becomes corporate self-interestedness (essentially a form of show-business bluffing); in the latter it is far more deeply embedded in the whole institutional psychology of reporting and the 'inferential structures', the systems of inference making, which it employs (see Halloran *et al.*, 1970). Nearly all reporting has to be organised by reference to anticipation of one sort or another, especially so large-scale live broadcasts which involve the pre-planning of how an event will be 'covered' in space and time. Lang and Lang's critical attention is drawn to this anticipatory factor and to the resultant 'blocking' of the real events' nature. Though it is seen not to be conspiratorial, the precise matter of causes and intentions is left open in a way which finally softens the force of their comments on television's *political* consequences. For uncertainty about cause makes it difficult to assess the degree of *inevitability* involved in the 'effect' analysed, and therefore difficult to speculate on what action might be taken to *prevent* it or *reduce* it. As later chapters will suggest, this is by no means an unfamiliar problem in media research.

Narrative Form and Selective Mobility

The form which the anticipatory framework took was that of a *story* cast within the terms of classically 'strong' news values; a story about a great day when a great man visited a great city and something very special happened. This specialness required scale and intensity – a very large crowd and an enthusiastic one. It was, among other things, the very *coherence* given to the details of the event by the story format – connecting them as interrelated parts of a strongly projected narrative – which gave the anticipated version of events such controlling power, as a way of seeing (as a *schema*), over perception and description of the actuality. Before the event had occurred, its script had already been written. In their discussion of the day's reporting itself, Lang and Lang bring out just how far this 'story power' was locally operative within the visual and verbal discourses of the reportage in a way which was at once both seductive and deceptive. It was seductive insofar as the television cameras were able to bring the viewer an almost continuous spectacle of 'MacArthur in Chicago' in contrast to the live spectators' brief, and perhaps only partial, experience of personal witness as a member of the crowd at some point and time in the day's events. Television viewers were thus accessed to a mobile and multi-viewpointed perspective on the day. A 'deceptive' one, too, insofar as this very mobility transformed aspects of the event quite apart from *any intention* to do so.

For instance, as the authors point out, the fact that the primary focal point for the visual coverage was MacArthur himself meant that he was nearly always shot against a backdrop of a cheering crowd, creating the impression of a vast and *continuously cheering* assembly, whereas in fact only that portion of the crowd which MacArthur was passing at any one time cheered, the vast majority of the crowd being always either silently awaiting his arrival or dispersing following his passing. Such observations on the way in which television visualisations worked a theatrical transformation upon events are complemented by the remarks the authors make on the commentary. By its exclamatory utterances (the 'most enthusiastic crowd ever in our city...You can feel the tenseness in the air', p. 6), this attempted to cue viewers into a particular interpretation, in line with the pictures. The reporters were projecting their own, professionally 'over-heated', version of public feeling through to those private rooms in which the television viewers watched, hoping thus to hold them more firmly within television's framing of the event. This projection of intensity, the authors argue, had the effect of fusing together the *civic* dimension of the event and its potential character as a demonstration (by MacArthur, civic officials and the crowd) of *political partisanship*. If these were kept as separate dimensions of 'what happened', it was possible for the viewer to accept one but to question the other. With both fused in the celebratory imagery and commentary, however, critical discrimination of this kind became a good deal more difficult for the viewer to perform.

Personalisation

The degree to which the television pictures concentrated on the General, particularly on close-up shots of his face, led the authors to comment on the heightened sense of *personal* relationship which viewers were encouraged to feel with him. This is in contrast to the difficulties of experiencing such a relationship as a member of a crowd only catching a distant, and perhaps brief, glimpse of the person around whom the day's events were organised. A visual opportunity for 'para-social' relationship was offered [to use the phrase from Horton and Wohl's classic, contemporary study of 'intimacy at a distance' (Horton and Wohl, 1956)]. It was supported once again by exclamatory statements from the commentary (e.g. 'look at that chin! Look at those eyes!', p. 8) and by the routine framing of the image of MacArthur by the image of a large, enthusiastic crowd. The implications of such a personalised view of the General for any *political* assessment of him by the television viewer are not directly addressed by the authors, but it is clear that they regard personalisation as a mode likely to close down the space available for a viewer to make a critical judgement. In this view, television's projection of the 'personal' attempts to elicit from viewers a highly subjectivised and empathetic viewing position, making it more difficult for them to get back to the objective distance necessary for assessment. More subtly, the authors point out how there is a powerful paradox at work in this combination of the large-scale and the personal. 'In this way' they note, 'the *public* event was interpreted in a very *personal* nexus' (my italics). Once again, the continuing relevance of the study is underlined, for few topics are currently receiving more research attention than the ways in which television variously constructs a 'personal nexus' for construing 'public' matters. Furthermore, the authors see this combination involving not only a paradox, but a transference of attributes:

> The cheering crowd, the 'seething mass of humanity', was fictionally endowed by the commentators with the same capacity for a direct and

personal relationship to MacArthur as the one which television momentarily established for the TV viewer through its close-up shots.

(Lang and Lang, 1953, p. 8)

Here the point of view, and the potential 'point of feeling', of both television viewer and crowd member are fraudulently aligned through the mediation of the report. The viewer not only gets scale *and* intimacy, but also *unity* with the crowd.

Primary and Secondary Participation: The Terms of Discrepancy

Lang and Lang's study is predominantly concerned with the organisation and the consequences of the 'secondary participation' in the event provided by the television coverage. But the evaluation of this secondary level is achieved chiefly by contrast with the primary participation of those who attended as members of the crowd. The terms of such a contrast raise important questions both of theory and of method but I shall leave such questions to a later chapter, where they can be related to the whole set of issues affecting study of audiences. Here I want simply to note how the authors go about this strand of the study and to what end. Data on the experience of primary participation was collected by a small group of participant-observers distributed at key points throughout the day's ceremonial schedule. These observers were instructed both to record their own direct experience of the day and also to report the experiences of the crowd insofar as these could be elicited through observation, overhearing, conversation and interview. Their accounts converged around four main points. First, that the expectations of the crowd were high. Many of them had anticipated a 'wild spectacle' with the potential for disorder. Second, that the primary source of these expectations was, indeed, the media commentary on MacArthur's visits to other cities and pre-publicity for the Chicago visit. Third, that attendance at the event and the degree of disruption to the city's daily routine (e.g. to traffic) were on a much smaller scale than the television coverage had predicted and then reported. Finally, that a great many people in the crowd were disappointed with their experience. One ruefully commented, in a phrasing which has acquired a global familiarity over the intervening forty years, 'This turned out to be a lousy spot. I should have gone home. I bet my wife saw it much better over television' (p. 9). According to the researchers, television offered not only what might be judged as a 'much better' view of the event but a very different view of it. Indeed, to follow the implication of their research findings, it might be better to say that it offered a different event.

Displacement and Conflation

The principal thesis of the Langs' study, the extent to which the 'media version' of events drew extensively on anticipation and displaced the realities of the day, requires that the researchers differentiate between televised version and real event and also between primary and secondary perceptual involvement. But the study does not pose the relationships involved here simply in terms of a 'secondary' phenomenon misrepresenting a 'primary' one. In yet another shrewd conceptualisation which prefigures later research and argument, the Langs point to the degree to which aspects of the primary event were themselves organised spatially with the requirements of the secondary (television) event in mind. This organisation required the intrusion into 'primary space' of television vehicles and equipment on such a scale that crowd members sometimes found them an obstacle to a clear visual and aural sense of what was going on. This was particularly true of the static moments of ceremony which the day involved. Here, the primary event itself was not simply being 'deceptively depicted' by television but was, in some of its central features, being transformed by television *prior to its depiction*. A more trivial illustration of this is provided in the authors' observation that for many in the crowd, the chance of appearing on television and the possibilities of 'acting up' to the camera if it arose, formed an important part of the attraction of live attendance in the first place. This interpenetration of the 'live' and the 'mediated' within the psychology of the spectators is also attested to by comments which showed that some of those attending had done so having been thrilled by television coverage of previous public events and in the (for many, mistaken) belief that the 'live' experience would *add* to this thrill the excitement of 'being there'.

The Resonance of the MacArthur Day Study

Although it is about the phenomenon of a major public event, I think we can see how this early study of television connects with many issues which have subsequently figured in the debate about politics and television. In its general emphasis on the transformative character of the medium and on its 'relay' functions (points discussed in relation to Hall's work in Chapter 1), it also has a much broader relevance. It identifies the work of inference making in reporting, together with the anticipatory, self-fulfilling factors involved. It notes the transformative, personalised character of the coverage itself and both the difference between 'primary' and 'secondary' events and yet also the interplay and, at times, fusion and confusion between them. In this way, the study reaches its pessimistic conclusions about television and contemporary political life. What strength do these conclusions have, both as propositions of their time and in the context of television today? And what kind of evidence can be adduced for a counter-case, one to the effect that television, far from restricting or debilitating democratic politics or weakening the data-base of public knowledge, has extended the sphere of democratic action and positively transformed the conventions by which political life is conducted?

Any full assessment of the Langs' study needs to pay some attention to the research design and the methodology employed. Questions of research method are not a main concern of this book, but clearly the 'findings' upon which many arguments about the political character of the media are based cannot be easily removed from the manner of finding out. In the case of the Chicago study, one would like to know more about what a range of 'ordinary' television viewers made of the coverage – how they made sense of it and how it figured in their political understanding of the event. While the Langs are methodologically cautious about the way in which their data on the 'real event' were collected, both in its objective and subjective aspects (what happened and how it was experienced) the account of the television coverage remains largely at the level of content-analytic description. This imbalance is reflected in the fact that although the active, critical character of crowd membership is documented and discussed, the passive, vulnerable character of television viewership follows directly as a presumed consequence of the content analysis (a presumption endlessly repeated in contemporary media analysis). Lack of knowledge concerning audience response does not invalidate the Langs' thesis, but insofar as the 'landslide effect' depends on what happens during viewing, more is needed on viewers' own experiences and understandings.

The focus on a 'live event' transmission also clearly puts limitations on the general significance of the findings. 'Live' broadcasting certainly remains a feature of television, including importantly the coverage of political events.[1] But the vast majority of public affairs' output, both then and now, does *not* conform to the conventions of 'live' broadcasting. Most of it occurs within the various forms of prerecorded television journalism. It places the 'spectacle' of recorded political action within the context of journalistic and expositional discourses. However much they have viewer engagement in mind, these have to work within terms other than those of the continuous single narrative.

Nevertheless, the Langs' project provides us with an early and cogent instance of television's political character under close scrutiny.

Processes of Political Order

To summarise, we can identify four related processes which lead the Langs to their conclusions about the effect of television upon political life. They are of different orders of generality but they all appear extensively in the literature of research on political communication since the 1950s. The most general are the processes of *anticipation and inference*, within terms of which the event gets reported. Secondly, there is the idea of the tele-mediation process being one of *selective transformation* across space and time. Thirdly, there is the idea of *narrative unification*, whereby the visual and aural terms of this transformation work to produce continuity, strong causality and a high level of 'story values' in relation to phenomena which may well have a multiple and contradictory character, as well as elements radically discrete in space and time. Finally, there is the depictive grammar of *personalisation* at work within these unifying conventions (a grammar able to project intense renderings of political persona). However, we should add to these four a process which the Langs document but do not directly engage with, since to some extent it undercuts aspects of their research design. This is the phenomenon of *reverse transformation* by which 'TV reality' comes, not so much to *displace*, but to install itself *within*, the terms and conventions for organising everday, empirical reality. Insofar as this occurs, it then becomes more

difficult to argue about a process in which one kind of reality (empiri-
cally grounded and pre-televisual) is displaced by another (selectively
televisual) one. Clean differentiation cannot be easily achieved and the
very basis of comparative analysis is threatened. Critical research is
pushed into a more speculative mode in which the critical datum is essentially a hypothetical political reality – what it (the election, the conference,
the argument, the war) *would* have been like if television had not been
there as a constitutive factor in its making.

Over the forty years since the Langs' study was published, the majority
of media research has tended to support the general pessimism of their
findings, whilst broadening out its range of inquiries well beyond the
specific kinds of circumstance they investigated. Anxiety about the health
of a democracy operating within the terms of televised 'political reality' has
run alongside anxiety about the health of public morality within the terms
of televised sex and violence. Indeed, the two kinds of anxiety have been
a primary dynamic (and a rationale of funding) for the enterprise of media
research.

I want to sketch out some of the main features of this 'tradition of
anxiety' and to examine the alternative, more optimistic, accounts which
are also to be found. At many points, echoes from the 1953 research will
be heard.

Television and Democracy: Two Inventories

In the Langs' study, the negative political consequences of television's
'unique perspective' are not seen as part of any direct intention, either by
broadcasters or by government agencies, to manage or distort the political
process. The 'landslide effect' is primarily an unwitting structural consequence of the way in which journalistic coverage is organised in relation
to television's (commercial/industrial) need to attract and keep an audience
and the emerging conventions of depiction and commentary for doing this.
Implicit in such a position there is thus the possibility that changed conventions of use might reduce the threat which the medium poses. The Langs
do not explore this idea, and perhaps one reason for their lack of attention
to it is not only that their immediate interest is in the way things *are*, but
that their understandings of the industrial dynamics of the medium, even
at this early stage in its development, do not suggest much likelihood of
significant change.

Later critics, however, have often judged what they have seen as the
anti-democratic character of television communication to be, in good part,
the result of strategic *intentions*. 'Television' as an institutional and formal
practice has, in this view, to be placed firmly in relation to two spheres of
self-consciously exercised power. First of all, the sphere of control
exercised by national governments in their attempts to manage public
opinion and sustain legitimacy. Secondly, the sphere of control exercised
by corporate, private interests, in their quest to maximise and naturalise
their own power and profitability and to marginalise threats to their
continued operation.

Clearly, national variations in the funding and administration of broadcasting radically effect the extent to which state power can be regarded as directly implicated in the organisation of tele-politics. In the same way, differences in the extent to which a society's economic order, including its national communication system, is organised according to market principles and mechanisms, will affect the probability, nature and scale of the strategic use effectively made of television by corporate interests. That said, debate within the British, European and American spheres of media analysis has been intensively concerned with perceived 'distortions' originating both from governmental and corporate activity, sometimes in combination.

Perhaps the most widely cited general perspective on current media/politics relations (and the one most often applied in recent work on television) is that articulated in a number of works over several years by the German critical theorist, Jurgan Habermas.[2] Habermas, working from intellectual roots in a European tradition of 'mass society' critique, has described the general political consequence of electronic media as one of effective 're-feudalisation'. This striking phrase suggests a post-enlightenment decline in which the very historical agencies of democratic emancipation – the public media (in the shape of a thriving, pluralised and critical public press) – have become in their electronic form the agencies of a discreet but pervasive system of centralised 'knowledge control'. The pathological character of this turn in polity is sharply registered against Habermas' central and most influential notion – that of the 'public sphere'.

It is on the organisation, scale and communicative character of a society's public sphere that Habermas assesses its democratic health. The public sphere is the space within a society, independent both of state power and of private, corporate influence, within which information can freely flow and debate on matters of public, civic concern can openly proceed. The concept is therefore central to Habermas' idea of the rights and duties of citizenship. However, in developing his account of the rational–critical citizen working within the undistorted communicative space of the public sphere, Habermas does not simply posit an ideal towards which radical change can direct itself, but also an historical precedent, albeit an 'imperfect' one. This precedent is the small but active sphere of civil debate among literary–political intellectuals in eighteenth century England. Organised around the reading of newspapers and the discussion of public affairs in the London coffee shops, such a sphere of discursive critical practice seems to Habermas to provide a suggestive model by which to guide critique. This, despite its being limited to a small elite in a period of extensive public illiteracy well before the enfranchising of the majority of the population.

The essayist and editor Joseph Addison, founder of the journal, *The Spectator* and one of the key figures in the history of English political journalism, is representative of many of the values which Habermas is evoking here. A sharper sense of these values can be got from this quotation from the edition of *The Spectator* for the 8 August 1712. Addison is talking of the newspapers which he reads in the coffee houses and on the kind of critical cross-reading made necessary by their differences of account:

They all receive the same advices from abroad and very often in the same words; but their way of cooking it is so different, that there is no citizen, who has an eye to the public good, that can leave the coffee-house with peace of mind, before he has given every one of them a reading.
(*The Spectator*, p. 452, 8 August 1712, cited in Smith, 1978, p. 185).

The key terms here, 'citizen' and 'public good', clearly connect directly with Habermas' ideas about how the media *should* be used, though it is important to note that the reading practice described by Addison is made necessary precisely by the inadequacy of each newspaper, on its own, in supplying the accuracy and general soundness of account upon which civic judgements might be securely made.

Implicit in Habermas' historical precedent for a critical public sphere is the notion of print as the ideal medium for political communication. In the many commentaries which have been influenced by Habermas' thinking, this has tended to produce harder or softer versions of a kind of 'abolitionist fantasy', in which engagement with television as an inescapably central feature of modern mediated democracy is replaced by a pervasive wistfulness about what politics would be like *without any television at all*. Together with the exceptionally limited socio-political conditions attending the eighteenth century model (in terms of the basic literacy requirements for entry to the 'public sphere', the amount of free time required to participate in debate and the lack of any popular democratic *rights* through which judiciousness might have an outcome), this gives to Habermas' notions a dubious character both as terms of critique and as terms of reform. A number of recent commentaries have identified and discussed this.[3]

Can a more direct engagement with the present modes of television-within-politics and politics-within-television develop the argument beyond the kind of generalised pessimism which Habermas' work appears to bring to a head?

We can get closer to an answer here by attempting to identify those factors which would count as most salient in any debate about whether television had hindered or aided the development of democratic politics. To simplify further, in the interests of cutting a way through to the core of disagreement, what are the three strongest points to be made on either side of the case? Taking the negative side first, I would select as follows:

1. Television has become, among other things, a sphere of intensive and sophisticated *knowledge management*. This has been carried out for the most part by official agencies and the more powerful private institutions. It works to regulate access and (increasingly) to accord privileged terms to those able to fund well-resourced publicity and media relations activities. The high costs involved in producing 'professional standard' broadcast television, and consequently the kinds of industrial infrastructure needed successfully to support it, make it difficult to break this pattern of inequality by an increase in the number of publishing points (this contrasts with print and, to some extent, with radio too). As the primary system of public communication in most modern societies, television (particularly at network or national channel level) thus becomes prone to imbalances in its sourcing, its accessing of individuals and in the

socio-political character of the definitions and conventions within which its policy is framed and its output produced.[4]

2. Television has turned the sphere of politics into one which is dominated by *strategic personalisation* (and here a connection can be made with the terms of the Langs' analysis). Increasingly, political issues and choices are projected within a theatricalised framework which emphasises the personality and personal qualities of key political actors, thus displacing a direct address to questions of policy and practice. Complex issues become condensed into simple and dramatic moments of trust or crisis in 'leadership'. Instead of being addressed as active citizens by television's depictions of the political realm, therefore, viewers are positioned as consumers in relation to the various 'decision packages' which they might be prepared to 'buy' by their electoral choices or simply to acquiese in by their non-opposition. This trend extends into a 'vicious circle' whereby the media relations' staff of political parties work to 'personalise' their party's appeal not only through concentration on its leading figures but by the setting up of suitable 'activity contexts' within which these leaders might be reported in a positive light by the media. The 'photo opportunity', an exercise involving not so much the allowing of media access to a politically significant event as the construction of a 'politically significant event' specificially for the media, is a key feature of strategically personalised politics.[5] Again, the Langs' study is relevant as an early indicator.

3. Television represents the world through visual and aural conventions which work to invoke *realist credibility* rather than critical engagement. The veracities of recorded vision and speech, edited for overall flow or continuity, generate a pervasive 'illusionism' in television's depiction of the political by which general and sometimes highly tendentious propositions, either explicit or implied, appear to be grounded in reported particularities. The technically advanced means of self-confirmation combine with the normative pervasiveness of television – its extensive colonisation of space 'inside' everyday life – to make it an extremely difficult agency from which to get a critical distance. It thus becomes well suited to *ideological communication*, forms of representation in which there is a mystification of power relationships and an affective, implicit rather than rational, explicit organisation both of description and evaluation.[6]

All three of these positions are open to dispute in respect of the evidence that might be found in support of them as well as in the cogency of their argumentation. However, versions of all three occur frequently in the academic literature as well as in more generally circulated commentaries.

So what of the opposing case, then, that television, far from being a block to democratic development, indeed an instrument of political regress, has actually served to extend popular involvement in political activity? As I noted earlier, outside of broadcasting circles this position is far less often expressed than the first one, though perhaps it is heard more in Britain than anywhere else. Nevertheless, it is not difficult to find three points upon which a case might be based.

1. Television, in many respects following the communicative direction set by public radio, has massively increased the proportion of the population who have regular political information which they are able to place within a broad framework of national, and international, political understanding. Since television requires little literacy, its visual and oral representations have been relatively little affected by those educational barriers to communication which have acted as a block to democratic initiatives, particularly in developing societies. However fragmented and superficial public political understanding may be, and however much television might be seen to be susceptible to information controls (see above), no previous period has seen citizenries larger, better informed or more regularly updated.

2. Television journalism, despite the countervailing force of public relations, news management and censorship, has in most modern societies been able to exert considerable pressures of accountability upon politicians and government officials. These have been increasingly required to explain and justify their policies and actions through a communicative convention which has now arguably become the central form of public political knowledge – the interview. This form was first developed in radio but when taken up by television it developed, internationally, an increased discursive range and popular appeal. While many public figures are adept at negotiating the hazards of the television interview (a key aspect of professional competence for a modern politician), it remains the case, as much to maintain commercial competitiveness in the news market as for the public good, that most modern television systems place national and international politics under more wide-ranging scrutiny than has occurred at any other time in history. In performing this function television frequently both feeds and uses as a resource other media, including the press, as well as international television networks.

3. The very speed of global electronic communications makes it harder for a national government to 'manage' its media output with any sustained tightness. Quite apart from the tendency for different governmental agencies (and different media) to be involved in 'leaks and smears' campaigns which threaten unified control no matter how over-arching the strategic design, there is the increasing 'uncertainty' factor introduced into patterns of coverage as a result of international satellite links and international news agencies. A good example of this is provided by the Gulf War of 1992 when, despite tight supervision of the news emanating from the Allied war zones, the presence of television crews in other countries, including Iraq itself, frequently required that the official position on information for disclosure and on the agendas and conduct of press conferences be revised at short notice.[7]

It is clear that these two sets of points are not just selecting different things upon which to focus attention but are in considerable interpretative and evaluative conflict with one another. For instance, whether one chooses finally to see the dynamics of journalistic inquiry as outweighing the trend towards skilled political PR and 'stagings' of national political performance, is a judgement which has to be made in the recognition that *both* are incontrovertibly present in the current television/politics relationship of many countries. Moreover, some of those broad consequences of television which have now become a sociological commonplace – for instance, the increasing blurring of the borderlines between 'public' and 'private' life – remain very much open to argument in respect of their specifically *political implications*. Here, it could be argued that British broadcasting's rhetorical construction of a 'national community' out of the listening and viewing activities and the projected common interests of its disparate audiences, was a positive opening up of the possibilities for collective identity and debate against the privilege, prejudice and exclusions of previous versions of the nation and its people. However, it has also been argued that such a development's primary purpose was that of a strategic reworking of popular sentiment which masked the continuing reproduction of economic and cultural inequality.

This example illustrates a point I made earlier, that arguments about television's consequences often and necessarily have a strongly national character – a factor not always recognised amidst the current academic fascination with television as a global phenomenon. As a further point of qualification, I would want to note, too, how both the points 'pro' and 'con' can vary in the extent to which television is seen either as having the *potential* to produce certain political consequences or as having already *produced* them. In the latter case, the argument moves from being about threat to being about damage. This then raises (or begs) questions about *evidence*.

Arguing the Case

To bring these kind of issues out more fully, I want to look at two recent analyses of television's effect upon national political order. One looks at the recent consequence of the medium for U.S. politics, the other looks more broadly at British broadcasting.

In his recent study, *Television and the Crisis of Democracy* (Kellner, 1990), Douglas Kellner advances an argument very much in line with the points 1 and 2 'against' above and very much counter to point 2 'for'. In a central chapter, concerned with the making of a conservative hegemony during the 1980s, Kellner comments that:

> My argument here will be that television did not provide the information necessary to produce an informed electorate and that the media actively helped forge a conservative hegemony rather than impartially mediating among competing social forces.
>
> (Kellner, 1990, p. 134)

Kellner's thesis is that this hegemony was partly, if not largely, achieved by skilful packaging of the President, Ronald Reagan. Through the strategic deployment of PR tactics – including political advertising, the 'photo-opportunity' and the pre-designed 'sound bite' for network news as well as the routines and ruses designed to protect Reagan from close critical questioning – a myth of presidential popularity became, according to Kellner, 'self-fulfilling'. Here, yet again, we can see a direct connection with the Langs' discussion of how the 'unique perspective' of television transformed popular perception of General MacArthur.

Kellner's theory about television's influence is partly a theory about the formal processes of television representation but it is primarily a theory about its function as an agency of (dis)information within a given framework of institutional practices under specific economic conditions. Against a critical reading of the relativism he finds in postmodernist commentary, Kellner develops his own account of the 'politics of the image' as part of a thesis about the essential contradictions between capitalism and democracy. He offers his study as a confirmation of Habermas' pessimism about the fate of the 'public sphere' under the conditions of the modern capitalist state. Indeed, from his analysis of contemporary U.S. politics, he sees the situation to be even worse than that outlined by Habermas in his most influential writings.

In contrast to this view is the position taken up in Paddy Scannell's widely cited article 'Public Service Broadcasting and Modern Public Life' (Scannell, 1989). Within the historical account of developments offered here, Scannell explicitly opposes theories of broadcasting as ideological representation and argues instead for a much more positive view of broadcasting's political impact on public life:

> In this article I wish to revalue broadcasting's social role against its devaluation in arguments that regard it primarily as a form of social control, or of cultural standardization or of ideological (mis)representation. To the contrary, I wish to argue for broadcasting in its present form as a public good that has unobtrusively contributed to the democratization of everyday life, in public and private contexts, from its beginning through to today.
>
> (Scannell, 1989, p. 136)

Scannell notes how, in broadcasting, there emerged 'a new public culture of the studio', within which a variety of programme formats 'created new forums for the debate of matters of general concern and new forms of shareable pleasure and play' (p. 153). It is important to note that Scannell's argument is not only specifically national–historical (with a focus on the BBC) but that, within this argument, the development of television services within Britain is largely seen as a continuation of the public project of radio rather than a shift to a different set of aims and audience relationships. At the end of his essay, Scannell also refers to Habermas. Like Kellner, he regards the theory of the 'public sphere' to be a useful one for the analysis of television but it is Habermas' principle of 'communicative rationality' which particularly interests him. He judges Habermas' discussion of this to be suggestive, but to be based on too narrowly academic and unrealistic a model of reasoning in the public domain – society as seminar, so to speak. Scannell wishes to put more emphasis on the idea of *cooperativeness*, on the sociable contexts and communicative skills upon which *reasonable* exchange (including political exchange) can be based. He uses the notion of 'communicative entitlements' to indicate what citizens may claim within a democratic framework of 'communicative rights' – 'a minimal notion of guaranteed communicative rights is a precondition of forms of democratic life in public and private' (p. 160). Far from developing these ideas as part of a critique of the existing broadcasting structure, he goes on to comment:

> I believe that broadcasting has enhanced the reasonable character and conduct of twentieth-century life by augmenting claims to communicative entitlements. It does this, as I have tried to show, through asserting a right of access to public life through extending its universe of discourse and entitling previously excluded voices to be heard: through questioning those in power, on behalf of viewers and listeners, and trying to get them to answer. . . . All this has, I think, contributed to new, interactive relationships between public and private life which have helped to normalize the former and to socialize the latter.
>
> (Scannell, 1989, p. 161)

Once more a connection back to the Langs can be made. For what Scannell is claiming is that the terms of *secondary* public participation' have (in British broadcasting) developed a democratic character which would have been inimical, where not simply impossible, within the earlier, pre-electronic sphere of 'primary' public activity (the premediated, the direct, the face to face). This is part of his more general argument about the extended sphere of socialised life, and of sociable life, which broadcasting has introduced, partly by interfusing private and public levels to the point where the terms 'primary' and 'secondary' would have to be used with very great care if used at all.

The introduction of these more detailed points on both sides of the argument, shows, I think, that any polemical claim about 're-feudalisation' is far too simplistic to be useful. Such a claim is likely to be based in a highly questionable act of generalisation – the taking of specific items or genres of output as 'typical television', denying variations here as well as the often extensive differences between national systems. Worse still, the *influence* of the medium is simply assumed. It does not figure as an *argument* at all (for instance, in the form of explicit propositions about the audience's level of dependency and restriction, about the processes by which these are sustained and about the kinds of experience and self-consciousness which members of a modern public have available to them). These limitations weaken the theory even where economic and organisational factors are least conducive to the pursuit of democratic principles and practice within a television system. Whilst there is ample evidence that tightly controlled state systems, such as those which operated in Eastern Europe, were consistent in their projection of a monolithic and highly censored view of political affairs, there is little evidence that they were particularly *successful* in winning for this managed output a significant degree of credibility, compliance and loyalty from their viewing publics. The non-democratic character of the political system was maintained by state coercion, not by state television. In fact, a subculture of deep scepticism and 'black humour' concerning all official communication often appears to have flourished.

Several recent commentaries have re-emphasised the importance of economic and organisational factors in any analysis of the relation between media and democracy.[8] I accept this emphasis as a necessary one – differently articulated, such concerns form a key component both of Kellner's and Scannell's engagement with the Habermasian question of political order discussed above. The need to retain a 'political economy' perspective, seeing the medium in its relation to the state and to commerce, is particularly urgent in circumstances where radical shifts – technological, economic and directly (sometimes dramatically) political – are occurring to public communication both nationally and internationally However, notions of democratic television cannot be addressed simply by 'working in' from models of funding and structure. I want to conclude my discussion by pursuing a line of speculation broadly consonant with the focus on the 'unique perspective', retaining the emphasis on the interpenetration of television form and civic culture, and on the processes of reality shaping, but paying attention to the kinds of politics which the medium might have the potential to enable.

Promotional Politics

So Kellner and Scannell see television's political consequences as a matter finally as much to do with its economic and institutional character as with its communicative profile. Nevertheless, they have important and, again, contrasting, points to make about this latter area. These points are suggestive both for a sense of the current *direction* of television/politics relations and for a sense of available *alternatives*.

For Kellner, it is television's potential as a device of comprehensive political image management for use by those in power, and therefore as a device of strategic anti-democratic practice, which is the focus of analysis. U.S. television, for him, achieves this potential by having those qualities of the medium which I discussed in Chapter 1 – qualities which follow from its electronic, visual, mass/domestic character – institutionalised and active within the political and commercial dynamics of the U.S.A. Although his account is therefore nationally specific, many of the features he notes – the increased sophistication and scale of political marketing, the emphatic personalising of political choice, the move ever further down the road both of 'showbiz' politics and 'showbiz' coverage as a consequence of the spiralling mutual demands of politicians and broadcasters – have been detected on an international scale.

In his provocative and pessimistic study, *Promotional Culture*, Andrew Wernick (1990) regards this tendency as the political instance of a much broader shift, a shift which is slowly changing the basis and conventions of public communications and of public life itself. I will examine Wernick's thesis in more detail later, in a chapter looking at advertising – the key promotional format – but its relevance to the specific question of politics and television is clear.

I want to note the emphasis which this view of television as a 'promotional' vehicle places on its capacities for *visualisation*. It is primarily through a particular strategy of imaging the political world (images of persons, of actions, perhaps of pseudo-events) that the promotional discourse works. That kind of symbolism-within-naturalism which television's visual language can project, combining a way of being evidential and immediate with ways of being implicatory and metaphoric, provides precisely the conditions for performing the promotional trick. It is not that speech is unimportant in such a strategy – its own referential and connotational capacities are indispensable – but that promotional speech on television mostly gains its effect within a context 'guaranteed' by the image.

Anxieties about the consequences for political culture of this technologically enhanced potential for duplicity has not been restricted to academic debate. For instance, a recent programme made for British television, *We Have Ways of Making You Think* (BBC2, 19 November 1992), presented a potted history of the development of image-driven promotional communication within the United States. Examples from contemporary U.S. political marketing were taken as an awful (if also fascinating and occasionally bizarre) lesson in the decline of political culture. After a scene in which a class of trainee political consultants watch a piece of negative political advertising and discuss various tactics for countering its influence, two academics offer brief comments on the more general situation. The first is Neil Postman, a notable and longstanding critic of the social effects of the medium:

> If that's the new perception of politics and these people are in on the ground floor and they're exploiting it, I don't know how much we want to yell at them about that. They're making a living. What I would object to is their trying to claim that this new kind of politics is good for us. It isn't. It degrades us. It causes people to be cynical about, and indifferent to, the political process.

At which point the programme cuts to a clip from an interview with Larry Sabeto, Professor of Government at the University of Virginia:

> So in the end what you do is you increase cynicism. And this electorate is already the most cynical in American history. The post-Watergate period has seen a deepening of the cynicism, it's gone well beyond scepticism, it's well into corrosive cynicism.

These quotes are interesting because they take the 'fact' of television as a tool of market-researched political manipulation and produce a theory, not about indoctrination or even about effective opinion management but about cynicism. One may well question the value of cynicism as a political principle, and judge its enabling capacities to be severely limited, but it is at least as likely a result of the increasing scale and intensity of political image management on television as those suggested by theories of persuasion or of opinion control. It also requires a different kind of engagement and response.

But what does this mean for the kinds of significance we can draw, the kind of trajectory we can plot, from Scannell's account of television's political consequences? For in his version of the television–politics relationship, drawing on the British case, this direct play-off between promotionalism and cynicism does not figure greatly. Instead, politics is articulated through the conventions of broadcasting's own self-identity as a social agency, a self-identity informed by its public commitments to that dispersed community of the citizenly reasonable, at once both 'public' and 'private' in their identities, which it is its communicative project to sustain. Here, television's possibilities for the uncritical portrayal of a flattened-out, self-evidential, watchable world, for strategies of spectacular misinformation and for a personalising dominance (powerful persons being seen to be personally powerful) are modified, counterpointed, held in check, by the discursive primacy of *talk*. The *monologic* properties of images (indispensable in the rendering of physical realities, potentially oppressive in the presentation of ideas) are complemented by the strongly *dialogic* conventions of *speech*. By creating a sense of dialogue through its routine modes of address (modes which seek to *exercise* viewers as parasocial participants rather than *fictionalise them* as such) television can, in Scannell's view, extend participatory political community. A further key component of television, for him, is the existence of a television journalism which has a relative independence, within the broader framework of state regulations and commercial imperatives, to follow a policy of public interest inquiries. I shall explore the question of television news in Chapter 3, but the kind of journalism indicated here is one which, in its news gathering practices, acts as a sieve in relation both to state and corporate promotionalism. It is also a journalism which visualises and narrativises the world for its viewers by reference to criteria of civic entitlement, even though other criteria have weight too.

By seeking to develop those forms of programming which offer viewers an opportunity for speech and perhaps for self-imaging, television can also provide further, more substantial, measures towards a genuine and effective 'conversationalising' of politics, in the process reducing the levels of political cynicism and the cultural space available for political image management. Whilst 'promotional' versions of tele-sociality develop around certain forms of political journalism – high-profile interview shows, television campaigning, advertising, the celebrity chat show etc. – the more 'conversational' forms have emerged around network phone-in programmes, 'feedback' programmes focused on television's own output, studio debate formats and the newer kind of 'access' programme, including the increasing use of home-shot camcorder material in series such as the BBC's *Video Diaries* and *Teenage Diaries*, both begun in the early 1990s.[9] Where these new forms are produced within a television system moving away from a centralist model of 'public' television towards one more pluralised in its funding and its sites of production (as it is, rather precariously, in Britain), any risks involved in the institutionalising of 'public' representations are considerably offset by other, profoundly privatising, tendencies in the political culture. The risks in projecting a 'public' imagery and language, well evidenced historically, almost always follow from the rhetorical and often authoritarian affirmation of national/public unities – political and cultural – against the facts of inequality and difference. An effective 'public' television today will have to build its dialogues of community across dispersed and various groupings, and to be sure that those differences which it regards as unacceptable inequalities are registered as such on the screen and not imagined away by sentiment, idealism or embarrassment.

We can make one final reference back to the ideas and findings of the Langs' study 40 years ago. In the 1990s we can register the threat of a commodified politics of the television image, trading off its mobility, contrasts of proximity and magnitude, much more clearly than the 1952 study allowed. But we can also see how the sphere of political action which the Langs believed to be threatened, the social–critical interaction of 'primary' groups, might be transformed into new and extensive varieties of mediated public engagement.

In this chapter I have attempted to identify and discuss some of the major factors which bear on the relationship between television as a medium and the broad character of the political process. The treatment has been heavily selective and sometimes all too brief, though continuity in engagement with the principal issues has been my aim. A central question has been the way in which the mediation of politics through television (as we have seen, something which involves a complex and varied set of transformations) affects the nature of democratic activity by changing the conditions of public knowledge and participation.[10]

An appraisal of Lang and Lang's early study provided a useful basis for this exploration, connecting us back to a formative period of political television and, despite the tightly specific focus of the primary data, opening out usefully on to some of those general ideas about 'political television' which, in the radically altered television systems of today, still remain contentious. Taking my cue from this work, I attempted to schematise the issue by drawing up an inventory of the 'good' and the 'bad' aspects of television as a political agency, exemplifying some of these aspects as they appear in the work of critical theory and in current media analysis. I noted how, while the development of 'public service' practices, modes of address and formats had increased the grounds for optimism (at least within some national systems), the international spread of promotionalism had created new forms of political–televisual relations which have lent support to a more pessimistic analysis.

Finally, any assessment needs to be set off against the emergence, within national, regional and local television, of new programme forms and relations of viewing. A good number of these continue in the directions identified by Paddy Scannell. The attempt here, marginal though it may sometimes be, is to direct the 'perspectives of television' in ways which not only maintain but develop the contribution of the medium to active and popular democracy. Engagement, recognition and exploration rather than varieties of displacement and alienation are the goal.

In other chapters, this present uncertainty concerning the potential of television as a political and social agency will be taken up in respect of different kinds of programme and arguments about their social effects.

3

'SEE IT HAPPEN'[1]

Over many parts of the world, television has become the dominant medium of journalism, routinely used by viewers as the primary and most trusted source of public information. In the schedules of television stations and networks, the main news programmes are 'flagship' productions, sharpening channel identity and playing a strategic role in attracting the audience for other programmes. Television news is the single most important route through which the medium directly impacts upon international and national public life.

One consequence of this has been a change in the character of newspaper journalism, increasingly less able to act as a 'news-breaker' and therefore pushed by market requirements either in the direction of more background analysis, more feature work (a route taken by most of the 'qualities') or in the direction of popular entertainment (the route most obviously open to popular tabloids). Although radio journalism continues to have a strong presence as a source of regular bulletins at a regional and local level (in many places, including Britain, it also continues to have a strong role within a national network), the agenda of international and national news is one very much set by networked television coverage, with occasional investigative 'scoops' by newspapers providing some movement in the other direction, especially around 'scandals' of various kinds. A clear instance of this hierarchy is provided by the Gulf War of 1992, an event of such magnitude that the intensive (and sometimes live) television coverage created an 'extraordinary' period of time for the international audience. During this period, the routines of everyday life were reframed, and everyday experience was substantially affected by the television schedules and their news content. Exceptionally high viewing figures and average viewing hours were recorded and both radio channels and newspapers were widely used as sources of further commentary, background information and associated stories.[2] The immediacy (and simulated immediacy) made possible by international satellite links, together with the extent to which international diplomacy was itself caught up in responding to the coverage and articulating its responses within it, prompted some commentators to see this conflict as the first 'television war'. Although such phrases contain an element of apocalyptic over-statement, hiding as much as they reveal, the way in which television figured in the Gulf War certainly had the effect of refocusing attention on the scale, speed and public impact of international television news. Not suprisingly, this has been the topic of much recent study, and I shall refer to some features of Gulf reporting in what follows.

My main concern in this chapter is with the communicative characteristics of television's way of providing news and comment and with some of the more important aspects of those debates about news presentation which have occurred both as part of public and political controversy and within media research. The line of discussion is selective rather than comprehensive, with relation between news form and news principles providing the backbone, and other factors, such as news gathering and newsroom practices, merely referred to. This selection does not indicate a concealed theory about relative importance, only the relative interest of issues within the intellectual scope of the book. In following this line of inquiry I shall refer to an extended example of 'controversial' news broadcasting which, despite the need to register its specific, national context, bears usefully on more general questions and problems.

First of all, it is worth standing back a few paces from the immediate object of interest and asking some questions about what 'news' is, about what purposes it is supposed to serve and about why people watch it on television so routinely and in such large numbers.

Any attempted definition of news which takes account of the way in which the term is used in everyday life will register that when people talk about 'the news' they mostly mean the particular events which have been described and depicted *in* news output.[3] In that sense, 'the news' as the particular set of professional operations which produces *descriptions and depictions* enjoys a measure of social invisibility, being perceived as so closely related to the events themselves as not to warrant separate identification. This usage derives from the meaning of 'news' outside of journalism (e.g. 'I have some good news for you') where transparency between the substantive circumstance and the form of the mediation in which it is conveyed is conventionally assumed. In fact, viewer research and common experience suggests that the application of this usage to professional news services does not block public understanding that what journalists do is routinely open to question and to the variables of 'point of view'. Nevertheless, as I shall show, the double meaning of 'news' has significance for the conduct of public debate about broadcast journalism.

Registering this duality, news might be defined something along these lines – 'regularly updated information about, and depictions of, significant recent events within a particular geographical area or sphere of activity'. As for the principal purpose of such a function (that is to say, leaving aside its appeal as entertainment or its satisfying of a general inquisitiveness), it might be defined as part of general citizenship rights, 'to provide knowledge and understanding about circumstances of consequence to readers, listeners and viewers, to contribute not only to their understanding but also to their capacities for judgement and action'. Immediately, the potential for news services to be highly controversial becomes apparent. By what criteria is the 'significance level' of items to be decided so that they can be included or excluded from 'news'? What presumptions are made (both by journalists and by viewers) about the comprehensiveness of the surveillance and sourcing activities from which a 'full' range of possible items becomes available for selection? Clearly, *selectivity* is a major issue for journalists, for readerships and audiences and for those people who do not find in the news what they want or too much of what they don't.[4] It is also a factor operative at every level of news production, from the origination of news items through the various news gathering routines and practices (e.g. the deployment of news teams 'in the field', the use of agency material, the press conference, the telephone contacts, the intermedia cross-referencing) through to the visual and aural elements by which reported accounts are rendered on the screen. Like some other factors which are the focus of controversy about the news, selectivity is also *inevitable* as a general feature of news production. This is to make the obvious point that no news outlet, print or broadcasting, can give 'all' the news (whatever one might choose to understand by that), nor can it give 'all' the information relevant to that news which it chooses to provide. Argument about selectivity is therefore always and essentially about *criteria*, about the principles of selection, and a good many public debates about news distortion would gain cogency if they focused on this directly and explicitly rather than using terms (e.g. 'but it wasn't the whole story', 'it was highly selective', 'it was taken out of context') which appear to be self-evident points of criticism but which, by themselves, lack argumentative force.

However, before looking at the issues raised by television news as a form of social knowledge, I want to examine it as a set of particular conventions.

News as Genre

Although a number of recent commentaries on television form have emphasised the way in which news programmes share characteristics with other kinds of output, including serial drama, it remains the case that the core communicative features of most television news have a distinctive look and sound. Around this core, internationally established, connections with other forms of programming provide a source of possibilities for innovation and for variations related to channel, schedule positioning and to types of audience expectation and appeal. In analysing this distinctiveness it is helpful to note those basic combinations of sound and image from which most news programmes are constructed.

a. Studio Modes
  1. Presenter's to-camera speech (from behind newsdesk and perhaps with background image).
  2. Presenter voice-over used with stills, film or graphics.
  3. Presenter interview with interviewee at newsdesk or, via link-up, at another location.
  4. Archive film with presenter voice or original sound.

b. Location Modes
  5. Reporter's to-camera speech in 'stand-up' exposition (with varying framing, composition and shot types).
  6. Reporter's speech and actuality sound in ongoing participant-action sequences (e.g. reporter in flood relief boat; with emergency convoy; trapped in ambush; attempting to gain access to premises).
  7. Reporter's voice-over filmed sequences in which reporter is not shown.
  8. Filmed sequence, actuality sound, no speech. Such sequences may involve visual effects of a non-naturalistic kind, for instance rapid, associative editing and various forms of 'symbolic' shot.
  9. Reporter's voice over still image (telephoned report; the convention here is reporter's face superimposed in the corner of a shot of the report's location).
  10. Reporter interview with both speakers in shot.
  11. Reporter interview with only interviewee in shot and reporter's questions edited out.
  12. Interviewee voice-over used with film.
  13. Interviewee seen as social actor, carrying out activities with relevant dialogue and/or interviewee voice-over.

These modes are only the basic units out of which news programmes are constructed. Not only are there more possibilities, even the ones I have listed can be brought together to form new options. Furthermore, several of them are open to further subvariations in respect of the manner of composition and editing (the interview allowing a range of realisations, for instance variously exploiting visual and dramatic potential). Each mode offers the viewer a different 'way of knowing' about the subject of the news report, a way which has an informational but also an imaginative character, as we shall see later.

Taking these units as providing a basic communicative reportoire for television journalism, the distinctiveness of what is then produced can be analysed under three broad categories, each pointing to a different aspect of news form. These categories are narrative, visualisation and talk.[5]

Narrative – News as Story

Journalists routinely refer to their items as 'stories', but however much the creative, interpretative aspect of news (journalist as author) needs to be stressed as a counter to any idea of it as straightforwardly 'factual record' (journalist as technician), the 'stories' told by journalists differ radically in form from those told by novelists and dramatists. The only exception to this is provided by those self-licensed (and self-conscious) flights of pure imagination now to be found in certain kinds of tongue-in-cheek feature writing in popular tabloid newspapers (for instance, 'Elvis is alive and living on Mars'). Even here, although the analogy with fiction is an instructive one, the journalistic 'tale' is still produced according to a different recipe (one in which a key ingredient is the tension between the conventions of fictional and factual accounts). In television, this difference from the fictional is much more clearly marked.

For a start, the possibilities for the development of 'character' and 'plot' are severely limited. This is a consequence not only of the available detail about the nature of newsworthy events and newsworthy persons, but of the relative inability of conventional news modes to organise what data *are* selected with any comparable degree of imaginative depth, interiority of viewpoint and continuity to that found in fiction. The 'stories' told in the news are often very brief (although they may form only an episode in a much longer, 'running' narrative). They frequently lack: (a) the classic devices of fictional plot movement (though they may well contain puzzles and conflicts), (b) continuity of action (though they may contain action sequences of considerable dramatic power in themselves) and (c) narratively developed characterisation (although 'strong characters', including those familiar from previous news reports, will appear and be projected as such within them). In most cases, moreover, their endings, though shaped by conventional journalistic devices of closure (e.g. stock reportorial phrasings, cadences, 'finishing shots'), do not usually involve any 'satisfactory' resolution, either aesthetically – in terms of the status of reports as artefactual constructions – or referentially – in terms of the events which they describe and depict. An exception here is the convention of the 'happy' closing story as established, for instance, in ITN's evening bulletins.

In what way, then, given these differences between news production and conventional forms of 'story telling', is it appropriate to see a narrative element at work in television news? I think the answer is that story forms are to be found in television news as one part of a principle of organisation in which two different notions are yoked together. This produces a *dual aesthetic*, one of *narrative/exposition*, and the movement between the two phases, far from giving the smoothly managed flow which a fictional narrative is able to produce, gives a distinctive discontinuity and disjunction to televised news accounts.

Narrative ideas exert an influence by bringing about a shaping of sense and significance around an underlying *unity* of account. They do this in terms which shadow (even if they cannot reproduce) the terms of fiction, thus giving the report a measure of cultural resonance and something of the pleasingness produced by self-contained expressive form (as in books, films and plays). The principle works primarily to give a totalising if condensed apprehension of events which is strongly *affective* – directed at the sensibilities of the viewer as well as offering a scheme for organising comprehension. Although the term 'mythic' has problems of imprecision, the idea that the news appeals to deep and subconscious cultural patterns of fear and fantasy is one which relates directly to its organisation along narrative principles.

The exposition principle pulls reporting in the direction of the incomplete, the complicated, the multiple and the propositional. It works primarily to give a fragmented apprehension of events which is strongly *cognitive* – directed at viewers as the material for knowledge and assessment. If the risk of narrativised news is of simplistic, personalised and overly affective appeals to the viewer, the exposition principle, when pursued excessively, risks collapsing the 'story' into incoherence either in part (too much detail) or in whole (relations between parts too implicit or uncertain).

It is clearly possible to overstate the extent to which the two principles can be separated in analysis, yet I would argue that the tension between them, and then the varying 'resolution' of this, is one of the clearest markers of television news discourse. One quite recent example of its general occurrence across a whole range of news reports is at the start of the air bombardment phase of the 1992 Gulf conflict. A widespread assumption among editors and reporters (both in the United States and in Britain) was that the commencement of hostilities was the start of what would be a very short, intense event. This assumption, in which past events like the 'Six Day' Arab/Israeli War of 1967 were placed as models, carried with it certain implications about appropriate intervals of news update (where possible, hourly) and of the 'threshold of significance' to be used in deciding what was newsworthy (initially, very little knowledge that became available was thought too insignificant to be included). The news frame thus constructed, with the expectations it projected to viewers, then had to come to terms with the fact that following the first two days of conflict there was very little sign of an early resolution to the event. The installed criteria of significance and the frequency of reporting (both leading to extensive repetition and a shift away from 'hard' news towards speculation – the only way to keep the narrative moving) were unable to register *development* and to meet those viewer expectations which their introduction had encouraged (compare the Langs' study in Chapter 2). In some frustration, a number of editors and reporters in Washington and London complained at press conferences about the war 'dragging on', turning the inappropriateness of their own reportorial assumptions into a criticism of military management. Eventually, and after strong criticisms of early news coverage by both the U.S. and British governments, a revised news frame emerged, one with a less urgent narrative tempo and one more discriminating as to the significance of different levels of expositional detail.[6] Nevertheless, some degree of mismatch between, on the one hand, the narrativised time-scales of a coverage which was always partly trading off war fiction and, on the other, the pace, complexity and contradictoriness of real events, was a feature of coverage until the end of the fighting. In the examples I shall draw on later, other instances of the relationship between the narrativised and expository phases of news accounts will be given.

Visualisation – News as Pictures

The images of television news have been variously celebrated as a major contribution to popular knowledge (and a proper object of public trust) and criticised as a key means of ideological manipulation. There has frequently been concern expressed within the broadcasting industry about the extent to which the 'picture power' of the news reduces its capacities for explanation and exercises an unacceptable influence over the selection of items. It is therefore interesting to note that, in Britain, television news images had a slow development as a distinctive generic feature. The BBC's *Television Newsreel*, started in 1948, was initially based on the model of the cinema newsreel and its essential news mode was presenter voice over film. In 1954, with competition from commercial television an imminent threat, the BBC shifted to a *News and Newsreel* format, with the main news read out, followed by newsreel items. It was only with the emergence of Independent Television News, following the starting of a commercially funded network in 1955, that the visual aesthetics of television news – offering a distinctive kind of anchored worldview to a domestic audience – began to be developed, drawing extensively on the model of ABC and CBS journalism in the United States.[7] This model included extensive use of reporters on the spot, location interviews and a new mode of visualisation with sound. Resulting from the use of location camera teams, this mode was increasingly able to offer proximities, immediacies and kinds of involvement very different from the distanced, self-conscious modes which had been conventionalised in the depictive style of newsreel cinema films and then adopted by early television news.

Although the offer of 'seeing' is absolutely central to the project of television journalism, to its impact, memorability and public power as well as to its commodity value (e.g. in 'scoop' film), it is important to note the limitations that stand in the way of any visualisation of news events. These modify the visual character of news in very much the same way that I argued its expository function modifies narrative shaping and closure and, like that modification, they serve to pull news away from dominant styles of fictional portrayal, whatever discrete fictional elements are worked into the visual ingredients of news recipes.

First of all, most 'unscheduled' news events, especially events where *action* is central to their significance, have happened by the time the journalists arrive on the scene, so in these cases news typically recounts *what happened* against images which show spaces and places *after* the event. The reporter is on the 'stage'; the spaces and places of news occurrence can be viewed and can generate their interest and significance (often more symbolic than informational), but the principal action is over. Though the reporter's presence then allows follow-up investigation, including that through interview, the *evidential* qualities of the visualisation itself – as a means of 'seeing it happen' – are negligible. Such limitation, affecting both the credibility and the affective power of the treatment, may well be partly overcome by news teams resorting to a variety of ruses. Reconstructions, 'stagings' (the asking of people to perform actions before the camera), the use of previously shot material, including library film, and the mixing-in of visuals from related but different stories can all be deployed in an attempt to make up for the deficit in actuality footage. In one of the most thorough studies ever to be made of television news practice on location, Richard Ericson and his colleagues (Ericson *et al.*, 1987) showed how a Canadian news crew routinely adopted the above devices, involving greater or lesser duplicity, in order to provide items with visual 'presence', with a measure of depictive continuity and, where possible, with an imaginative/narrative appeal which gave them a resonance with other forms of cultural representation (e.g. the thriller movie, the police series). Clearly, the topics which news teams are sent to cover vary considerably in their possibilities for visualisation, even allowing for ingenuity and professionally licensed 'faking'. At one end, there are stories – even physical action stories – which offer no direct visualisation at all, save perhaps for still shots (for instance, from the family album of a murder victim) and for in-shot interview sequences (for instance, with relatives of the victim). At the other end, teams covering ongoing events such as wars and major civil disturbances may produce a variety of detailed depictions of events, shot from different vantage points and entering the space of the action as it unfolds. In between, there is the familiar visual recipe for portraying scheduled, national or international political and diplomatic events. Here, a repertoire of highly conventionalised depictions of the events' 'official' physical occurrence (arrivals at airports, limousines drawing up outside state buldings, entrances and departures from conference rooms, handshakes on steps etc.) provides something over which a *spoken* exposition can be delivered. Such exposition frequently serves to *establish* the event in a way which can then lead on to consideration of its outcome and significance via press conference questioning and perhaps the taking up of the item by specialist correspondents for more detailed studio-based commentary.

It was the perception of these constraints on news visualisations which led Howard Davis and Paul Walton, in their detailed case study of a political assassination story (Davis and Walton, 1983), to talk about news images as being essentially 'symbolic' rather than 'iconic'. By this they wanted to point to the secondary nature of many of the images:

> In television news, in fact, a relatively small proportion of the total number of shots is iconic or directly representative of the people, places and events which are the subjects of the news text. A far greater proportion of shots has an oblique relationship to the text; they 'stand for' the subject matter... symbolically.
>
> (Davis and Walton, 1983, p. 45)

As I shall discuss below, this question of direct and indirect visual representation, of the relations between the two modes and the *shifts* between them, is of considerable significance in debates about news bias.

Given both the interrupted or fragmented nature of television news visualisations and their extensive use as other than directly referential/evidential indicators within an item, their function can be seen to be frequently that of providing the journalism with a continuously viewable plane, an interface with the realities of a 'world in action', one *external to the news talk*. At one level, this equips reports with what in effect is a repertoire of 'props' by which descriptive speech can routinely connect with forms of particularity and embodiment, even if the connections are indirect and associational. In doing such work, the visualisations act as reinforcing marker points around which other components of the news discourse are organised, 'levels' over which exposition can be laid and 'surfaces' upon which the meanings of these other components (voice-over, interviews) are condensed and construed by the viewer. Where they *do* contain images and sequences of a strongly evidential character or of a strongly affective kind, this broadly demonstrative function becomes more particularised and intense, radically altering the image/word balance and the grounding of news *truth telling*.

When sufficiently strong in revelatory/dramatic character (high in its impact upon the viewer, 'self-evident' in it significance) such picturing may serve to crystallise the whole report and to enter public circulation with a force no other form of contemporary journalism could possess. The examples of the first pictures of the mid-1970s Ethiopian famine, broadcast all over the world, are often cited here. Other, more recent, examples having international significance would be the scenes of the Baghdad shelter following the Allied bombing in 1991 and the scenes of the Serbian-run internment camps in Bosnia, shown by television in 1992. In both cases, and in many others, the television pictures attain a 'nodal' status for subsequent public debate about the circumstances depicted, and often for political responses to them too. By 'nodal', I mean that the power of their particularisations (not necessarily directly proportional to their yield of 'new information' – see my discussion of this in Chapter 1) sets up a datum which all subsequent reporting has to recognise and to which all claims and counter-claims about 'what really happened/is happening' are forced to refer in order to cross the threshold of public credibility. The relation between pictorial form and viewer psychology involved here, together with the implications of both for public knowledge, are issues to which I will return in a later chapter.

As well as variously imaging the reported world, however, television's pictures also importantly present the viewer with an imaging of *the process of reporting itself*. This is simultaneously a spatial, social and personal imaging (who, where, talking to whom?), linking the viewer to a seen source of information and allowing the personalised investment of a trust in the visible processes of inquiry, of the search for truth. This trust is not available in the same way for other kinds of journalism and other kinds of journalist do not become 'stars' in the way that high-profile television reporters frequently do.

Talk – News as Words

Although images can be combined in such a manner as to articulate complex and abstract ideas without the assistance of words, it is very rare to find symbolic work of this 'advanced' kind in news material, and then it is usually within the more expansive and less immediate feature items. Given the logistics of news picturing (compared with, say, that of documentary) and the particularistic, informational requirement of news, this is not suprising. The main sense of the news is carried by various forms of speech. Words carry the burden of naming and description, of interpretation and evaluation. It is through them that conflicts of opinion are articulated. I want briefly to consider news speech under two headings, speech–viewer relations and speech–image relations.

Speech–viewer relations
News provides television services with one of their routine 'live' moments. Although reports are often recorded, news programmes are always 'anchored' live and the direct-to-camera speech of the presenter is perhaps the strongest single identifying feature of the news genre [thus Fiske and Hartley (1978) see its rhetorical function as 'bardic' in relation to its community of viewers]. Such speech places viewers as the 'seen recipients' of journalism. Although news conventions in many countries have shifted towards more informal styles of presentation, 'anchor' speech is still most often projected in a strongly public address mode, the newsdesk itself acting as a marker of its 'official' character. The speech of reporters on location is also direct address (both to-camera and voice-over) but a wider range of tones and registers becomes available to location reporters. This is a result both of the more extensive possibilities available for self-visualisation in location settings and the shift in the basic talk form from 'reading' to 'reporting', with the validation for what is said now being grounded in the personal experiences and inquiries of the speaker. It is in the context of this direct speaking by broadcasting professionals that the *indirect* speech of others, either of those observed within the news–event frame (e.g. politicians) or of those interviewed within or in response to this frame, is fitted. These latter speakers do not, conventionally, establish direct eye contact with the camera, speaking instead to the on-screen or off-screen reporter/interviewer. Some television analysts, drawing particularly on coverage of industrial disputes, have pointed to the negative implications of the indirect interviewee–viewer relationship thus established (for instance, Ellis, 1982), but these do not follow of necessity. Although the terms of interviewee speech are subject to interviewer management and to subsequent editing (as are the terms of interviewees' visual portrayal), viewer evaluation of interviewed speakers, while it is clearly influenced by matters of general format, is by no means exclusively determined by them. It will vary with topic and with the specific content and manner of the speakers' talk. Nor will people and groups named in professionalised direct address (as various 'theys') necessarily be placed subordinately to the 'us' relationship implied in the direct-address bond between broadcaster and viewer. The formal configuration of speech in news privileges the talk of broadcasters over kinds of 'accessed talk' (see Hartley, 1982), but this potential has to be realised in relation to specific subject material (e.g. foreign wars, political conflict, social issues) and the various self-identities and dispositions which audience members possess in relation to topics. The projected alignment of broadcaster and viewer carried by direct address speech (strongest, perhaps, in the more informal, chatty registers) may simply be overridden by more substantive factors. Analyses of news language, while opening up a usefully complex, schematic sense of the social relations at work in news discourse, have often tended to foreclose on the whole issue of the social meaning of news

by implying that this is entirely a product of the discursive forms employed.

Speech–image relations

News speech and news image are related to each other with varying degrees of directness, as indicated above. Images *do* work to 'show' what is being described, but this function is less frequently performed than more indirect ones, where what is shown is an imaging of something associated (or *to be* associated) with what is being said. Since part of most news reports includes speech about *abstractions* (opinions, consequences, implications) and images are necessarily of the *physical world*, whatever their abstract connotative force, some degree of indirectness in speech–image relations is inevitable.

If we watch the news with the sound turned down, the meaning of the images (at the primary level of what precisely they are images of) will quite frequently be impossible to determine. So, for instance, *who* these people are, *what* is on fire, *where* this building is, may be unresolvable from the visuals. Therefore, one aspect of speech–image relations is the use of speech as an intepretative guide in reading the images. Speech of this kind (either by a presenter or a location reporter) will usually draw extensively on information not pictorially available. Given that the 'seeing' and 'hearing' components of television communication are hard to keep apart in the viewing act, this raises the possibility of a *transfer effect*, whereby viewers assume they have 'seen' something when in fact key items of this 'something' were heard in speech and then fused with the information received visually. Uncertainty and confusion as to precisely what was *said* and what was *shown* is a key feature of many disputes about the news. But leaving aside the more obviously controversial occurrences of 'transfer', the processes by which speech works to fill up images with an often crucial measure of meaning, additional to that carried by their own 'iconic' or 'symbolic' properties (see above), is a standard feature of news communication.

If, however, we watch the television news in sound only, another aspect of the speech–image relationship is foregrounded. For many items, this procedure will actually work quite well, certainly producing a lot more sense than the vision-only experiment. But sections of the account, particularly in the location reports, will contain demonstrative pointers (e.g. 'this square', 'these boys', 'here') which will simply leave us with holes in our sense making. Moreover, the whole movement of the reporting, its narrative organisation and changing tones, will be grounded in a seeing experience from which we have excluded ourselves. Although often not directly image dependent, television news speech is addressed to a 'viewing' audience in such a way that even its most verbally self-contained elements are designed to be heard across and within images, designed to be read against and through realities made 'tele-present' to the viewer.

The shifting, interpenetrative nature of speech and image in television news gives discussion about its objectivity and balance a distinctive complexity. At the same time, the very popularity and institutional dominance of the form makes this discussion inevitable.

News Form and Controversy – Impartiality and Bias

No debate about television news services has been more intense and confused than the one about 'impartiality'. In Britain, it has been a debate which has been engaged in by all major political parties as well as by corporate concerns, campaigning organisations, individuals and, of course, by media researchers and the broadcasting institutions themselves.

The 'impartiality' principle is institutionalised within the professional codes applying to news in many broadcasting systems. Though its precise framings differ (in Britain, the BBC is required by charter to show *'due* impartiality'), it broadly enjoins that news collection, presentation and interpretation be 'fair' in respect of all legally expressable political and social viewpoints (so, for instance, as a consequence of U.K. race relations legislation, there would be no obligation to give fair coverage to *openly* racist opinion). In applying such a principle, television journalists, newsreaders and editors are expected not to seek to promote one body of opinion over another or advance a view of their own in their accounts. This 'fairness' requirement contrasts with the situation generally obtaining in the newspaper industry, where, although guidelines for journalistic conduct cover matters such as 'accuracy', it is generally regarded as being within a newspaper's rights to offer assessments linked to party political affiliation and to broader, social viewpoints. Such judgements are by no means limited to editorial columns. They may inform not only the selection but also the treatment of a large number of items carried in the news pages (including headlines and use of photographs). In doing so, they may offer themselves as indistinguishable from, as blended into, the primary news account. This is not a covert practice; the socio-political complexion of newspapers is part of popular knowledge and is one factor (but only one) in readers' purchasing decisions. In certain countries, broadcast news services work with something of the same kind of license, but where they do not it is for a mix of reasons which generally includes at least one of the following. First of all, that the broadcasting system is publicly funded in whole or in part and therefore needs to maintain independence in respect of any one sector of political or social opinion. This is an obligation grounded directly in economics, in *who pays* for broadcasting. Secondly, that the scarcity of channel availability and/or the high costs involved in national television production means that the 'free market' conditions under which the press supplies news cannot apply and therefore that television news has responsibilities grounded in the limited range of alternatives. This is, in essence, a *public dependency* obligation. Thirdly, that requiring television journalism to be impartial is, in fact, the best way of gaining a circulation of information and opinion adequate to the maintenance of the 'public sphere' (see Chapter 2) and the democratic political process. This is a *public interest* obligation, less tied than the others to the particular contingencies of ownership and the systems of distribution. In practice, of course, all three positions are often interrelated.

Against this can be set the example of what we might see as the 'viewpoint' principle of the news, one largely unfamiliar in the U.K. This argues that television news is inevitably the product of a 'point of view' and that the best arrangement for television services is therefore to have a multiplicity of outlets (national and local) each of which is able to declare the broad political and social assumptions informing its news production, allowing the viewer to choose and judge as they wish. The 'point of view' model can either be regarded as a matter of institutional affiliation, with particular stations or programmes having openly stated political and social perspectives (usually in direct relation to their funding source) along the lines of some European channels, or more problematically, as a matter of the perspectives of individual journalists and news teams.

Both these models of television news turn on assumptions about 'impartiality'. In the former case it is assumed to be possible and desirable. In the latter, although the view that it is possible but undesirable could, theoretically, be advanced, the usual argument is that it is impossible, and therefore undesirable to pretend that it is not so by taking it as a principle of conduct. In order for arguments about the 'fairness' of news to be properly assessed, these assumptions need further examination in relation to points about the form of television news brought out earlier.

The Impossibility of Impartiality?

As a journalistic principle, 'impartiality' needs differentiating from three other notions with which it is regularly associated and often confused in debate. These are 'accuracy', 'objectivity' and 'balance'.[8]

I take 'accuracy' to refer to the correctness of primary elements of the news account such as dates, names, places, numbers of people, durations and attestable actions (e.g. quoted statements, legal consequences, injuries received). The 'attestability' of a news item will vary from topic to topic and at some point its range will become so attenuated in its evidentiality as to blur questions of 'accuracy' into questions of 'opinion' and to make the 'facts' increasingly an indeterminate construct of variant interpretation. So there is no clear dividing line. But no one doubts the possibility of a journalist being 'accurate' about a lot of things for a lot of the time as agreed by the very widest spectrum of political and social opinion and very few people doubt the desirability of them being so. *Accuracy* is certainly a problem for journalists, greater or lesser according to the kind of fact-base of the item they are reporting and the sources upon which they are able to draw, but it does not raise the same kind of questions as those posed by 'impartiality'.

I take 'objectivity' to refer to 'that which is external to the mind' and, more tightly, to 'that which is unaffected by subjective mental operations' (*Concise Oxford Dictionary*). It is a term with a long pedigree in discussion of journalistic principles and since it is safe to assume general public support for the idea that television reporters should address themselves to matters outside their mind, this is not suprising. But it seems to me to suffer from three limitations as a criterion for news production. First of all, it is an absolutist principle. Either you are objective or you aren't, and the amount of falling short tends to be registered as relatively insignificant once failure has been established. Secondly, and most unfortunately given the above, at the level of perception and of image and language use it is quite clear that total objectivity is as impossible for journalists to achieve as for anyone else and that it is, philosophically speaking, nonsense to suggest otherwise. Thirdly, there is evidence to indicate that, contrary to the implications of both my earlier points, the use of the term 'objectivity' within journalism and schools of journalism has tended to go along with a degree of complacency. The term's categoric, 'scientific/professional' ring rather too easily suggests a level of *routine accomplishment* which can mask the real problems of reporting and the formation of a proper response to these. In that sense, 'objectivity' is a term which serves to desocialise journalism, to pull it away from its *contingencies of practice*.

I take 'balance' to be ambiguous in its usage in debates about news. Either it points towards a general reflexive disposition on the part of the journalist, a synonym of 'fair minded' ('a balanced presentation'), or, even more unhelpfully, it implies some kind of proportional formula in which 'both sides' of an issue get an airing. This is then a recommendation effectively limited to issues on which defined positions can be identified (better if there are only two) and weighed (better if they are roughly equal), a recommendation showing the influence exerted upon British journalism by the tradition of Parliamentary reporting, covering both Government and Opposition opinion. 'Balance' also has a well-documented tendency to fall victim to its metaphoric origins by encouraging a reductive concern with the measurement of the airtime given to interested parties in coverage of a given topic, often to the exclusion of other factors.[9] However, 'balance' does direct our attention to the multivocal aspect of television news – its function in providing the space for non-media professionals to have public access within news accounts, as providers of facts and of opinion. This contrasts with its *univocal* role in privileging the journalist's own words and images. I want to return to this point later.

A further, subspecies of 'balance' argument occurs when it is claimed that the obvious point of balance between two points treated as equal is in the middle, and that 'the middle ground' is therefore the spot upon which journalists should aim to alight. Such a claim is most often offered in 'bad faith' by those wishing to show the banality and timidity of the principle, so it does not merit the attention given to other variants. But significantly, it too follows the restrictive Parliamentary model of reporting and, even in its own limited terms, was considerably disadvantaged in Britain by the emergence of a strong centrist party in the 1980s, wanting to set up on exactly the same site.

Where does this leave 'impartiality'? It certainly leaves it as a debatable term but I think debatable in two ways. It is a 'soft' enough term to be vulnerable to general scepticism but but it is also a term open to debate, flexible enough to be used productively as a tool of argument in public and professional discussion about the principles and practices of journalism. Its being defined against what it is *not* (not partial, not prejudiced) is a help here. A social principle of impartiality will be *contingent*, certainly. It will be contingent on context, on the broader debates about the legitimacy and the salience of those political and ethical viewpoints from which the journalist is required to keep the report free. More riskily, this will make it contingent, too, on the balance of power among the various political and moral discourses at work in the realms (politics, economics, crime, home affairs, international diplomacy) upon which journalists report. However, these contingencies seem to me to be addressable ones, ones which can be *made open to account*, within the terms of impartiality conventions. That they have not routinely been so in the past does not count as adequate grounds for taking a different view of the public propriety of broadcast journalism. They are not so addressable within the terms either of the 'objectivity' paradigm (because this is too inflexibly absolutist) or within the relativism which some have seen to be the only appropriate alternative to this (because the tendency here is towards an 'anything goes' approach).

If 'impartiality' is a socially contingent principle for television news then this is also true of any useful idea of 'bias'. Where 'bias' is used to mean 'not totally objective' then the argument is immediately over since no meaningful charge can be brought against journalists for not achieving the impossible. If, however, it is used to mean 'significant departure from fairness' then the basis of an argument and, indeed, the basis of possible redress and remedy, are available. This is not to underestimate the considerable difficulties, in the context of the structural inequalities to be found in most societies, of achieving equity of representation purely by force of argument. It is, however, to register the importance of retaining the means to argue publicly about the status of variously sourced social knowledge.

Whilst it will frequently be possible to determine levels of accuracy with a good degree of inter-subjective precision, measurement of 'bias' raises more difficulties since there is not likely to be any yardstick which can be appealed to independently of interpretative evaluation. Whether an accident happened on the morning of 17 July or on the afternoon is a matter which one might expect in most cases to be quickly established (although, as I noted above, the ascertaining of basic definitions and facts in relation to an event *can* be problematic). Whether or not the use of a particular sequence of film, a certain phrase from a reporter, or the omission of certain statistics from an account constitute 'bias' in a news item is more difficult to *ground* as a charge, as the extensive literature of both academic research and public debate shows. One response to this difficulty is, as I have already indicated, to limit 'bias' to quantitative factors (e.g. duration of certain kinds of footage, number of appearances of given speakers). Though these factors are not unimportant they fail to connect fully with the way news works as communicated meaning, and therefore the way in which any 'bias' present becomes socially consequential. Another response is to relativise the idea to the point where its critical usefulness disappears.[10] This repeats the stalemate position arrived at by one kind of response to the 'impossibility of objectivity'. It involves pointing to this impossibility in order to claim that 'we are all biased', broadcasters, viewers and researcher/critics. If news accounts are being both produced and comprehended within such a hotchpotch of variously biased perceptions, then bias may be finally judged to be 'in the eye of the beholder', and disentangling the perceptions of the journalist/beholder from those of the viewer/beholder or the researcher/beholder is a futile business.

Once again, such a position gives up on the idea of an *arguable fairness*. For it is not necessary to have uncompromised access to the 'truth' of circumstances in order to advance a reasonable and cogent case for a report being biased in a way which is detrimental to journalism's public function. Here, an uncompromising philosophical scepticism does not make a helpful guide, since it is that which is realisable *in practice* which requires attention. The omission of *arguably* significant details, perhaps ones published in other national news sources, the treating of an interviewee to hostile questioning in a way which prejudices their expression of opinion, the suggestion of causality which is not substantiated, the use of certain labels to define groups in a pejorative way, these are all grounds for a claim of bias. Moreover, it has been shown that although they are ones which may be contested, they can also receive widespread public support and are ones to which editors and journalists can respond constructively. Unlike *assertions*, which can only be 'strengthened' by emphasis and repetition, *claims* of this kind can be strengthened by evidence and argument.

In most studies of broadcast television news, bias is seen not as a function of an individual intention to distort by the journalist, but as a 'skew' produced in an account by the institutionalised activities of the news-making process itself, as its routine practices and assumptions are shaped in specific political and social contexts. In some studies, such 'skewing' is regarded as widespread and indicative of a larger systemic skew in the general representation of the capitalist economy, one which is politically and institutionally strategic even if it is not a product of individual intention (see the discussion of Habermas in Chapter 2). Whatever the view taken, the nature of television news form, analysed earlier, is a key factor in argument about impartiality and bias.

A good way to illustrate a number of the points made above is to take an example of a major controversy over news.

The 'Tripoli Bombing' Story: News Language and the Politics of Impartiality

This event provides a particularly illuminating instance of conflict around 'impartiality' in television news and of debates about the language of television journalism and the pictures it uses. Although it happened in the mid-1980s and a number of more recent events have provoked controversy as strong (notably, again, the 1992 Gulf War and the coverage of the fighting in former Yugoslavia in 1992–1994) it still repays analysis. Not only does it directly involve political factors, but most unusually it shows a television news organisation responding in detail to charges made against it.

On 15 April 1986, United States bombers operating from British bases attacked targets in Libya, including Tripoli, causing damage and casualties. Among the civilian casualties were members of Colonel Gadafy's own family. The raid was in reprisal for what was claimed by the U.S. government to be Libya's continuing role in international terrorism. In the British coverage of the raid, two television reporters based in Tripoli featured prominently. Kate Adie, of the BBC, produced a filmed report on the day of the bombing, as did Brent Sadler of the independent network news organisation ITN. In both reports, film of bomb damage was presented and the reporters concerned offered to-camera assessments and voiced-over commentary.

On 30 October of the same year, Conservative Party Central Office submitted a 21 page document to the BBC complaining in detail about the BBC handling of the coverage and asssessing it unfavourably not only in respect of the principle of 'impartiality' but in relation to ITN's coverage on the same day. The document also made points about related 'Libyan story' coverage on subsequent days. It was signed by Norman Tebbit (now Lord Tebbit) who was then Conservative Party Chairman and a member of the Cabinet in the Thatcher government. Among the points noted by Central Office were the following:[11]

1. The BBC in the opening lines of its 9 o'clock bulletin referred to the 'world-wide condemnation of the American air strike on Libya'. The Conservative document noted that 'the BBC gave particular emphasis to the Libyan case. The BBC made the principal feature of its news the "world-wide condemnation" of America – a subjective and emotive description which is repeated but never substantiated throughout the broadcast.'

2. The BBC gave undue emphasis to civilian casualties, 'one of Libya's major propaganda points'. This included sequences of damaged buidings to which the camera team had been taken by official Libyan guides (see Fig. 3.1; interestingly, a Libyan official appears to be objecting to filming in this shot). The document complained that whilst this 'Libyan-controlled footage' had been indicated as such in the ITN report, 'no similar qualification concerning Libyan control of news coverage was forthcoming from the BBC'.

Fig. 3.1. BBC *Nine O'Clock News* on the Tripoli bombings: Scenes of Devastation.

3. In a subsequent broadcast on 17 April, the BBC reported on the 'terror-ist' shooting of three hostages in the Lebanon. The terms of this report are criticised by the document as follows 'Strangely, whereas ITN said the hostages had been "murdered", the BBC merely said they were "shot through the head" and "killed", neutral terms which decriminalised the act.'

The document concluded its case by describing the overall impression which it found the bulletins left in the mind of the viewer, supporting its assessment that 'two different stories were being reported'. For ITN, the document said, the story was:

> 'that the Americans had carried out a raid on Libya, which they defended as a timely and necessary demonstration that the USA would not tolerate state terrorism, that the raid had been attacked by many others as a savage and unjustifiable use of force by a superpower against a small country and that by allowing British bases to be used for the raid, the British government had created a political storm at home'.

For the BBC, however, it was:

> 'that the Americans had committed an act of unjustifiable aggression which had resulted in the deaths of many innocent civilians, which had attracted world-wide condemnation and which had greatly increased international sympathy for Libya, and that by supporting the Americans the British Government had put British lives at risk.'

A week later, on 5 November, the BBC responded with a 24 page document prepared under the direction of its Editor of Television News, Ron Neil. In general, it was a detailed rebuttal of the Conservative charges. Many of the terms of this rebuttal are instructive for the links they have with the more general problem of the news as a form of socially situated authorship. They are best linked in with the points of criticism itemised above.

1. The BBC found that the phrase 'world-wide condemnation', used in the headlines of the 15 April news, was 'thoroughly substantiated during the broadcast'. It had been reported that only Canada, Israel and Britain supported the action. Comments deploring the action from France, West Germany and Spain were reported in the broadcast. The BBC notes that 'altogether about 100 countries throughout the world were to associate themselves with condemnation of the raid'.

2. The BBC assessed that the amount of time given to film of civilian damage was greater in the ITN bulletin than in the BBC one. It defended the integrity of its reporter, Kate Adie, who, it said, had regularly made reference to reporting restrictions imposed on foreign journalists in Tripoli and whose report on the night in question indicated quite clearly the limitations placed on her movements.

3. The BBC judged the Conservative report to be inaccurate in its description of 'shot through the head' as a neutral term:

'Shot through the head' is not a 'neutral term'. It is a horrific and graphic phrase describing to the audience the chilling nature of the murders...The [Conservative] document accepts that the phrase 'murdered' was used in the BBC closing headlines. Oddly [it] fails to mention that ITN's closing headlines use the word 'shot'...

Altogether, this selective list of matching points raises a number of questions which are not directly addressed by either party to the dispute. They can be brought out best by running through the points in sequence again, this time attending to the more general significance they have both for the idea of 'impartiality' and its realisation within the conventions of television news practice.

1. Just how many countries have to declare their disapproval of an action for it to be justifiably described as 'world-wide' is a matter of interpretation rather than determinate measurement, but it would appear that the BBC is able to document and defend its usage convincingly in this case. The use of generalising phrases serving to intensify the effect of a description (as, for instance, in describing the effects of industrial disputes) has been a frequent cause of complaint and dispute about news language. It does not usually receive such an explicit justification.

2. The way in which the voice-over accounts of a presenter cue viewers into a particular interpretation of 'controversial' images (here, controversial both in their degree of preselection by the Libyans *and* their likely effect) often results in a spoken discourse which 'moves around' a good deal, variously reading with and against what might be thought of as the self-evident meaning of the pictures. It is worth quoting the relevant passages of both BBC and ITN reports here, both of them offered over roughly equivalent sequences of damaged buildings (as in Fig. 3.1), wrecked cars and casualties on stretchers:

BBC:
Foreign journalists were confined to the hotel. Then as dawn broke, we were taken by officials to a residential district in the centre of the city. At least half a dozen bombs had been dropped in this area, flattening one apartment block...

ITN:
The Libyans are now trying to use the American raid as a propaganda weapon for themselves by concentrating news coverage on the civilian and not the military side of the attack. But these scenes of residential carnage can hardly do President Reagan's case any good.

The two journalists adopt contrasting approaches to the business of indicating the status to be given to the pictures. In the BBC report, their 'conditional' status is implied by the opening comments. The report then goes on to describe events in alignment with them. In the ITN case, the conditional status becomes fully explicit at the point the pictures are used, but the return to an aligned reading is marked by heavy irony and the use of one word ('carnage') the negative force of which (in terms of common usage) is a good deal stronger than any single descriptor in the BBC report. Clearly, the Conservative monitoring team were alarmed about the effect such pictures might have on public opinion (precisely the same situation arose in British discussion of the visual coverage given to the Baghdad shelter bombing during the Gulf conflict).[12] They want the power of the (in their view, misleading) pictures 'contained'. In their judgement, the speech in the ITN account does this sufficiently, displacing attention temporarily *on* to the propagandist motive, the BBC speech does not. In my earlier discussion of news images, I noted how television's ability to *particularise*, to show *embodiments*, was an important aspect of its communicative power. This often involves a part-for-whole relationship whereby the viewer is placed as witness to a particular scene, 'striking' or otherwise, whose significance is nevertheless to be read as much more general. Not suprisingly, this part-for-whole link, as here in the connection between specific scenes of devastation and an overall assessment of the raid, often becomes the focus of contention.

3. The question of whether or not 'shot through the head' is 'neutral' or 'horrific', 'graphic' and 'chilling' can only be decided contingently, in relation to the pattern of viewers' own responses. My own assessment, grounded in a sense of common usage, is that whilst it unlikely to be understood to 'de-criminalise' the act which it describes, neither is it likely to cause such a strong affective response as the BBC document indicates. How particular phrases work, evaluatively and affectively, at the level of their implications, is of course at the core of many disputes about news language but also of interest here is that *what is seen as a neutral usage is being criticised and what is seen as a negatively evaluative one is being defended*. This seems to reverse the accepted convention of arguments over impartiality, where it is most often evaluative usages which are the source of the complaint. What we see here is an indication that broadcasters themselves regard evaluative language as appropriate when they perceive no significant controversy among the audience over the nature of the evaluations. More speculatively, we also see an indication of a strong desire by the party of government to reduce evaluation where this is likely to run counter to government decisions and explanations and to encourage it where it is likely to be supportive. This position, essentially a strategic version of 'due impartiality' (or 'due partiality'!), often becomes the general policy adopted, whether explictly or not, by governments in time of war. Recent research suggests, however, that it commands less support among viewers than *open* defence of it as a news principle would require.[13]

The Tripoli study brings out aspects of the debatableness of news accounts with instructive sharpness. Its very untypicality in being an attack on news practices from the political Right, an attack thought serious enough in its implications for the BBC to warrant a quick and thorough response from them, puts into focus aspects of impartiality which do not usually 'go public'. Alongside the most influential academic case studies, notably the Glasgow Media Group's analysis of industrial relations coverage in the mid-1970s (Glasgow University Media Group, 1980), the Conservative claims lack quantitative soundness (many of their basic statistics were refuted by the BBC) and they move too swiftly to the level of hyperbole and speculation. Though the Conservative team had clearly been influenced by the concepts and methods of previous academic news analysis, their approach was seriously flawed in a number of ways, not least in its setting up of the contrast between BBC and ITN coverage (a contrast, one might guess, central to the desired effect of the report on the BBC and on public perceptions of it). This became extremely difficult to demonstrate in the context of the full transcripts.

The dispute also concerned what I earlier called the *univocal* and *multivocal* dimensions of impartiality. Univocal requirements are made upon the discourses of news teams, in framing, naming and picturing the elements of a news item. Multivocal requirements are made upon a news teams' accessing of non-professional views, mainly via reported speech, direct quotation and interview. In many official statements about impartiality, it is the multivocal dimension which is seen to exemplify the general principle ('give both sides' etc.), yet reporters themselves have to incorporate and synthesise information and viewpoints in their own accounts as well as describe what they have directly seen and heard. Although it would be wrong to underestimate the difficulties of achieving a 'fair' multivocal mix, it is the journalist's own privileged univocality which is most often the primary focus for dispute, as here and as in much of the concern over the reporting of major international events. Clearly, in any interpretation of a whole news item, multivocal and univocal elements will frequently be closely related factors, with the univocal working most often as the dominant mode in the opening and closing phases of an item and in the linking of elements within it.

Finally, the Tripoli instance bears upon debates about journalistic 'fairness' in respect of the assumptions which debaters make about the influence of news not only upon viewers' understandings of the specific matters being reported but on their grasp of more general features of politics and society. Thus, for instance, the Conservative monitoring team seem to fear that pictures of civilian damage in Tripoli will work to turn viewers against the American raid and perhaps against the British–American alliance. During the Gulf War, it was thought by some critics that the regular screening of 'target video' footage would have the effect of displacing the reality of the bombing ('sanitisation') and securing greater alignment with war aims at the same time as encouraging a broad desensitisation to military violence. During the British miner's strike of 1984–1985, it was widely assumed that the routine depiction of picketing miners from a camera point behind opposing police lines would have the effect of predisposing viewers against the striking miners' case, with perhaps more general consequences for political disposition. In none of these instances is it being proposed that the depictions are in any clear sense 'false'. It is their distortive effect upon viewers' overall understandings, their status as defective or insufficient 'part-for-whole' representations while being *credible merely as parts*, which is most often the source of anxiety and complaint.[14] Although it is true that the *effect* of the news upon viewers cannot confidently be predicted from an analysis of its form and contents, it is also clearly true that neither television journalism nor debate about it is worthwhile unless it is assumed that what is shown has some consequences for public understanding and belief. This assumption is best examined alongside more general theoretical issues concerning media influence and the character of viewing activity, and such an examination will form a principal part of Chapter 6.

Television News as a Form of Knowing

I suggested that the distinctive communicative forms of television news, constructed according to what is now an international 'recipe book', are a primary point of interconnection for the televisual, the social and the political. It is through the regular schedule of news that a particular configuration of 'public' and 'private' receives daily reinforcement, that public life becomes routinely accommodated within the domestic frame and the domestic setting at the same time as assumptions about this frame and setting inform the news-making process. Some commentators have seen one consequence of this as being that news 'normalises' life, by reporting events from a position of assured normality in a way which may serve to reproduce the interests of those holding economic and political power. Just how far this is the case will partly be a matter of the institutional relationship which news agencies have with political and economic interests, but certainly the kind of surveillance which the news offers has the potential to foreshorten perspectives within its own national optics and to 'integrate' that which is potentially too contradictory or too disturbing to be handled on its own terms. As part of their much-discussed analysis of the medium in *Reading Television* (1978), Fiske and Hartley saw this as a 'claw-back' function, by which 'out there' realities (particularly those of international affairs) were transformed into the terms of a domestic/televisual 'here'. In this sense, television is a *centripetal device*, and nowhere more obviously than in the news. Against this, however, has to be set the real efforts made by many television news teams to address the specificity and necessary otherness of the events they cover, in so doing often developing accounts quite strongly and explicitly refusing centripetal tendencies. As I write, some of the television coverage of the conflict in Bosnia would provide an example.[15]

The imperatives of television news and the forms through which these are realised turn on the nature of news as a commodity. In many national systems, this issue is very much part of the wider problem of popular journalism, a journalism that is able to retain its serious objectives whilst also retaining, and perhaps developing, its market attractiveness. One example of a shift away from seriousness and integrity in recent British news has been the attempted enhancement of narrative appeal by the insertion within some news reports of brief, dramatic scenes (for instance, parents watching the television announcement of the release of their daughter from a foreign prison), presented as 'live events'. This construction of certain aspects of the news into a theatre of self-performance follows precedents in the popular press and takes journalism more deeply into the territory of 'staging' than most previous conventions allowed for.

In this chapter, I have concerned myself primarily with the form taken by news programmes. There is, of course, another major area of journalistic output on television, linked closely to news bulletins. This is 'current affairs' programming, which grows out of both the newsroom model and the wider depictive and social range of the documentary. In certain formats, it is actually merged in with one or other of these.

The basic remit of such programmes has been to provide 'in depth' background to events in the news on a regular (including sometimes daily) basis. This has normally involved a mix of both extended studio interview/discussion and filmed reports, often constructed as short, self-contained documentaries. Where such output takes the form of a single topic treated by filmed report, it essentially becomes part of the loose genre of television documentary (so, for instance, Granada's *World in Action* is frequently placed in this category). Where several items are handled from a studio base, the connection back to news practice is obviously stronger.

Both in the United States and Britain, a further split here has been between the more serious forms of programme (the BBC's *Panorama* would be the classic example whilst its daily *Newsnight* would provide another, current model) and the more relaxed form of the 'news magazine', of which the BBC's *Tonight* was a pioneer in Britain. Magazine formats have become the focus of much recent development in the competition for 'watchability' and the search for successful blends of journalism, features and 'chat'.[16]

Internationally, shifts in provision and scheduling (for instance, the relatively recent arrival of 'breakfast television' in Britain) are making distinctions in this area even harder to maintain. The changing formal character of 'current affairs' output and its (still) distinctive occupying of a space between news and documentary, grounded in the agenda of the one yet possessing something of the scope of the other, deserves more attention, including historical analysis. Although not usually having the popularity of the main news programmes, 'serious current affairs' has frequently had a considerable impact upon the discussion and management of political and social issues.

I have suggested that the 'look' of the news is one of fragmentary narrativisation, caught as its discourse is between a narrative and expositional aesthetic, between its informational function and being 'pleasing'. News visualisation, though it may offer the promise of 'seeing it for yourself' is, for reasons which I have outlined, often a matter of discontinuities and indirectness, despite the ingenuity, licence (and occasional downright dishonesty) of news teams. The problems of 'impartiality' in principle *and* in practice are great but, I have wanted to argue, they are not terminal and the notion needs to be defended at the same time as the constraints on its realisation need open recognition. In the next chapter, I shall look at an area of television, 'documentary', which has sometimes been seen as a form of expanded news, but which is also frequently regarded as a special sub-branch of drama.

4

CIVIC VISIONS: FORMS OF DOCUMENTARY

A narrow definition of 'documentary' might indicate that, assessed in terms of their frequency and positioning in channel schedules and the audience figures they routinely attract, documentary programmes are not a major area of popular television output. However, a broader definition would see 'documentarism' as one of the medium's defining modes. Programmes which offer depictions of actuality, with or without exposition, have always been central to television's appeal. The popular 'documentarism' of the travel programme, certain kinds of sports footage and the wildlife series has now been joined by that of the 'video diary' or, as we saw in Chapter 1, of the 'real life drama' series, to constitute an outer ring of documentarist production, surrounding a core of non-fiction output to which the generic label 'documentary' is routinely applied by the industry itself. As I suggested at the end of the last chapter, 'current affairs' programming is sometimes uncertainly placed between having its own identity and being a subgenre of documentary. Core documentary on television, however entertaining it is also required to be, almost always works with a 'serious' expositional (and frequently journalistic) purpose and, in Britain at least, this purpose has often been that of social inquiry set against a recognised (and visualised) context of economic inequality, social class difference and social change, together with the consequent 'problems' thus produced.

The term 'documentary' has widely been regarded as an unsatisfactory one since the pioneer film maker John Grierson first used it of *Moana* – a film made about life on a South Sea Island – in 1926. His coinage was partly derivative from the French 'documentaire', a term frequently used of travel films. However, although the extraordinarily wide range of different production methods, forms and intentions which it now covers often makes it a hazardous classification, there is enough 'family resemblance' discernible between the different types of film-making activity subsumed under its label to ensure its continued use both within the industry and amongst the public and critics. While in cinema studies, given the dominance of fictional work, the use of a term like 'non-fiction film' may be a useful, more forthright alternative, the idea of 'non-fiction programming' is far too broad to be usable as a critical notion in relation to television.

Grierson himself recognised the term lacked precision but, like everyone else since, he had difficulty in coming up with anything better. 'Documentary is a clumsy term, but let it stand' he wrote.[2] 'Documentary' meant that a particular film was to be regarded primarily as a 'document', a text whose interest lay in its referentiality, in what it indicated about the world through its sounds and images. Within Grierson's critical vocabulary, such documentation was in contrast both to the form and the content taken by the majority of acted and scripted feature films, with what he viewed disapprovingly as their elaborately 'escapist' appeal and their often marked unreality of setting. Film can, of course, 'document' through dramatic reconstruction, through interviewee accounts or through the speech exposition of a presenter, all of which are communicative modes widely used throughout the history of documentary film and television. However, the core mode of documentation from the 1930s through to today is the employment of the *recorded images and sounds of actuality* to provide the viewer with a distinctive kind of 'seeing' and 'hearing' experience, a distinctive means of knowledge. Documentary was grounded in an appeal to *sensory evidence*.

Various ideas of 'truth' and 'reality' have gathered around definitions of documentary principle and practice, sometimes attracting counter-ideas of 'deception' and 'artifice', but the notion of the 'evidential' provides the best place from which to start an examination of this type of programme making. As we saw in Chapter 1, the evidentiary properties of television and of film are related to their capacities, as recording technologies, to produce a 'trace' of the physical world in sounds and images. They thereby have an 'iconic' status which (though it is being undercut by the electronic technology of image processing) carries with it a level of *referential guarantee*. Within many documentary productions, this iconicity is used to implicate the viewer, both imaginatively and cognitively, as a witness to a heard and seen 'real'. It is on the basis of this relationship to apprehended realities that the other discourses of documentary – commentative, investigative, evaluative – are built. The way in which the base is established and the building work done across the broad range of documentary methods and styles involves a *series of transformations*. 'Transformation' was the term Stuart Hall employed as a central idea in his analysis of how television worked as a *medium*, acting as an agency of change as well as of continuity and of connection. It is a notion which is well suited to an analysis of the phases of documentary production.

Documentary Production as a Series of Transformations

In the diagram below, the documentary process is depicted as one occurring across four stages, linked together by three moments or phases of production.

realities → pro-filmic events → recorded material → programme

    ↑   ↑   ↑

scripting/organisation   shooting   editing

If we take the three production phases in turn, we can examine how each does its transformative work.

Phase 1. Scripting and Organisation

Out of the range of possible kinds of reality open to documentary treatment, a topic is chosen as the subject of a film or programme. But how will this topic be depicted in particular images and sounds? The initial decision here concerns what to film, who to film and what kinds of sound (including speech) to record. No matter whether the topic is an abstract one (for example, loneliness in student communities) or a physically grounded one (for example, the problem of heavy traffic in rural areas), a _strategy of representation and of visualisation_ is required. Within this strategy, certain people, events, places, etc. will be selected for filming as being somehow 'typical' of more general circumstances, even if this typicality is only implicit in the programme rather than a declared premise of it. Unless the programme is to consist entirely of interview segments linked by commentary, the selection needs to be thought through in terms of the pictures (of places, of things, of actions) which will best objectify the abstract and instantiate the general. What results from this set of decisions, once availability and practical considerations have been taken into account, is a selection of entities from the physical and human world at which or at whom the camera and the microphone will be pointed. This is the basis of what can usefully be identified as the *pro-filmic* stage of documentary making, by which time much creative selectivity has already been exercised. The expansiveness of 'the real' (even around a quite specific topic) is already being got into shape for its transformation into coherent data, grounded in 'the seen'.

Phase 2. Shooting

Although previous (Phase 1) work will have established what to shoot, where and when, the direction of the shooting itself will also usually involve some management of the pro-filmic. So, for instance, an unemployed man might be 'directed' in the timing and movements involved in a trip to the postbox with a job application letter or a refugee mother might be 'directed' as she prepares and serves a meal for her family. The degree of spatial and temporal management of pro-filmic activities (ostensibly activities which are only 'observed' by the documentary team) will vary considerably in relation to their nature and complexity and to the type of depiction of them which the programme seeks to offer. Its projected naturalism and continuity, its duration and its possible intercutting with other material or its mixing with voiced-over speech will be factors here. Certain sequences may have to be rehearsed and, as in fiction filming, many actions may have to be repeated in order for a one-camera production team to get visual continuity by combining shots taken from several viewpoints. The people being filmed are thereby positioned as 'actors of themselves' within these adjustments, designed to fine-tune reality for photographic or electronic 'capture'. Almost certainly they will be encouraged not to recognise the camera's presence, since the illusion of unseen onlooking is central to conventional documentary aesthetics.

All these activities can be regarded as contributing to the realisation of pro-filmic events and circumstances, the initial features of which were decided in Phase 1. However, the principal business of Phase 2 is that of 'recording' itself. Here, a whole range of decisions about the position, angle and movement of the camera, the type and number of shots to be taken, the lighting to be used and the kind of sound recordings to be made will be implemented. It is at this point that an *aesthetics* of representation becomes active, as a (by now, managed) reality-in-process is turned both into data and expression; a stabilisation, on film or video, of sights and sounds and also, inscribed within the making of the likenesses, a *way* of seeing and hearing. Perhaps the most important, creative (and often most controversial) stage is still to come, but a fundamental and irreversible translation has occurred and bits of reality are now in cans and boxes as *raw material*.

Phase 3. Editing

This phase, more comprehensively regarded as 'post-production', leads up to the final, transmitted programme. The various shots taken on location are selectively worked into sequences, with synchronised sound or voice-over and, in some cases, with a music soundtrack. Any pre-shot material (e.g. library film) is added, as the overall communicative organisation, already there on paper, is implemented, often with considerable amendments in the light of the 'strength and direction' of the material obtained. The proportion of argument to evidence, the movement across space and time (the latter perhaps involving chronological sequences), the introduction of conflicting viewpoints, the 'weighting' of the programme, explicitly or otherwise, in its findings and evaluations, all are interlinked matters of concern here. Final decisions are made about how to deploy material across the length of the programme (certain scenes perhaps being returned to; interviews perhaps being 'sliced' into sections and dispersed to several points). In particular, the question of how to 'open' is posed. What resonant shot or section of interview comment or phrase of spoken commentary provides the most engaging way in? And then, how to close? Where to leave the viewer at the end, in terms both of knowledge and of feelings about the topic as it continues to exist in the world, outside the temporary, intensive framing of the documentary 'window'?

Such a broad outline ignores the often radical differences of method and form to be found in current documentary, but it brings out well the elements which are common to many and it highlights some of those aspects which have made documentaries so controversial a form of programme making. In fact, the scheme could be extended beyond the fourth stage – the screened programme – to a fifth – the understanding and significance given to it by viewers. This would involve a further phase of transformation – the interpretative activities of the viewers, drawing on their previous knowledge, dispositions and values. That programmes 'mean' different things to different viewers, both at the level of primary comprehension and at the level of attributed significance, is well established in media research (Chapter 6 discusses some of the implications of this). Many disputes over the 'fairness' and truthfulness of documentary programmes involve differences of opinion as to actually what was being 'said'. As we saw in Chapter 3, this is also true of disputes about news. However, documentary is a more symbolically expansive form than news, able to develop a range and density of depiction which becomes more open to interpretative variation as it extends beyond direct exposition into the implicit and the associational, often in the process touching on imaginative territories more closely associated with narrative fiction. I shall say something about the characteristic form taken by public disputes over documentary portrayal at the end of this chapter.

I want to consider both established and emerging aspects of documentarism by using a number of subheads which help to identify some its interrelated components. First of all, though, given its lineage in cinema and radio, it is worthwhile considering briefly the social history of documentary as a major genre of public communication.

The Formation of Television Documentary

Documentary on television now draws on internationally familiar conventions. These conventions constitute a subgeneric system of socio-aesthetic 'recipes', each of which carries its implications for the particular kind of 'hearing and looking' experience offered to the viewer. The nature of television sound and image and the character of the medium as a domestic service most frequently operating through scheduled programming have influenced the way in which the documentary has been able to develop within it. However, the precedents of cinema and of radio documentary were strong ones in the formation of television work and they still show through in contemporary developments.

The Precedent of Documentary Cinema

The British documentary cinema movement of the 1930s, centred on John Grierson and the team of directors who worked with him successively at the Empire Marketing Board, the GPO Film Unit and at the Crown Film Unit, provided what was undoubtedly the most powerful direct influence on television documentary.[3] Although it could be disputed what precisely should be included in the 'canon', major pre-war films would include *Song of Ceylon* (1933), *Industrial Britain* (1931), *Coalface* (1935), *Housing Problems* (1935) and *Nightmail* (1936). The 1930s movement has been the subject of intensive recent scholarship and any analysis of its work is obviously beyond both the scope and purpose of this chapter. It may nevertheless be useful to identify the principal aesthetic and social principles which it established as central to the 'documentary approach', principles which have so often been cited, defended and attacked in relation to subsequent films and programmes as well as in relation to these pioneering productions themselves.

The films made by those involved in the 1930s 'movement' were the result of what now seems a rather strange mix of motives, very much of the period. There was, first of all, a very strong interest in developing film as an art form, and (following European examples) in doing so by taking 'real life' subjects as the basis for 'creative interpretation'. This aesthetic impulse, broadly realist in orientation but also influenced by modernist form (so not at all committed to the idea of a simple 'transparency' and quite prepared to use the images and sounds of the real as the elements of a 'film language'), was related to a belief in film's capacities as a medium of social revelation and of democratic development. Film could engage people with, and *in*, the political and social adventure of modern industrial society, an adventure which involved recognition of new levels of economic interdependency between social groups and which brought with it the need for a revised sense of national community. There was a new respect for the various work skills by which a modern society sustained itself, and a declared belief in modern citizenship, unprejudiced by older, class hierarchic values and newly committed to exploring 'ordinary life' as part of a proper representation of community and nation.

However, yet another element in the mix was an interest in the new role played by promotion and publicity within the modern political and social order. One aspect of this is apparent in the use of film as an agency of popular, civic education. Such films were to be devices not only of instruction and revelation but also of persuasion, they were to be *propagandist* in the cause of democracy. But the interest in promotional communication, together with the broadly optimistic perspective on national development held by many of the film makers ('a modern Britain in a changing world'), also fitted in well – perhaps too well – with the requirements of the funding base which the movement relied upon. This base was essentially provided from organisations (including those of the State) seeking to promote their product and their corporate image through the films, albeit indirectly. So the overall socio-aesthetic character of the documentary movement was partly made up of tensions, ones not always successfully reconciled in the films themselves. Realist in general philosophy yet also interested in modernist 'experiment', ethnographically exploratory yet didactic, democratic yet propagandist, egalitarian yet often condescending, analytic yet often celebratory – the tensions are multiple. They are also often productive in giving many of the documentaries an ambivalence which is one source of their continuing distinctiveness and interest, putting them at some distance from the dullness and complacency of standard 'official information' films of the period.

But perhaps the most important tension at work within the movement (one that gets implicated in most of the others) is the one between 'documentary as art' and 'documentary as report'. The play-off between form-led aesthetic experimentation and a topic-led concern to address social reality and social problems (a play-off with implications not only for communicative form but for communicative aims and intended audiences) was a major factor in determining differences of directorial practice. Finally, it figured in disagreements which developed between group members about overall documentary direction (the contrast between an aesthetically self-conscious film like *Coalface* and a 'reportage' work like *Housing Problems* is illuminating here). This issue, though rarely so pronounced, has been a continuing one in the formation of documentary television, negotiated in various ways in relation to technological change and the shifts of generic development.

Radio Features and the Accessed Voice

The film documentaries made under corporate sponsorship during the 1930s, and then as part of the Government's Home Front propaganda during World War II, thus provided television with a number of models for turning the camera into a 'public eye', for its visualisation of the social world. Many of those who had worked in documentary film subsequently became members of the BBC's documentary department after the war and, at least initially, saw the television documentary as continuing directly in the tradition established by the film movement. The distinguished film maker Paul Rotha, appointed Head of Documentaries in 1953, noted the 'paramount importance' which nightly access to a mass audience had for 'those who still believe that documentary has a specific social job to do'.[4]

But there was another important influence at work in early television documentary. During the 1930s, members of the features department of BBC radio had developed ways of building programmes around actuality sound and speech which were finally to be as important a point of reference and creative stimulus for television documentary as the cinematic precedent. With few exceptions (*Housing Problems* being notable here) documentary cinema had not used the interview as a primary informational device. This was largely due to technical limitations, and consequent practical difficulties, in the recording of synchronised sound on location. However, the result was an aesthetic of documentation which, while it sought to *depict* social realities, was unable to explore social experience except insofar as this could either be visually rendered or reported at second-hand. A degree of 'distance' inevitably opened up between depicted world and viewer, a distance which could only be further underlined by the use of a spoken commentary coming, as it were, from 'outside the frame' and objectifying that which was seen within it.

By the very need to work primarily through speech, radio features' producers had pioneered location interviews and had, within a variety of innovative programmes, placed 'ordinary talk' recorded on location right at the centre of their programme design.[5] Even though such early examples of the interview (often broadcast as direct 'testimony') sometimes sound nervous and stilted alongside the speech of broadcasting today, the use of participant talk realigned the relationship between portrayed subject and listener. It allowed the mediation of a world which was at least partly described and reflected upon in the terms of those portrayed rather than those of the portrayers. The documentary perspective moved from one model (the cinematic), which was emphatically visual and external to another (radio features), which had a degree of access to the 'interior' of social process, including ordinary experience. The public character of the relationship between portrayers, portrayed and audience underwent a change as a consequence; 'access' of one kind or another became written into expectations about what broadcast documentary did. Many of the important developments in television documentarism, in the formative period and since, differ from the cinematic tradition in that, like radio features, they too are grounded in the use of ordinary speech, either in forms of interview or in 'overheard' exchange.

The Generic System of Television Documentary

Quite quickly, the conditions of documentary production within television established an aesthetic order different from that of cinema. Programmes were frequently made within a series format. Along with this went the use of regularly scheduled spots, a named reporter/presenter who appeared (and often 'featured') within the programme, a style of more personalised, intimate address and a recognition of the fact that most viewers were sitting at home and, depending on the placing of the programme in the schedule, might be pleased to see the topic treated in a 'lively' way as well as informatively. The arrival of competition in 1955, with ITV's network being available to viewers as well as the BBC, pushed the development of documentary television further into innovation across a wide range of different formats and styles, creating inter-generic links with drama, with news and current affairs, and with the various 'magazine' programmes then being devised as a way of mixing 'serious' and 'light' elements.[6]

One of the most important determinants of the social and aesthetic range of documentary in this period was the extent to which it was regarded within broadcasting institutions as a form of journalism. Seen thus, certain kinds of news-related subjects began to seem more appropriate than less topical themes and documentary styles organised around the 'quest' of a presenter/reporter, often delving 'behind the headlines', became dominant. For those who regarded the documentary as essentially a director's form, as a space for authoring a kind of 'visual essay', the aesthetic limitations imposed by journalistic conventions were often regarded as a threat. Two subgenres which created space for extending documentary language beyond the journalistic were drama-documentary and the 'fly-on-the-wall' style of observationalism, the latter developing (with considerable modification) out of the 1960s' *cinema verité* movement in France.[7] Both gained large audiences and critical prominence in the 1960s and both relied extensively, though in different ways, on the extended opportunities for 'location naturalism' which lightweight 16 mm cameras brought with them.

Though no longer so controversial *per se*, partly because of their development into a conventional subgenre, drama-documentaries still find a regular and high-profile place in the broadcast schedules. 'Fly-on-the-wall', on the other hand, is the broad designation (less pretentious than *vérité* though perhaps equally misleading) for one of the most successful and long-running strands of documentary television. It is a strand which has gone through a number of phases of innovation and development. These have left its basic communicative idea and appeal largely unchanged however, if a good deal less novel than when the first such programmes appeared on the screen.

I have outlined briefly the general transformative processes involved in producing documentary television and noted some of the influences at work as the distinctive identity and range of television documentary came to be established. I now want to explore further five aspects of communicative principle and practice – observation, interview, dramatisation, *mise-en-scène* and exposition – which have given documentary work such public appeal, influence and controversiality.[8]

Elements of Documentary

Observation

The idea of unseen observation, and then the communicative organisation of this through a variety of devices, are central to documentary aesthetics. Such an idea has implications both for the pleasure of watching documentaries and for the kinds of knowing which they generate. Unseen observation is, as I shall argue in more detail later, the 'enabling fiction' upon which many documentaries depend. Sequences of observation are common to most kinds of documentary programme, whilst in some an observational mode becomes the principal if not exclusive means of portrayal. Grounded, with few exceptions, in the pretence that those portrayed are unaware of the camera's presence, the observational mode provides viewers with a vicarious experience of the real – an experience of witness – against which to form a response. This does not require that they believe that somehow the camera *was* unseen (although the watching of observational sequences certainly encourages the temporary illusion that this is so, together with some of its voyeurist consequences). What they have to believe is that nothing significant would have changed had the camera not been there, thereby legitimating the way in which its absence is pretended. This is a belief in the event-which-might-have-been, one which the very production of the 'pro-filmic' makes a matter solely for speculation and trust since what *might* have happened had the camera not been there is not available and never can be for a television audience.

What would be the consequence of *allowing* the recognition of the camera by participants? First of all, it would have the effect, in many instances, of de-objectifying the documentary 'look' at the world, thereby implicating the production team and, via the camera lens, the viewer, in an uncertain relationship of mutual subjectivity with participants. Within a framing of mutual observation, the action of the participants would implicitly take on an aspect of 'display' such as to render certain observed activities (for instance, casual asides in a shop whilst making a purchase, an exchange between two policeman on the beat) awkwardly false, an act in dissonance with a pro-filmic which, elsewhere, was openly proclaiming its status *as performance.*

Paradoxically, the observational mode places the viewer in relationship to 'real action' much closer to that of screen fiction than to that of primary perception. In most cases in everyday life, the *acknowledgement* of an observer by the observed would very much be expected, to the point of stopping ongoing behaviour or changing its nature. The 'trick' of observationalism thus allows distinct kinds of opportunity for depiction. The director can choose either to let significance be delivered self-evidently (perhaps with recorded speech between participants framed as 'overheard' and naturally occurring within the observed scene) or to run voice-over speech across the image track, thereby inserting a 'bridge' of direct address between observed scene and viewer. This latter procedure increases the informational productivity of the sequence at the same time as it reduces the spectatorial intensities of observational viewing, risking a diminishing of what is shown to a mere illustration of what is being said. Another option, the use of participant voice-over across observed sequences, is less intrusive insofar as it has a generation point within the frame, though it, once again, risks compromising the space for scrutiny, and the space for viewer self-sufficiency, ostensibly made available by unaccompanied observationalism. However, whereas presenter voice-over further reinforces the objectification of depicted persons and events, making them a matter of openly 'public' scrutiny, participant voice-over can powerfully subjectify and interiorise what is in the image, perhaps displacing it from immediacy and making it a basis for speaker self-reflection.

Visually, although the plane of the observed action shares features with the plane of action in narrative fiction, there are important differences. In much observational documentary, all persons are equally objectified by the camera, precisely as objects of observation. In narrative fiction, extensive use of close-up, shot-reverse-shot in conversational exchange and the use of the point-of-view shot to align viewing with the gaze of one of the people within the action, all work to subjectivise aspects of setting and circumstance. This has often powerful consequences for the viewing relationships which viewers develop with those portrayed on the screen.

However, despite the gap between documentary representations of persons and the portrayal of 'characters' in fiction, some recent observational programmes have attempted to construct visualisations which draw on modified elements of fictional language. There are clear points of risk here. For instance, to bring the viewer too comprehensively into the space of observed action, dispersing viewpoints and shots in accordance with its movement, would be to break precisely with that sense of 'onlooking' which certifies what is seen as evidential (not manufactured for the cameras) and which is necessarily experienced imaginatively as viewing 'at a distance', however small this distance may sometimes be. With large public events (for instance, a rally or a riot) the question of how onlooking distance squares with the evidential trustworthiness of what is seen hardly arises. The more intimate the sphere of life made available to the public gaze however (for instance, a family argument in a kitchen), the more this relationship becomes a potential problem. So although observational scenes of domestic life are now routine on British television, scenes between observed subjects taking place in cars, for instance, or in bedrooms, would raise to a possible crisis point the question of the credibility of the image.

Similarly, to adopt too striking a *styling* of the observational image, using tracking shots, slow pans, zooms, etc., works against the idea that the image has been 'captured' adventurously and perhaps somewhat furtively from the ongoing real. Short observational sequences in documentaries constructed within a spoken, direct address structure can develop as highly stylised 'little scenes from life' with more impunity than programmes whose primary mode is observational. Within the former structure, the 'little scene' becomes illustrative (secondary to the exposition; a kind of moving tableau) rather than evidential (the actual basis for exposition and, perhaps, self-sufficient as communication without it). In a structure grounded in observationalism, depictive integrity (the grounds for viewer *trust*) is certified in the uneven, awkward framing of action; the slight delays in following its movement; the necessary distance from it and the general unavailability of cutaway shots to anticipate what is to come (e.g. doors, hands, objects to be used). That the viewer is intermittently aware of a camera at work in the production of their 'view' does not disrupt engagement with the viewed. But too frequent a noting of just *how* this 'view' is being constructed may well do.

As I noted earlier, the observational mode has become central to a whole range of documentary styles (and also to the documentarist elements in other forms, for example in news reports and in travel programmes). Its apparent discursive minimalism provides programmes with a strongly 'evidentiary' or possibly 'illustrative' (see above) level of visualisation. Around this core, secondary elements, interpretative and evaluative, can be organised. What it offers for viewers is the spectatorial appeal of observing present-tense realities from a 'safe' position (a position whose presence has been aesthetically erased from the plane of observation). This an experience which gives distinctive onlooking pleasures, of a kind related to those involved in attending to dramatic performance, as well as the satisfactions of independent judgement in relation to presented evidence.

Observation is both a 'direct' and an 'indirect' communicative mode: 'indirect' in its placing of viewers as witnesses of speech and action which they are largely left to construe into significance through their own interpretative work; 'direct' insofar as, assuming an 'intention-to-mean' on the part of the production team, such a method might be seen as merely a strategy of 'soft sell', avoiding the risks of perceived partiality carried by more direct exposition but nevertheless effectively supporting certain evaluations and prompting particular ways of classifying and relating what is said and shown. To take this latter approach, however, assumes a more self-consciously propositional 'core' to depiction, a narrower agenda concerning both the topic and the materials of its representation, than most documentarists working in this way declare themselves to have. Notwithstanding such denials of implicit 'point making', wherever observationalism is used *illustratively*, embedded as a sequence within an exposition using other modes of address, the suspicion will linger that the requirement for it to 'fit in' with what is proposed more directly elsewhere is one which overrides all other criteria brought to its selection, shooting and editing.

The observational mode, variously combined with expositional forms (interview, voice-over, to-camera presentation), becomes the central principle of *vérité*-style programmes, to the point that in many such programmes all discourses external to the plane of observed action (for instance, presenter speech of any kind and speech in response to interview questioning) are excluded. Additionally, directors working within such formats, though they vary considerably in philosophy, have generally eschewed any directorial management of the action to be 'observed', thus imposing quite strict limitations on the kind of scene which is likely to be available for recording (unlike in the more conventional, short 'observational' sequences of mainstream documentary which, as I noted above, can be, and often are, fully managed and rehearsed for the camera).[9] As many commentators have observed, the 'purist' approach, when sustained across the full length of a programme, may run into a number of difficulties with its viewers. Dependence on the close observation of the particular without expositional support increases the possibility of incoherence and boredom, in relation both to observed particularity ('what is going on here?') and to the significance of *this* particularity for the general *topic* (for instance, 'loneliness', naval training, the operations of the vice squad) into which it is an exploration. Ironically, anxiety about this may drive the 'purist' production team into putting greater emphasis on the hidden transformations of post-production, using high ratios of film shot to film screened (30:1 is not uncommon in this kind of work) to edit the piece into coherence and watchability through a set of practices which are finally every bit as *authorial*, if differently so, as those of heavily directed shooting.

Perhaps it is for this reason that recent British television *vérité* has begun to introduce both presentational and interview elements into the flow of its observational depictions, sometimes affording them a degree of 'naturalisation' within the frame of observed action (for example, in-shot interview speech whilst the interviewee is driving a vehicle, thereby avoiding the problem of their own 'look' and also embedding their speech, directed out of frame, in a context of in-frame action).

As I write, the most recent attempt to rework observationalism in Britain is the BBC series *The Living Soap*, in which students sharing a house are filmed in their weekly activities. This draws on precedents for domestic *vérité* (such as the BBC's *The Family*, 1972) but introduces elements of 'access' programming too, insofar as the students themselves voice-over much of the material and also do short to-camera pieces from a room in the house rigged for this purpose. The mixing of modes, involving varying kinds of relationship with what is going on but implicating the subjects deeply in their portrayal, has received a mixed reception by critics and audiences. As a result of its year-long run and the transmitting of earlier episodes whilst later ones are being made, the series has begun to feature reactions to itself. Not only have some of the students developed self-consciously 'star'-like personas (along the lines of soap celebrities) but local prejudice against them has resulted in abuse and attacks on the house. All in all, this has turned out to be an extremely awkward venture in the revision of documentary viewing relations.

Interview

Interview speech is a major mode of television documentarism. It contrasts directly with the observational mode in that it is openly interventionist. This intervention is signalled both verbally and visually. Speech is elicited by questioning and the speaker usually either addresses an in-shot inter-viewer or looks 'out' in three-quarter profile. When interview speech is used as voice-over across sequences of participant action, the talk relates to (and perhaps describes) what is in the pictures. Nevertheless, the communicative address is still outwards, as direct address to a viewer. But although the interview breaks with the idea of a plane of ongoing action simply present to an unacknowledged camera, its general mode of presen-tation depends on a sensitive play-off between its status as public speak-ing and its status as an overheard exchange between two individuals. In respect of the latter, the fact that is *calculatedly and self-consciously* overheard makes it communicatively different from speech in the obser-vational mode, where no such calculation is presumed and, indeed, where it would undercut the efficacy of that mode were it to be so. Clearly, inter-viewees will vary in the extent to which they feel able to move from supplying 'answers' produced within the professionalised conventions of overhearing to supplying answers which attempt a more direct commu-nication with the audience. Private citizens questioned on matters of direct personal concern are far less likely than politicians to make such shifts, which can either be carried out as an implicit 'tactical switch' or explicitly marked as a temporary and partial reconfiguration of the communicative relationship (as in phrases like 'I'm sure many people listening to that question will want to ask. . .').

The interview as a *method* for eliciting speech for documentary is not the same as the interview as a mode of discourse within the finished programme. The relationship of the one with the other varies and with this go variations in the kinds of social relations obtaining between speak-ers and viewers. At one extreme, there is the use of fragments of inter-viewee utterance at several different points throughout a programme, with no indication of the kind of questions used to prompt such talk and little sense of the context in which the talk was produced (no sense at all in the case of speech being used entirely as voice-over). At the other, there is the presentation of the interview itself as a social episode within the documen-tary, involving an initial encounter (perhaps an exchange of greetings) between interviewer and interviewee and a full depiction of the setting and circumstances within which subsequent talk takes place.[10] This latter mode of presentation moves towards a modified form of 'observational-ism' although, unlike the kinds of production in that mode discussed above, it is one in which what the viewer is invited to observe and is essen-tially a 'television event' (the status of which is grounded in the visible presence of the presenter) rather than extra-televisual reality. However naturalistically such an interview may be depicted (location settings, continuity of action, markers of the passage of time etc.) the question of television's intervention exerting a modifying effect on behaviour (including speech) does not arise at all. It has no grounds for doing so, given that the action is television initiated from the start and there is little or no behaviour depicted which has its immediate motives *outside* of television's own requirements.

It is interesting to consider what alternatives exist to the duality of the interview as public speaking organised as private exchange. Two options present themselves immediately. First of all, a reporter could simply give an account of what people had said. This would deny visual depiction to those whose speech was used, present difficulties of communicative organisation (for instance, judging the length of such accounts that viewers would find it acceptable to listen to) and pose questions not only about the accuracy of reported speech summary but, if citation of direct speech were used, about the accuracy of this to the original utterances (the pauses, the stressing, the cadences etc.). It would also radically, and perhaps catastrophically, reduce the evidentiary status of the material. Alternatively, the interviewee could be invited directly to address what they say to the camera and the viewer rather than to the interviewer. But this option runs into two problems. First of all, 'ordinary' interviewees usually have no *specific* communicative project other than their willingness to answer questions about their experiences or views. In this sense, their utterance is 'dependent speech' and its obvious and most appropriate form is an answer to the person who asked the question. Secondly, the delivery of speech to a camera lens requires an interviewee to have an ease and competence in a kind of professional public address which would frequently be found wanting. This could serve only to reduce the effectiveness of what was said and, in most cases, it would act as a considerable constraint on the interviewee's expressive opportunities. So the 'duality' of the interview, together with its semi-fraudulent aesthetics, is likely to remain a central feature of documentary language and thereby an indispensible element of public communication.

This allowed, the precise form of the conduct and representation of interview sequences has been the focus of recent development. For instance, the visualisation of interviews raises a number of pressing questions about *personal* depiction in documentary. Amongst these are questions about the communicative status of interviewees within the documentary as a whole, the settings in which they speak and the way in which they are established and shot as speakers within these settings.

In strongly presenter-led programmes, interviewees can be heavily subordinated to the exposition, appearing merely to lend eye witness or brief experiential corroboration to an account fashioned essentially from other information sources. Such programmes sometimes give the impression of simply 'appropriating' the speech of the interviewee for a project grounded elsewhere, a project of which the interviewee is unaware. Given the scale of revision to which treatments are sometimes subjected in postproduction, it is not hard to see why interviewees are occasionally suprised and angry to find themselves speaking on screen within the framing terms of a topic or subtopic other than that which they had been invited to believe provided the grounds for their interview. It is important for the public integrity of the form that documentary makers do not routinely become agents of interviewee interests (an impossible task anyway, given the various directions these might take within any one documentary). However, the emergence of 'access documentaries', in which the expression of ordinary and often marginalised experience becomes the primary directorial goal, has considerably developed the aesthetics of interviewee portrayal (for instance, in respect of settings, compositions and forms of editing) and, at the same time, 'access' approaches have tried to be more open about the social relations of the interview method. Such films frequently feature a sequence of caption-identified interviewees right at the start, establishing them as central within the structure and aims of the piece.[11] Depending on the subject of their speech, a reinforcement of their status is achieved through allowing what would, by convention, be regarded as 'extended' periods of talk, with opportunities for self-correction, repetition and the exercising of a local control over the direction of the topic not normally extended in mainstream shooting and post-production practice. Moreover, the visual framing of the speaking itself often works 'with' rather than 'upon' what is said, eschewing that kind of objectifying surveillance of the face, tightening up around emotional display and 'meaningful' cutaways (nervous hands, awkward posture) which are to be found in many mainstream productions.

It is likely that some aspects of this kind of more supportive representation of accessed speakers will become assimilated into a broader range of output. As I remarked earlier, however, it would clearly be a mistake to suppose that the public project of documentary is best served by privileging accessees over any sense of the independent integrity of the topic or of responsibilities to the viewer.

In my scheme of documentary transformation, I referred to the way in which the use of interviews within the structure of a programme can vary considerably, even given the same practice at the time of preparation and shooting. The edited interview can be used in its entirety at one place in the programme or it can be divided into a number of sequences, even down to one-phrase units, placed at different points according to the logic of exposition being followed. The more it is used in dispersed form, the less opportunity there is for what is said to achieve a significance which is informed by the *terms of the interviewee* and the more likely it is that interviewees will regard their final 'performances' as, intentionally or otherwise, to be taken 'out of context'. However, preserving the integrity of interview-as-method in interview-as-screened, by eschewing 'slicing' and only using an interviewee once, dictates a logic of structure in which the sequential treatment of multiple themes, or the development of a chronology of events across a number of witnesses, is seriously restricted in its portrayal. Subordination of interviewees to programme logics is a continuing requirement in documentaries other than those in which 'access' is the principal communicative goal. Even here, of course, subordination may well occur.

Dramatisation

'Dramatisation' is a level of nearly all documentary production in the sense that it is a consequence of that 'enabling fiction' referred to above, by which things appear to be occurring naturally in front of the camera and unaware of its presence. Within this routine dramatisation, there occurs what the documentary scholar Bill Nichols has called 'virtual performance' (Nichols, 1991, p. 122), as people play themselves before the cameras with greater or lesser degrees of motivated adjustment. However, the idea of 'dramatisation' is most often associated with programmes in which the generic conventions of documentary *exposition* are put in some combination with those of dramatic *narrative*. Although there are now a number of 'recipes' for drama–doc combination established on both sides of the Atlantic, it is useful to distinguish between those which give primacy to a documentary base, which then receives a dramatic realisation (dramatised documentaries), and those which are primarily playscripts, receiving a treatment drawing variously on documentary's depictive conventions and the viewing relations associated with these (documentary dramas).

The latter became the centre of much academic and public debate in Britain during the 1960s and 1970s, when a number of politically radical writers and directors were involved in different kinds of realist drama production, all of which projected politically and socially controversial themes. Given the general adoption, in this work, of a 'heightened naturalism' of shooting style, acting and scripting, together with frequent imitation of newsreel and *vérité*-style sequences, the precise nature of the truth claims being made in the dramas was turned into an issue by politicians and by some television critics.[12] Since the content of most programmes was left-wing in general orientation, there was inevitably a certain amount of disingenuousness about Conservative complaints that it was primarily the *form* of such productions which was unacceptable.

At the centre of such complaints was the charge that drama–doc mixes were likely to lead to confusion among the audience about precisely what they were watching. Anxiety about this was the reason given for the Government banning Peter Watkin's BBC drama–doc about nuclear disaster, *The War Game*, in 1966, although concern about the likely impact of the programme on 'deterrence policy' seems to have been more decisive. It is also the case that many of the programmes which were found so controversial either concerned historical events (a notable instance was the *Days of Hope* series of films about working class experience, directed by Ken Loach, scripted by Jim Allen, and first broadcast by the BBC in 1975) or involved the portrayal of quite intimate ongoing action and speech between characters (as in the 'classic' Loach/Sandford *Cathy Come Home*, 1966). It's hard to see fundamental confusion as a real risk here. Certainly, a 'playing' with established conventions, pointing up the inadequacies of sharp generic distinction, was generally part of production aims. This was designed to rub up against audience expectations and to generate a fresh kind of response. But for viewers to believe that they were watching actuality footage of Great War trench conversations or contemporary marital argument would have required a quite astonishing naivety about what television documentary can do. However, an uncertainty about the *extent* to which what was depicted was 'based on fact' is more understandable and more likely. In the case of *Cathy*, for instance, just how far one particular real incident had been the model for the script (in other words, whether there was a 'real Cathy') seemed to be a matter of concern and confusion for a number of viewers at the time and continues to be an issue with student audiences today, despite the explicitness of the closing captions.

Whilst, as I have noted, it was precisely part of the whole project to call into question the neatness of the convention that fiction was 'false' and documentary 'true', the tactic of mixing depictive conventions to produce an account indeterminate in its specific referentiality is one which still produces public argument and is by no means settled by pointing to the inadequacies of conventional categorisation. Many drama-based productions used documentary-style presentation in order not only to put the socio-aesthetic conventions of television under stress but also to get the double benefit of documentary credibility and creative licence. For unlike mainstream documentary, documentary-drama operated with a playwright's freedom to construct characters, dialogue and action precisely as wished, and then placed these within a strongly developed context of historical or contemporary realities, sometimes including the portrayal of real (and 'famous') people.

The move in the other direction, towards the dramatisation of material initially researched within the documentary frame (and often in documentary departments), has a long history in television, being one of the methods used when the lack of lightweight equipment made access to certain kinds of location impossible for orthodox documentary representation.[13] There are considerable variations in the means and models adopted for dramatising the documentary 'core' material, which is often of a kind – papers, tape recordings, private interviews – not visible to the audience at all. But the overall style of such programmes is generally very different from that of documentary drama. The claim to documentary credibility is based on the specific referentiality which the script, via research, has to actually occurring events (a claim whose strength may vary from programme to programme) and so there is no need for the producers to go for a documentary 'likeness' in the manner of portrayal itself. Indeed, in some recent examples in Britain [*Lockerbie* (Granada 1990) about the PanAm/Lockerbie disaster, and *Valdez* (BBC 1991) about the Alaskan oil spill] the international thriller and the disaster movie have provided the stylistic model.

It is interesting that 'based on fact' films continue to be a major genre in cinema but they do not arouse anything like the heated debate which has followed many drama-documentary programmes (of both kinds discussed above) on television. This is partly due to the particular, public character of the 'truth ethics' of television, and the way in which both dramatised documentaries and documentary dramas play off the strong presence in television schedules of mainstream documentary output. In the cinema, the public anticipates a film which is primarily concerned with delivering a form of dramatic entertainment, whatever historical referentiality it also wishes to claim. Therefore even when questions of accuracy arise in public discussion [as for instance in relation to *J.F.K.* (1991) or *Malcolm X* (1993)], they generally do so in a climate which shows considerably more tolerance towards the film maker's licence in the context of a fully commercial entertainment industry.

The types of research and documentation upon which drama-documentary forms are based continue to be a point of development in contemporary television, as do the different possibilities of dramatic form which are employed in turning the result into screen narrative. The various approaches to documentation and depiction also continue to present research with a key intersection point of different television practices and kinds of realism. As I illustrated in Chapter 1, drama-documentary is now to be found as a part of programmes using other conventions. In Britain, the United States and Europe, dramatic reconstruction has been assimilated within many different genres to become an accepted, if still sometimes controversial, component of public television.

Mise-en-scène

The term *mise-en-scène* is taken from the critical language of fictional cinema (and before that, of theatre), but it has always been useful for the analysis of work in documentary and is particularly relevant to recent developments in television. In cinematic criticism, it means 'putting into shot' and describes the way in which a director organises the composition of a scene and the placing of people, action and props within it. Although the expressive opportunities for non-fiction directors have often been more limited than for their counterparts in feature film making – a matter of budgets and production time as well as of generic convention (the relatively narrow circumscription of documentary discourse in relation to 'topic' as opposed to the expansive possibilities of 'story') – *mise-en-scène* points to an important dimension of documentary assembly. In the self-consciously experimental films of the 1930s, realist settings were often combined with more symbolic renderings of place and space [the depiction of the mining village and its surrounding landscape in *Coalface* (1935) would be a good example, whilst Humphrey Jennings' wartime classic *Listen to Britain* (1942) works from a base in realist representation to make emblematic certain parts of wartime Britain, particularly the buildings of London].

The emergence, and then the dominance, of the journalistic in television documentary depiction had consequences for visual treatments. It encouraged containment of the range of visualisations within the terms of the literal and the naturalistic. Often, the visualisation of setting offered no more than a framing for inquiry, for interview, for observed social action. There has always been a place (often under the aegis of 'arts' output) for documentaries taking a more indirect route to their subject, allowing the play of associations and giving visual depiction (sometimes accompanied by music) a dominant communicative function, but this place has often been marginal. The work of Denis Mitchell for the BBC and Granada is notable here [particularly in prize-winning films like *Morning in the Streets* (BBC 1959), about aspects of working-class life in the inner cities of Manchester and Liverpool].

Recently, this established television tendency towards a 'literalisation' of the documentary image, the visual rendering kept flat and spare, consonant with the terms of an observed, objectifed and mundane social reality, has given way to the emergence of much more symbolically dense ways of rendering place and action, and relating them both to the human subjects of the documentary and to the development of topic. This shift, observable across a range of programmes, is one which seems to have been largely prompted by the influence upon documentary production of other generic forms, many of which have themselves undergone quite radical shifts in depictive mode. The newer approaches to visualisation in television advertising (for instance, towards the appeal of the 'strange' and the 'bizarre') and the range of image types explored by pop video are two of the most obvious sources of a rethought documentary *mise-en-scène*, although behind both of these are shifts in the set design, lighting and visual styling of mainstream cinema.

These influences continue to work their way into the production of the documentary image in a number of different ways, as part of a more general process of inter-generic blurrings, borrowings and adaptations within television. One of the most significant changes, first of all to be found in the work of small independent companies but now observable more generally, has been the use of a lighting style and mode of composition which produces what I think can best be called an effect of 'hallucinatory realism' or 'displaced realism'. The image is still firmly referential in its depiction, nor is there any rearranging of the pro-filmic to create supplementary non-referential effects. However, by 'theatrical' lighting and a camera style which holds and explores the scene with a more obvious, confident control than is usual in documentary (e.g. crane shots, slow tracking shots, the visual marking of certain things as 'significant') the setting is displaced from conventional referentiality and is (however lightly) 'defamiliarised' in the direction of the fictional.

Sometimes the use of colour filtering (particularly, the use of blue – widespread in television advertising) gives a further objectifying distance and coolness, a further suggestion of a level or dimension of artifice uncertainly placed between being somehow a property of the real itself and being a function of self-conscious depictive style. This may be the way in which a documentarism aware of post-modernist debate chooses to put its reality into inverted commas whilst remaining true to the physical contours of pro-filmic appearance. The result is often not so much a subversion of the normative, however, as a heightening of its interest. As I suggested, the newer, ironic styling of international television advertising and, behind this, certain shifts in the look and movement of feature film, seem to be factors in many of these revised practices of visualisation.

A concern with developing a semi-detached aesthetic for documentary (one which is not directly subordinate to what it represents but which still grounds its project in the depiction and exposition of a referent) can also be noticed at work in interview sequences, a point already touched on. For instance, there has been a move, though not yet a pronounced one, towards placing the interviewee in 'striking' or 'provocative' settings, as long as these do not break entirely with realist plausibility.

Fig. 4.1. When the Dog Bites: The Swimming Bath Interview.

A good example of this kind of shift away from the conventions of contextual literalism can be taken from the film *When the Dog Bites* (Penny Woolcock, Trade/Channel Four 1988), whose degree of commitment to the extension of documentary language was controversial when it was first shown. An unemployed man is interviewed in the local swimming bath, the camera portraying him with the water-line at midpoint in the frame, the submerged lower half of his body partly visible (see Fig. 4.1). The whole aesthetic of the shot is based upon this 'split' depiction, together with the uneven and shifting light patterns caused by reflections from the water. The effect of such an approach is immediately to strengthen the visualised context of speech, though whether this is complementary to what is said or a detraction from it is open to dispute. The introduction of a more symbolically expansive approach to documentary depiction increases the visual appeal of work in the genre (in contrast, say, to the minimalism and visual banality of much *vérité*), at the same time as it risks a similar kind of 'aesthetic displacement' to that which certain documentaries of the 1930s are sometimes accused of displaying. This is a displacement whereby the specific realities, ostensibly the subject of documentation, become secondary to the discursive effects generated from them.

It is interesting that at the same time as a more aesthetically ambitious, self-consciously stylised approach to documentary has been making progress in the British schedules, there has also been an attempt to revivify the appeal of the undermediated, or even of the apparently *un*mediated. This has taken the form of do-it-yourself documentaries (notably, the highly successful *Video Diaries* and *Teenage Diaries* series on BBC) and a number of experiments involving concealed cameras. The footage produced by such initiatives often sets a new standard for 'raw' television (undercutting in this respect the increasingly familiar repertoire of *verité* observation). To continue with the culinary metaphor (see Levi-Strauss, 1970), it is tempting to see its appeal as being gained by contrast with (though perhaps, finally, in complement to) the newer forms of the 'cooked' now available in documentary television.

Exposition

'Exposition' (description and commentary) in relation to a body of visualised evidence is what the vast majority of television documentaries provide. Frequently, this exposition takes the form of an inquiry, the conduct of which may be more or less explicit. I discussed earlier how, in programmes made primarily or even exclusively in the observational mode, exposition is indirect, implicit and open both to uncertainties of intention and to considerable interpretative work by the viewer.

But even in the most 'purist' of fly-on-the-wall documentaries, the imaged particularism of local action and behaviour, however fascinating and 'watchable' in itself, must be filtered upwards by the viewer to a more general level of significance, must be seen to 'say' something about the *kind* of events and people being observed. Action must be connected to topic. This 'saying' may, with varying emphasis, be attributed to the *intentions* of the programme makers.[14] Production teams working on such films edit them according to criteria of relevance and significance in relation to their revelatory yield at this general level (as well as to their 'watchability') however non-dogmatic and provisional such criteria might be.

In many British observational series, the focus for 'implicit exposition' of this kind has been an institution (series titles have a strong tradition of making this very clear, e.g. *Sailor, Police, The Family, The Duty Men, Redbrick, Murder Squad*). Bound by its procedures to the depiction of present-tense action and able to use only those forms of logic, explanation and argumentation which arise plausibly from such depiction, the observational programme can only work effectively where 'top-down' classifications of this kind can be used to organise local meanings. As a form for the revelation of contemporary social process, this 'weak exposition/strong evidence' format achieves optimum force and focus. But, of course, this is by no means the only type of communicative task which television documentary undertakes. It also requires to address topics (say, of an abstract or historical character) which cannot easily be particularised around present-tense action, or benefit from the constraints of space and time which provide observationalism with its density and power.

At the other extreme from the reticence of observational exposition is the continuous use of presenter voice-over to introduce, to describe and to connect parts of the account and perhaps to conclude it. This has been well-dubbed the 'voice of God' mode and, although it was extensively used in documentary cinema from the 1930s onwards, it has been sparingly employed as a structuring device in contemporary television. Risking a negative reaction from a viewer willing to be told things but unwilling to be the subject of continuous expositional address, full commentary inevitably closes down the possibilities for the development of a visual exploration of the theme, since 'under' its discourse there is a strong tendency for images to become merely illustrative and to be edited at a pace which does not allow room for the viewer to give much attention either to what they show or how they show it. The old cinema newsreels illustrate this tendency to what now seems an almost parodic degree.

One exception to the gradual shift away from commentary in television was the *World in Action* series, started on Granada television in 1962. From the start, the series made regular use of the commentary style. However, instead of those tones of authoritative knowing from which it was hard for the older style of commentary to escape, *World in Action* carried the clipped and urgent voice of a reporter, taking the viewer through a programme structured entirely in terms of investigative immediacy and imminent revelation (sometimes one directly visualised, sometimes not).[15] The voice issued from 'within' the inquiry (often using present-tense description) rather than from 'above' it, and its use differed from that of earlier styles of commentary film in the interspersing of commentary with sequences of interview.

Although many documentarists today prefer, where possible, to have a revelatory rather a descriptive structure to their accounts, the use of commentary voice at points within a programme is still indispensible for providing the viewer with certain kinds of information and explanatory background and for linking between sequences. By convention, the journalistic account (unlike the more indirect kinds of documentary exploration) often requires a summary and a reportorial assessment at the end. Here, the viewer is presented, if not usually with hard conclusions, then with pointers to what factors are important in *coming* to a conclusion. This kind of rational, argumentational work is best suited to direct speech, either in voice-over or camera address.

I looked, earlier, at the function of interviews in documentary discourse and noted both their variety and widespread use in television. Interviews are another way of organising exposition as well as being a component of it. The 'string-of-interviews' model is now more prevalent in television than the commentary-over-film model and just as common as the varieties of observationalism. A structure based on interviews produces a looser, more dispersed logic of development than either the focused particularity of observationalism or the highly defined, verbal order imposed on a documentary by a full commentary.

In documentaries seeking to develop a general theme primarily by a sequence of interviews, where there is some choice as to the interviewees used there is also frequently considerable effort put into selecting personable subjects, ones who will project engagingly to the viewer and who are able to give their responses in a way which will *seem* both authentic and coherent.

It is not uncommon in interview-based programmes for one or more of the interviewees to take on the role of a 'presenter substitute', being featured regularly in order to make key links and to offer voice-over commentary outside the confines of 'personal experience', the primary category of knowledge which interviewees are used to develop. In several recent films, speaking subjects who might have conventionally been placed in the programme as interviewees, have actually been shot in observational mode, delivering their accounts to groups. For instance, the Oscar-nominated 1992 film, *Liberators*, about the all-black U.S. Army units which fought in World War II, makes intercut use of a lecture to achieve expositional continuity. Such a method immediately allows a far more formal and explicit presentation than interview response and it also has the effect of 'socialising' the spoken testimony outwards to include, rather than the mediating figure of an interviewer, an actual audience. An awkward duality between the speaking requirements of the occasion and the speaking requirements of the programme may remain, however, making it difficult to classify the speech as being *simply* an address to a primary audience eavesdropped on by the camera crew. (I suggested in Chapter 2 that the management of this kind of tension is now a routine element of political speech making.)

Within the various combinations of image and speech deployed in recent documentary exposition, *archive* material has frequently been given a major function in the overall design. This function has often been a dynamic one insofar as it has not been to set up an authoritatively visualised 'then' over which the interpretative commentary of 'now' can be offered, but to raise questions about both 'then' and 'now' by juxtaposition, often interrogating both the forms of official memory and the character of popular experience in relation to this.

An influential example of this *diacritical* use of archive material as a primary component of structure is to be found in Connie Field's much-discussed film, *The Life and Times of Rosie the Riveter* (1980).[16] Throughout *Rosie*, which concerns itself with the experience of women working in different sectors of U.S. industry during World War II, footage from old government propaganda material provides an intercut contrast with the testimony of selected interviewees, talking of their own working lives. The promotional excesses and insincerities of the archive material provide the film as a whole with a number of devices crucial to its structure. They give a contrast by which the women's testimony is enhanced as well as the means by which the film develops an edge of wit and critical humour and by which the more general questions of propaganda and of gender inequality are raised. The couplet of archive/testimony, in its varying degrees of non-alignment and contradiction, is used by the film as the means through which to develop a critical historical narrative.

A 'light' form of dramatisation is brought into the combination at one point, resituating the film's respondents back in the historical moment which was to be of such significance in determining the pattern of their lives over the next few years – the Japanese attack on Pearl Harbor. This sequence begins with the in-shot testimony of an interviewee who tells how, serving as a maid at the time, she was asked by her employer to come into a room and listen to an important news flash being broadcast on the radio. As the news broadcast begins on the soundtrack, the sequence moves to a clip from an old feature film in which a couple listen in on their bedside radio, cutting to other feature film and archive shots of various groups of people responding to the broadcast in their cars and in public spaces. As the soundtrack shifts to a recording of President Roosevelt's speech containing the declaration of war, all five women interviewees are depicted in a series of shots which places them, too, as 'listening in'. The sequence finishes with archive film of Roosevelt making his speech. The effect is to re-enact 'then' within 'now', a depictive interfusion of the two times and yet also a recognition and underlining of their separateness.

Such a mixing of modes in post-production produces an expositional system which is able to achieve a wide range of affective as well as cognitive effects. The inter-discursive use of archive materials (their use as other than unproblematic historical *reference*) was pioneered in independent cinema. For instance, the U.S. documentarist, Emile De Antonio, explored recent archive footage as a tool of critical documentary in his Vietnam film *In the Year of the Pig* (1969), where much of the visualisation is constructed by the juxtaposition of archive clips, with their various soundtracks also providing a major contribution to the film's project.

I have already mentioned how 'mixed' expositional structures have started to appear more frequently in the British schedules. A good case in point is the series *Disguises*, launched by Granada in 1993. The basic idea of this format was the use of hidden cameras as an aid to reporting areas of public controversy. The 'core' footage, often taking up a small amount of the total programme time, was the *vérité* material thus shot. Since *this* was taken without the knowledge of those in shot, it had a referentiality of an even stronger kind than that obtained in conventional *vérité*: that of the 'poor image' – cramped, badly lit, lacking composition and consistent framing and often in unplanned motion, with accompanying actuality sound often so poor that speech has to be subtitled.

Around this point of innovation, another novel dimension was organised – that of reportorial disguise and reportorial participation. This was primarily a prerequisite for obtaining the clandestine shots, but it was also more. A reworked version of the reportorial quest became the principal narrative of each programme, a quest in which 'becoming disguised', 'being disguised' and sometimes 'removing disguise' became episodes of marked journalistic self-dramatisation, playing knowingly with the idea of uncertainty and risk as well as with the pleasures of 'dressing up', 'pretence' and 'spying'.

However, the programmes still required visualising from conventional sources (location camera teams) in order to provide an expositional context within which the clandestine material could fit and make sense. With some variation as to topic, they also required the use of voice-over, to render the events depicted fully comprehensible; and direct presenter address, to get the personalised 'out-of-role' alignment with the viewer upon which the thrills of 'in-role' disguise partly depended. In some cases, interview material was also used. In its combined expositional form, *Disguises* seemed in many ways to be very much a product of its times. It went for a new form of 'revelatory' account, a new form of documentation (inescapably action-based in its focus) and for a new kind of documentary appeal, a new 'buzz' for the viewer, drawing extensively on the fly-on-the-wall tradition and a kind of theatricalised reporting owing something to current styles in 'features' (as seen in the newer youth programmes as well as in a range of special interest formats being applied, for instance, to cooking, travel and motoring series).

My own judgement is that the *Disguises* mix was pushed too far in the entertainment direction and that the informational yield of the hidden camera material was often insufficient to justify the elaborate setting up of disguised behaviour. This produced a discordance between aims and means which sometimes showed itself as uncertainty of tone in the reporting itself. But the series, like the *999* series discussed earlier in the book, is best seen as indicative of some of the elements at work in what is only the 'first wave' of a broad and diverse movement towards rethinking the terms of television documentary. I suggested that this trend draws on a new intergeneric awareness, but in Britain it is also directly determined by the need for documentary to reconsider its relationship with audiences under the conditions of extended channel choice and increased competition for revenue and funding.

Contested Optics: The Disputability of Documentary Form

At the start of this chapter I discussed how documentary had its origins in ideas about progressive citizenship in industrial society. Some of these ideas were democratic and critical of an older order of informational inequality and political control. But the 'solution' which documentary offered to the problem of the limited availability of public knowledge and the increasing commercialisation of the press was itself shot through with authoritarian strands. Not for the first time nor the last, ostensibly democratic initiatives become less straightforward when it came to their implementation and the selection of means. It is also the case that pioneer documentarists, not unlike many contemporary broadcasters in this respect, had to keep their work within certain 'givens' compatible with regular and adequate funding.

However, as I noted, most of television documentary's accounts are institutionalised as 'public' by their proximity to the publicly accountable activity of journalism. In many countries, this is further underwritten by their production as part of a broadly 'public service' dimension to the national television system. It is clear that this latter context is now rapidly changing towards one in which market factors will identify viewers more strongly as 'consumers' (even allowing for the necessary, minimum 'public' status which journalism has usually to claim as a professional condition of its activity). Although the early 1990s has seen a remarkable amount of innovation in topics and treatments, the effects of these larger changes upon documentary television internationally may well turn out finally to be strongly negative.

The consequences for television documentary of having an institutionalised public identity have been both limiting and enabling. The limitations have followed from the relatively tight circumscription of documentary 'impartiality' within a code of practice drawn up without much, if any, direct recognition of the contexts of political power and of economic inequality within which television operates. To that degree, documentary television (particularly in Britain) has always risked being over-polite, cautious and complacent whilst at the same time being celebratory about its own boldness. It has also risked a degree of patrician condescension in its tones, echoing in this respect some of the pioneer documentary films. The history of explicit and of covert interference in documentary production by government agencies as well as by national television managers suggests that such limitations, and the 'climate' they characterise, are partly the product of effectively maintained parameters external to television itself.

The complementary strengths which 'public' status has bought to documentary have resulted from the need to engage the popular audience and to develop an investigative integrity of evidence, and of precision and clarity in its analysis, by which to resist 'official' pressures either during production or after screening. This has worked to give the best documentary teams and departments a discipline of thoughtful practice which has often served to trim stylistic self-indulgence as well as to restrain any moves towards an over-speculative use of data or the premature judgement of causality.

Both the limitations and strengths can be contrasted to the relative 'freedoms' of the independent documentary movement in contemporary cinema, far stronger in the U.S.A. than in Britain. Here, given the circumstances of distribution and exhibition, formal innovation has not felt so tied to the requirements of market popularity. The result has been that a far richer, more complex and more self-consciously authored language of documentary has been developed, one often matching the density and 'difficulty' of art cinema.[17] Along with this has gone freedom from the requirements of balance and impartiality, allowing film makers to develop expositions which have far more polemical edge and depth of critique. Self-identified as 'interventions' in the public arena rather than as 'commentaries' upon (mostly predefined) 'issues', the films of independent documentary cinema have no obligation to be fair and they can therefore generate a calculated *un*-evenhandedness of treatment which some have seen as a necessary corrective to the economic, social and communicative inequalities which broadcasting tends to reproduce as much as it questions.

The reverse side of this opportunity is the increased danger not only of 'preaching to the converted' (a matter as much of distribution as of form in the first instance) but of becoming 'promotional' in a particular cause to the point of losing the self-critical controls of argument. If a belief in the routine professional availability of 'objectivity' has been an obstacle in the development of an adequate level of self-reflection both in television documentary and in television news, the belief that 'objectivity' is an entirely illusory quality has limited the force and relevance of much work from independent cinema, reinforcing the marginality of its social significance.

Across both television and cinema, two simple notions which can be useful to a discussion of documentary's controversiality are 'openness' and 'closure'. In television, the origin of much documentary practice within the framework of current affairs' journalism means that many programmes are built around a spine of investigated circumstances presented as the factual basis for opinion and argument. This is 'closed' insofar as most viewers are unlikely to have access to alternative information with which to challenge its account, even though they might entertain scepticism as to its reliability.

A routine exception to this occurs where a programme concerns itself with a particular group of people, defined in terms of common characteristics such as socio-cultural background (for instance, London's Afro-Caribbean community, Liverpool Irish, first-year undergraduates), recreational interest (for instance, golfers, football supporters) or social problems (alcoholics, the homeless). The interpretations of the documentary fact-base made by people in the groups which form the subject of the programme are then likely to be actively critical (even if finally positive) when compared with those of other members of the audience.

It would be very useful to know more about the judgements made by groups or individuals who have been the subject (and, in one sense, the object) of documentary representation. This would not entail a simple privileging of their accounts against those of the documentarist – after all, their own anxieties about portrayal and closeness to the topic may well produce a version of what is finally 'fair' and 'unfair' at least as skewed as a documentary account. Where professional groups (for instance, doctors, teachers, police) have publicly complained about their depiction, it is often clear, despite declarations to the contrary, that a highly selective and positive self-concept has been used as the criterion for their judgement. Documentary makers need a way of maintaining responsibility for their own accounts (not routinely ceding this to subject groups out of some misplaced notion of representational democracy) while at the same time dissuading their audience from taking this account as unproblematic. They need to retain sufficient 'closure' on their material to present a clear and coherent exposition, underpinned by visual material, but sufficient 'openness' to allow viewers to exercise a critical independence.

These basic questions about the *democratic character* of documentary discourse do not easily and directly correlate with particular forms. For instance, a commentary film, ostensibly a traditional closed form in which discursive management is direct and often continuous, can be constructed in such a way in relation to the various other voices it uses, and in its combination with visuals, as to present viewers with a thoughtful and questioning viewing experience. On the other hand, a fly-on-the-wall programme, despite its apparent openness, can work with a very tightly managed sense of the significance of what is going on. This sense may have an implicit presence at every stage of the production process and be projected for 'sharing' by the viewer without at any time being a matter of explicit address.

Although critics have often overestimated the gullibility of viewers in response to visualisation, there is no doubt that one of the most effective means by which documentaries seek to naturalise their accounts, to remove them from the contingencies of their own production, is by the use of images to provide a level of self-evident support. This can have the effect of closing the account neatly down around its own selected data and classifications (e.g. 'types' of people', 'types' of problem, 'types' of circumstance).

Documentary television does not have available to it the space for self-reflexivity which independent cinema frequently allows itself. But there are ways of hanging on to the primariness of theme while being more open about the extent to which this is a construct of the production agenda and chosen form (of voice-over, of interview, of the observational scene, of particular combinations of sound and image). Developing these ways is one of the most important requirements for any reimagining of television documentary as a civic enterprise.

'A good documentary stimulates discussion of its subject, not itself' (Nichols, 1991, p. x). In his invaluable discussion of documentary theory, Bill Nichols cites this remark of a director, probing at the issues it raises. Clearly, in one sense it is self-evidently true – a 'good' documentary must always, by definition, have the primary aim of directing its viewers down its *referential axis* towards 'real world' concerns. Yet, as we have seen, there is an *aesthetic axis* too – a documentary 'poetics'. This does not merely comprise a set of presentational skills; it is centrally implicated in the production of the referential, and can be admitted to be so without distracting from the latter's primacy.

We return again to the documentary pioneers of the 1930s, for whom the debates about 'art' and 'reportage', the tensions and the complementarities, were fundamental. I have suggested that their attempted resolutions of this debate in documentary practice were often characterised by a certain ambivalence, a degree of instability and, indeed, of uneasiness. Given the nature of what is involved communicatively and socially, it may very well be that these qualities will continue to be present in much of the most imaginative and most socially engaged work in documentary.

5

ADWORLDS

Ideas about advertising have been at the centre of international media theory and media research for a long time. While the anxieties which I have considered in earlier chapters – about political mediation, news and documentary – have been grounded in a sense of the 'proper' public role for television in these areas, anxieties about advertising have often been grounded in a belief in its essential impropriety. In many commentaries, advertising has, indeed, been positioned as the quintessentially 'anti-public' form, a kind of anti-news designed to mislead rather than inform and to promote selfish emotion over civic reason.[1] Its nature, both as an economic and a representational practice, has thus been viewed pathologically, and much effort has been put into devising means either to regulate and reduce its influence or to develop the possibility of a media system (and an economy) which could manage without it. Yet, despite this tradition of critical concern (variously reflected in the political and public sphere as well as in academic analysis), advertising has increasingly become assimilated into everyday life as a basic constitutent of late modernity. In recent years it has become much more international, extending to societies in which it was previously either marginal or non-existent, while in those societies where it has an established place it has often become even more culturally pervasive and representationally subtle.[2]

One consequence of this move towards advertising as economically and culturally *normal* has been the emergence of a revised perspective on it within media theory. Such a perspective keeps up its connections with the earlier tradition of criticism but modifies this with newer, more accomodating, tones. For as well as it now being very hard to think *counterfactually* against the sheer penetration of advertising into social and cultural experience, the newer aesthetics which advertising has adopted have often had a depictive energy and social resonance which has prompted analytic interest more immediately than dismissal.

In this chapter, I want to examine some features of television advertising, paying attention to aspects both of the established critical debate about its forms and consequences and to revised versions of this. As in other chapters, my principal concern will be with the character of the communication itself, rather than the nature of advertising as an industry. Despite this tightening of focus, however, I hope that a concern with television advertising form can be made to connect with those more general questions about the relationship between advertising and society. Having first looked at the way in which advertising is placed within the aesthetics of television, sometimes initiating and sometimes reflecting changes elsewhere, I shall look at the distinctive way in which questions of aesthetics are linked to questions of 'influence' in advertising. Finally, some of the different and quite often conflicting evaluations which have recently been made of advertising's social consequence will be explored. Given the rapid turnover in television commercials and the now broad, international familiarity of their different types, I have not referred extensively to specific examples in my commentary, preferring to let readers test my points against their own viewing experience.

Advertising and Television Aesthetics

The 'commercial' is one of the most *intensive* deployments of television form. This is a combination of the extremely tight time constraints placed upon it and the need to develop within these constraints the significatory definition and power to 'get the message across' in a manner which will exercise some form of persuasion upon the viewer. Such intensity and such an explicit commitment to influence marks commercials out as an *extraordinary* form of television, but the basic devices which they use to engage and to 'woo' the viewer frequently draw on television's communicative *ordinariness*, its routine (by turns, dramatic, personalised, serious, comic, relaxed, hectic) kinds of representation. In this sense, then, commercials often work as a kind of *essential television*, using the generic system of broader television culture, with its grouped conventions of speech and image, and working their elements up into a range of 'micro-formats', where they appear transformed but nevertheless recognisable (often, in recent advertising, constructed as the subject of pastiche and parody). There are also strong indications of a movement the other way too, in which forms of mainstream television (for example, travel programmes, music shows, youth magazines) have reworked their look and their sounds so as to incorporate developments in television commercials. There has even been a shift in some television drama towards certain styles of lighting, ways of using settings or composing a shot and a manner of acting which have been seen by some critics as showing the influence of 'commercials' culture'. Cinema has also been an important source of ideas for the television commercial, offering its own distinctive generic range and visual styles. Many commercials are produced for both cinema and television screening (albeit in different versions). The number of cinema directors now also doing commercials work indicates that stylistic influences are partly the direct consequence of professional toing and froing.

The *contexts* in which television ads often appear, a 'break' in programming consisting of a sequence of commercials, clearly exerts an outer level of influence on their character and their potential for giving pleasure. As an interruption in programming these breaks are both welcome (a chance to make coffee, see to something in the house) and unwelcome (a blocking of continuity in the enjoyment of the programme). The way in which these two conflicting aspects of the setting in which ads occur affects the disposition of viewers towards them, especially in the context of multi-channel availability, is certainly worthy of further study.[3] However, the internationalisation of advertising-financed television has made such breaks a routine part of the modern viewing experience in many countries (the early use of the term 'natural break' by television companies was an attempt to anticipate this).[4]

The Television Commercial: Basic Communicative Elements

Clearly, advertising on television is communicatively different from advertising in other media. In poster and newspaper advertising, for instance, the advertisement is *static*, though, of course, it may well imply narrative action. The temporal element involved in the interpretative work performed upon it (connecting with basic questions about the nature of the product and its attractiveness as well as with the appeal of the ad itself) is very much determined by the viewer, by how long they wish to engage with the images and words. There may be external constraints on this time (e.g. posters at busy traffic intersections, designed to be seen briefly but regularly) and constraints imposed by routine (e.g. the daily browse through a newspaper, moving through the pages and returning to some for more detailed attention, in accordance with established habit). In television advertising, however, the temporal dimension is very much part of the advert's communicative structure and this regulates the intepretative time available to the viewer. In the making of advertisements, such a regulation of interpretative time allows, of course, for the possibility of the increased comprehension and pleasure consequent on *repetition*. It has also, increasingly, to make allowance for the possibility of the advert's status as a *video item*. Whilst, theoretically, this allows the viewer to rerun the ad at their leisure, giving it extra attention, it is much more likely to result in it being fast-forwarded so as to receive hardly any attention at all.

A number of studies of advertising have developed analytical accounts of its semiological character without due regard to the differences between media in which advertisements occur and to how these differences might bear on advertising's cultural consequences. For instance, Leiss *et al.* (1986) develop a very useful historical survey of advertising imagery, together with a typology of advertising structure, by focusing primarily on newspaper and magazine ads. Williamson's influential account (1978) of the ideological character of advertising imagery draws exclusively upon examples from magazines. Pateman's highly original attempt (1983) both to offer a critique of previous, semiotic, approaches and to develop an analysis grounded in linguistic ideas concerns itself, too, with examples from posters and newspapers. His conceptualisation of advertising as a certain kind of communicative act (following Searle's notion of the 'speech act') and his analytic vocabulary for discussing this are related exclusively to printed forms.

There are many things about advertising which can, and should, be addressed at a cross-media level, but a prerequisite for this general commentary is a recognition of the variety of distinctive media which advertising now uses. For television, this would involve attention to three basic communicative features not present in poster or newspaper formats – speech, action and music.

Speech

Speech gives to the television ad both a regulatory and a dramatic facility. The male voice-over pronouncing in sonorous tones upon the special qualities of the product is a cliché of television advertising, now much parodied both in television and in radio formats. But with the more 'serious' types of product (medication, for instance, or educational materials) or where it is assumed that a 'straight pitch' will work best, the direct address mode is still employed in a manner derivative of news or documentary practice – an authoritative presentation, strong in immediacy values, of 'news about the product'. Direct address, either in voice over or in-shot, allows a number of communicative functions, amongst which are:

i.   product identification (as in the emphatic and perhaps repeated use of the brand name).
ii. product description (key characteristics and use of product stated).
iii. product affirmation (evaluative claims as to product quality made).

These three functions can all work to *personalise* the address of the ad, situating it as social communication in a way which does not occur in print forms. This factor may be used strategically, as for instance in the use of a professional male middle class voice to sell car security devices, or the use of young woman's voice to sell a diet drink. Sometimes, rather than a subliminal appeal, a 'neutral' connotation is sought. In other ads, the use of pronunciation and accent is such as to project the social identity and/or character type of the speaker for the viewers' conscious recognition. I have talked in an earlier chapter about the social relations of direct address speech on television, in which it becomes possible for the speaker to adopt a conversational register and to assume a relationship of familiarity with the viewer. Clearly, the direct address speech of advertising is routinely used not only for the delivery of 'hard' product information but also for the 'soft' task of establishing sociable relations.

Speech also clearly serves the need of television advertising to offer dramatic representations. In the typical dialogue of the commercial, the dramatic requirements of the speech are in combination with the requirement for product promotion. 'Realist' portrayal often gives way, in dramatic exchange, to an emphasis on product quality and the repetition of the product name (sometimes requiring a marked shift from dramatic, indirect address to 'individual' or 'choral' forms of direct address).

Action

The possibility of showing action takes television advertising into areas of product representation simply not available in static depiction, however ingeniously this is organised. We can identify four main consequences of kinetic representation.

Dramatic
The potential of the television ad as micro-drama has provided modern societies with one of the most intensively developed promotional forms. Dramatic structure, even in so brief a format as the commercial, allows for a degree of 'character' development, with important consequences for the strength of viewer identification and for any personalising strategy – for example, that organised around a celebrity – which is used. It also allows for a much stronger representation of *sociality*, since the product can be set within the dynamics of social action, 'caught up' within the warmth, adventure or sensuality of social *processes* rather than 'located' within social *spaces* as in a photographic depiction (though one must not underestimate the power of viewer imagination here). The comic dimension of advertising is, of course, greatly increased by dramatic depiction, which allows generic imitation of both film and television comedy as well as the development of distinctive, 'condensed' formats of its own. The idea that ads have become another media 'product', whose relationship to the product which they promote is actually becoming less determinative than their own entertainment value for audiences, is very much premised on the relatively independent status which micro-dramas, both comic and serious, can achieve for themselves in audience estimation. Although recent ads have become a good deal less obvious in the ways in which products are placed within their scenarios, the micro-dramas of the commercial still typically close, if not with an old-style 'pack shot', then by using a strong (often 'frozen') image of the product in context.

Demonstrative
Another function of kinetic depiction is that it allows the product to be seen in *action*. For many products, this 'functional' level of representation is inappropriate but for others the appeal of demonstration can be considerable, even where objectivity is not expected (e.g. the perfect surface of the scratched table after the application of polish, the breaking power of the car on the airport runway test). The most traditional type of demonstration ads actually set themselves up as tests for viewer witnessing (e.g. blindfolded housewives testing margarine; two attempts at cleaning the bath,

one with the advertised cleaner) but, again, any rationally demonstrative function is now usually mixed with elements both of the self-consciously theatrical and the comic.

Symbolic

Symbolism, in the sense of a non-literal significance being generated by (and attributed to) words and images, is a key element of nearly all advertising communication. The classic analysis of its presence is perhaps that by Roland Barthes. In his essay 'The Rhetoric of the Image' (1977) Barthes uses the term 'connotation' and 'myth' to engage with this level of associational (often metaphoric) meaning, providing a case study which has become a major influence on subsequent academic commentary. A frequent assumption in such work is that the 'symbolic' level is in fact a 'hidden' level of textual meaning in the sense that it is not consciously registered by viewers even while it is being generated by them from the text. It has therefore been regarded by many analysts as the level at which advertising power is most operative and most in need of critique (this is in contrast to the 'literal' levels of speech and image, where questions of misdescription, fraudulent claims, misleading illustration etc. have provided a traditional point of address for consumer groups and regulatory bodies). I shall return to this point later in the context of conflicting arguments about influence.

The extension of overall symbolic field provided by the use of moving images and by speech allows advertising to deploy a rich aesthetics of movement and process. In early commercials the links with static forms of symbolic display were stronger, a matter of technical limitation as well as of imaginative convention (see Fig. 5.1). Commercials can either be developed on a base of realist depiction (e.g. the 'scene from domestic life'; the

Fig. 5.1. 'Fresh as Ice': Visualised Simile in the first ad shown on British Television (Gibbs SR, 1955).

comic sketch) or else developed directly within either continuous non-realist narrative (e.g. a fantasy scenario) or in mixed, semi- or non-realist and perhaps non-representational formats (the montage sequence; the abstract employment of sound and colour). In this latter area, developments in music video production have been a significant influence. There has recently been a marked increase in the number of adverts using non-representational shapes, colourings, sounds and movements. This provides an articulation of symbolic meaning which appears to have links with other shifts in contemporary cultural form, including these in the visual styles of magazines and computer games.[5]

Depictive
'Depictive' is an awkward term in this context, but I use it here to indicate the possibilities for *camera movement* which follow from the use of the television medium. That is to say, not the way in which the camera can represent action taking place in front of it but the way in which the use of zooms, pans, glides, tilts, tracking shots and so on can construct an ad within an aesthetic altogether different from that of the static image. This aesthetic clearly connects with all three of the above 'action' functions – dramatic, demonstrative and symbolic – but it also has a powerful use as a way of organising apprehension of the product spatially and temporally. We can think of the example of a car, notionally static within the frame of the shot. The camera will control our perceptions, organising them into a rhythm of shifts – part to whole; the low-angle 'journey' around the front; the zoom on to the wheel hubs; the marking out, through controlled perception both of product beauty and product power. This method of providing enhanced perception of a product's physical being – its 'thingness', replete with potential for use and for pleasure –is employed extensively in television advertising, with wide variations in the pacing and styles of disclosure.

The depictive scope of ads has been considerably increased recently by the use of computer graphic simulation and modelling. This has allowed perspectives, perceptual movements and 'transformation' scenes of a kind either difficult or impossible to achieve in relation to real objects and it has thereby enhanced the possibilities for visual pleasure.

Music (and sounds)

The function of music in commercials is more fundamental than it might appear to be. It may seem merely 'additional'. In many commercials cast in the dramatic mode, the music provides the primary indication of mood, very quickly establishing the 'correct' way of reading character and action. In commercials cast in other modes, music is often similarly important in establishing moods and in providing a strong reinforcement of product identity (the 'jingle' is, of course, a traditional form for the projection of brand). Given the brief and intensive character of many commercials, music is not only a *thematic* factor however, but also very importantly an agency of syntax and punctuation, serving to link together the various parts of a commercial, giving movement within shot and movements between shot an overall structural appropriateness and bringing the whole assembly to a strong conclusion.[6] Whether or not singing is used, music allows an element of *repetition* within the form of the ad. This frequently supports linguistic repetition, though it should not be confused with it, as the consequences of musical repetition for the aesthetic of the commercial are far more comprehensive. Clearly, not only does the use of music allow commercials a broader range of cultural cross-referencing (the use of pop music and rock music being particularly important here) but it also allows the sociality of commercials to be projected more effectively, emphasising 'togetherness', 'happiness' and forms of 'fun' as well as a range of more dramatically themed emotional states.

Sounds and noises are also included in many commercials. At one level, they are necessary to support action, whether dramatic or otherwise, as indicated above. But they also frequently exceed this literalist function. They are deployed as mechanisms of heightened realism, for instance, in order to develop a stronger sense of product identity (e.g. the crunch of breakfast cereals, the fizz of an opened can of lager). In some commercials, their use is designed to underscore non-realist actions associated with the product (the cartoon-like repertoire associated with speed, sudden stops, collisions, jumps etc.). Almost always, they are woven into a soundtrack of voices and music to give the commercial a firmer and more memorable structure, to punctuate it more attractively and add to its overall vivacity.

Genre and the Television Commercial

Many commentaries on advertising have offered a basic typology of the television commercial, identifying the principal kinds of communicative strategy. Among the more perennial of these are the 'testimonial ad', in which a celebrity of some kind endorses a product; the 'scientific–rational ad', in which the qualities of the product are 'proved' by some form of ostensibly objective testing, variously visualised in the commercial itself; the 'animation ad', in which the product or product name is represented within an abstract or cartoon format; and the 'slice of life' ad in which the product appears, or is mentioned within, a micro-drama of everyday life, presented within some version of realism. There are many variants and combinations even within this basic selection. For example, in detergent advertising the use of an 'ordinary housewife', either alone or in combination with a (male) presenter, has been used as a key testimonial form. This kind of ad has also frequently employed elements of the 'scientific–rational', insofar as it has 'shown the difference' between washes using the product and those using other brands. Two other broad kinds of ad which have been around for a long time but which have recently become more dominant are the 'comedy ad' and the 'fantasy ad'. In many contemporary comedy ads the humorous entertainment of the viewer is frequently undertaken in a way which may appear subversive in relation to the product itself (not merely to competing products). In advertising for all types of goods, there has been a movement away from the emphatic sincerity of earlier kinds of 'hard sell' commercials towards the more relaxed, oblique and ironic significations of product quality offered by comedy. As I have indicated, the parodying of 'serious' formats has been a feature of many new-style humorous commercials whilst the parodying of earlier advertising is also widespread in current British commercials, along with the use of elements from a broad range of television entertainment. A fashion for using archive footage (old black and white movies particularly) and intercutting this with newly shot material has been one of the most notable recent developments in comic commercials, though its force of novelty is quickly expended. Together with the broad tendency towards parody, this kind of mix is often cited as an example of just how 'postmodern' in sensibility advertising culture has now become.[7]

An equal, if not greater, amount of innovative effort has gone into the subgenre of the 'fantasy ad'. Fantasy (like comedy in this respect) has been a traditional component of television commercials, whose interest in generating viewer/consumer desires has obviously required a discourse able to stimulate notions of the ultimate, the ideal and the perfect and to place the *attainable* in a strategic relationship with the *unattainable* (as we shall see later, getting this 'trick' right is central to the efficiency of much advertising). What is new about fantasy in advertising is its degree of self-consciousness and of elaboration. In many recent commercials (I draw on viewing experiences in the United States, Britain, Sweden and Australia but imagine the tendency to be fully international) 'fantasy' is overtly signalled by the presence of an overt symbolism of location, of shot composition, and of action and speech. Here, one source of influence from the late 1980s has been the new science fiction cinema (for instance, 1982's *Bladerunner* or 1987's *Robocop*), where advanced cybernetics meets urban dystopia. Within some treatments, the level of directness and emphasis on fantasy desires has the effect of tipping such projections into the comic or ironic, often thereby giving them a social acceptability and enjoyableness which they might lack if taken 'straight'.

Perhaps an example might be useful to finish this section. The British ITV award for the best commercial of 1993 went to Levi's 'Creek' ad, devised by the agency Bartle, Bogle and Hegarty. This draws on a wide range of tactics for its appeal – many of which I have discussed above – its originality laying mainly in their combination. It is essentially a wry microdrama of awakening sexuality, putting the emphasis on the rugged charm of the outdoor male. Filmed in black and white and placed in nineteenth century America, it opens with a decidedly Puritan-looking family (Amish community) going out in their horsedrawn coach to picnic amidst the rocky setting of Yosemite valley (Fig. 5.2). The parents have the countenance of stern self-denial, however the expression of one of the two young sisters shows she is struck by the beauty of the landscape. After the picnic, the girls stray away from their parents and discover a muscular young man bathing in the river; the upper half of his body is unclothed (Fig. 5.3). As she observes from behind a tree, the looks of the older daughter show a developing and self-suprising sexual arousal (Fig. 5.4). Her awe at the sight of the man's body is comparable with her awe at the scenery. Jeans left on the bank suggest the man is completely naked. As he emerges from the water, this possibility is reflected in the girls' faces; they use the jeans as a part veil for their embarrassment/anticipation (Fig. 5.5). When his lower half is revealed, it turns out the man has been bathing in his jeans (Fig. 5.6),

Fig. 5.2. Levi's 'Creek': The Splendour of the Wilderness

Fig. 5.3. Levi's 'Creek': The Bather

Fig. 5.4. Levi's 'Creek': Awe and Awakening

Fig. 5.5. Levi's 'Creek': Modesty and Fascination

Fig. 5.6. Levi's 'Creek': Denouement

the ones on the bank belong to another swimmer. He wades out of the water on to the bank and, picking up his saddlebag, walks away towards his tethered horse. The Levi caption appears on the screen.

The period setting, the landscape, the typing of the characters and the storyline as well as the mode of shooting (which uses extreme close-ups both of the man's body and the older girl's lips and eyes) – all organise a response which connects together history, national identity, scenic splendour and the erotic on a cinematic scale. The musical accompaniment is organised around a steady development, starting off ethereally with choir and orchestra and then breaking into a familiar and crashingly loud heavy rock riff as the lower half of the man's body emerges from the water.

I now want to explore matters of form a little more by using the subheadings of 'knowledge' and 'pleasure'. These, I hope, will allow me to get further analytic purchase on the kind of communicative and aesthetic work going on in television commercials.

Knowledge and Pleasure in the Television Commercial

It is very hard to imagine a television commercial having any effect at all (that is to say either a 'good' one as seen by the advertiser or a 'bad' one as seen by critics of advertising) without some kind of 'knowledge' being generated in the viewer. I will leave aside for the moment the question of whether such knowledge is consciously held or not. It is also very hard to see how commercials can hope routinely to win the minimum level of attention necessary for their effectiveness if they do not set out to give pleasure to the viewer in some way, visually or verbally, through humour, parody, excitement, sexual appeal and so on.

The knowledge generated by commercials inevitably concerns information about product identity, product use and product qualities. That is to say, however minimalist their style, all ads indicate *what* is being marketed. In many cases, the *kind* of thing it is may be redundant information, given the presumed consumer awareness of the viewer, but some statement about quality is nearly always present. Even the methods of representing established brands, whose manufacturers may feel able to rely simply on pre-existing assumptions about 'quality', involve a degree of quality projection. The very simplicity and restraint of these ads are designed to work as a textual marker of quality. They show the ad to be more active in its *implicit* promotional work than its explicit discourse would suggest.

Of course, the taking of knowledge from ads is almost invariably done in a way which recognises their distinctiveness as a mode of *persuasive* communication and recognises, too, the sorts of communicative moves they are likely to make (including the use of selectively positive information, the use of exaggeration and the linking of the product, with varying degrees of directness, to established forms of 'goodness'). This interpretative fact about ads, that they are typically read within the cultural 'rules' for reading them, is sometimes forgotten by academic analysts, who have shown a tendency to regard them as texts to be related to culture-in-general directly, rather than via the mediations of such 'rules'. Here, it is interesting to note an erroneous assumption often made by students of advertising (particularly in school and media studies classes) about the 'promise of ads'. This assumption focuses on that which is put into the ad to lend a product desirability (say, an attractive woman sitting in a sophisticated-looking restaurant, clearly somewhere in Europe; a well-built, handsome man using an aftershave) and regards this as indicating a promise to the viewer along the lines, 'If you buy this product then you will be (more) like this person'. Whatever the psychological mechanisms by which a displacement, or an act of 'value transfer', is achieved between certain non-product features of the commercial and the product itself, this very rarely amounts to a proposition which could become an element of viewers' conscious reasoning ('Yes, I would love to look like that and do that kind of thing, so I'll buy that perfume right away'). The response is much more likely to be one which, interpreting within the 'rules', finds aspects of the product's depiction either thematically or formally attractive and desirable but continues to register the radical implausibility of any major *personal transformation* occurring as a result of purchase. Such a response is not likely to view the ad as fraudulent in its depiction, since it may regard the implausibility of personal change of this kind as just too widely accepted for people to be vulnerable to deceptive appeals. The 'rules' therefore permit ads to connect their products to 'goodness' in a number of ways without a promise being seen to be made.[8]

This is to move from an emphasis on knowledge to one on pleasure and to see ads, particularly perhaps those of contemporary television, as a kind of 'cultural game' played across knowledge/pleasure with the general acquiescence of the viewer. Advertisers have become extremely adept at making sure that they do not break the rules, particularly not their selective codification in the regulations governing television advertising practice (in which context, to be seen to be making a substantive promise to consumers which the product was unable to fulfil would be to risk a legal penalty). In a useful account (developed in the form of a classical dialogue) of how advertising messages work, John Thompson (1990) has suggested that the basic model is a 'rational core', which is read by viewers as giving 'knowledge of the product' and to which legal constraints on product description in merchandising apply, and a 'decorative periphery', to which viewers attribute little or no knowledge function at all, instead regarding this as a legitimate attempt by the advertiser to please them and to 'win them over'. This latter area is not the subject of marketing and consumer legislation but, instead, has to conform to a broader set of laws and 'public taste codes' concerning public representation through image and speech. For certain types of potentially harmful product such as alcohol and tobacco, the codes may be explicit and combined with restrictive legislation.

Thompson's distinction is a useful one in breaking with the more simplistic approaches to the 'advertising message' (hidden or otherwise) but the disjunction of 'core' and 'periphery' seems to me to be unhelpfully abrupt when applied to the textual organisation of most contemporary ads. The terminology also cannot help but attribute a representational primacy to the rational, although Thompson recognises that current tendencies in advertising are often productive of a minimalist, quite notional, 'core' and an extravagantly developed 'periphery'. My own view is that the inter-articulation of the propositional and the entertaining, of that which can be seen as a quality of the product and that which is there merely to sell it, is more a matter of movement across levels of interpreted significance within the *reading* of the ad as a whole, rather than a function of two distinct and detachable communicative schemes at work within it. Nevertheless, Thompson's rejection of the idea of unified signification, which either 'influences' the viewer or doesn't, is cogently worked through and it may be that his core/periphery model was devised primarily in relation to static adverts (posters and magazine display) where its binarism might prove less awkward than with the dynamic form of the television commercial. It is also true that many static adverts give far more time to detailed (printed) product information than could prudently be included in a commercial's voice-over or captioned text. For certain products, new hi-fi accessories or new models of car for example, it is sometimes the case that potential buyers require this level of 'technical' information about 'product performance' before making a decision about purchase. In such cases, the television advertisement can only act as a point of *attraction*, projecting product identity and value with sufficient force to push potential buyers on to the next stage of seeking printed information either in newspaper and magazine ads or through specialist publicity produced by the manufacturers themselves.

For other products, of course, such an emphasis on subsequent information seeking will not be necessary, since purchasing decisions will not be based on product performance to anything like the same extent. However, nearly all television adverts form part of a more comprehensive marketing strategy for a particular product. In this strategy, not only ads in other media, but also marketing campaigns in shops, mail-shot leaflets and perhaps a whole range of other promotional devices, will be employed. The television ad is usually regarded as being in the vanguard of the campaign. If it does its pleasure–knowledge job effectively, the other elements are means of support, amplification and extension. If it doesn't, then the product is not likely to achieve the minimum level of public visibility necessary for it to 'take off' on the market.

Mechanisms of Influence

I remarked above that the basic method by which many ads work to create positive evaluations of their product is through a process of *value transfer*. This term, sometimes to be found in advertising training manuals, is perhaps too mechanistic to capture adequately the complexity, and the degree of unpredictability, involved in the actual business of generating 'good feelings' around products, but it has the merit of clarity and pointedness. By locating the product in the context of what are, in one way or another, positive situations, people, events, other goods etc., a generalised positive feeling is produced which then becomes attached to the product. Value transfer can also seek to work through form alone, setting up a pleasure in colours, sounds, shapes and movements which then becomes the object of transfer.

As I have noted, where 'realist' scenarios of good living are involved, it is certainly not a part of advertising strategy to persuade the viewer that by buying the product they will actually gain an entrance to this world. However, it may well be part of the strategy to encourage them to play around with the idea of themselves in such a setting, to stimulate a daydream around this *im*possibility. Within such a circumstance, the product does not become the *agency of transformation* but a kind of *fantasy aid*. The viewer's recognition of the impossibility of a significant shift in personal circumstances goes along with an enjoyment of the reverie (and the possibility of positive consequences for the product's image). This is particularly the case with goods which are self-consciously marketed as *personal products* (bath salts, perfumes, aftershave lotions, soaps, cosmetics, shampoos etc.), in relation to which self-conscious fantasy about the 'improved self' is culturally conventionalised (a matter of everyday talk among friends and the subject of comic narratives in different media). I suggested that no purchaser is likely to feel cheated by an ad of this kind when the product does not act as an agency of real change.

In assessing the general relationship between product values and broader cultural values and the way in which the latter are deployed to determine and project the former, it is worth registering how talk about 'advertising influence' frequently collapses together two rather different lines of potential power, selling power and cultural power.

Selling Power

Ads are designed to sell goods and one very clear criterion of their success (maybe not so clear to measure *conclusively* but clear enough as a general guide) is their ability to increase sales. To do this, they must do two things. They must establish a brand name in the minds of viewers, so that the existence of the product becomes widely known and available to memory at subsequent moments of purchase (particularly so in the case of routinely purchased items of modest price, where 'giving X a try' is feasible). They must also, in most cases, provide the viewer/consumer with some reasons as to *why* they should make the purchase. With a completely new product this will require the projection of novel qualities and functions. In the far more typical case of a branded item in competition with many others, the distinct advantages available from *this* brand need clear articulation, which may or may not require implicit reference to other, 'lesser' brands.[9] As we have seen, in order to carry out both these communicative tasks, advertisers have recourse to two broad areas of evaluative discourse. Although the separation between these becomes at times purely notional, we can call these an *intensive discourse*, in which features of product design and performance are the subject of affirmation, and an *extensive discourse*, in which the product is situated within a whole range of much broader, cultural values. In this way, the product is projected both as a 'tool' (in the sense that a perfume is a 'tool' for personal enhancement) and as an object with a specific cultural resonance. Some advertisers regard this latter area of product projection as the 'value added' factor, giving the product (via mechanisms of value transfer) that degree of extra definition and/or attractiveness which makes all the difference to the selling power of the ad.

Critical anxieties about selling power have typically taken the form of a suspicion that viewers/consumers are somehow under an unacceptable level of communicational coercion from ads to buy things which they do not really need and which they do not really want. In an extension of this, some viewers/consumers are seen as living within an advertising-induced regime of purchasing aspirations which they have not the money to fulfil.[10] Although anything like adequate documentation of the real needs and wants being 'falsified' here is rarely provided [see Marcuse (1972) for a classic piece of question-begging on 'false needs'], the belief that unwarranted constraint on rational consumer choice is a primary function of advertising discourse remains a strong one. It is, understandably, frequently linked to theories about a *subconscious* level of advertising effect, one which therefore is exerted 'below' the level of the viewer's awareness. Such a view may also see impositions of this kind, not as the localised 'bad practice' of a particular industry, but as something which is perfectly functional for the larger socio-economic system. That is to say, capitalism requires excessive consumption in order to maintain profits, and one way (perhaps the only way) in which excessive consumption can be maintained is by persuading people to buy things in a quantity and of a kind which it is unlikely that a rational consideration of requirement alone would suggest was sensible. Advertising, from this point of view, is demonstrably a form of anti-public, anti-rational activity, and may be judged as generally illegitimate without recourse to specific arguments about its effectiveness.

Cultural Power

Cultural power in the form of strategically organised cultural resonance, including the evocation of various types of 'goodness' and 'badness' from images and words, is an important dimension of advertising's selling effectiveness. However, the cultural power of advertising has been regarded by many writers to reach well beyond that which is self-consciously deployed by the advertisers in order to sell the product. It has widely been seen as having a deep and general connection with the basic classifications and value system of social life, such that advertising reproduces and sustains the larger pattern of values, prejudices, anxieties and desires. This pattern is formed within terms broadly established by the dominant social and economic groups. Usually, this is much more than a theory about how advertising 'reflects' existing social prejudice, thereby inhibiting social change. Indeed, some accounts place the emphasis on the *constitutive* function of advertising's cultural character and regard this function as one frequently carried out in a deliberately *non*-reflective way. Here, it is precisely the combination of the *gap* between existing social realities and advertising, on the one hand, and the *influence* of advertising on cultural values on the other, which is the focus of anxiety. Children are often viewed as being particularly vulnerable to the broader cultural 'lessons' which advertising teaches.

The devices by which 'selling power' works usually involve a kind of *centripetal* energy, in which desirable aspects in the broader culture come to be focused on or around the product itself. Advertising has become strategically adept at picking up on, or in some cases prefiguring, cultural trends in order to carry out this 'culturalisation' of the product. Some of the most revealing studies of advertising in this respect are those of 'repositioning' campaigns, in which a product which broadly remains the same is 'moved' in its cultural associations. So, for intance, the glucose drink 'Lucozade', long associated with convalescence and the sick bed, was given a successful new image by being associated with sport and leading sports personalities. In shifting the connotations from those of illness to those of super-fitness, the advertisers were able to provide the drink with new connotations and a new 'use' (energy replenishment for the already healthy).[11]

In contrast, whatever 'cultural power' advertising possesses is generated by a *centrifugal* process. This is one in which the associations generated around the product work to sustain the desirability (or perhaps just the normality) of certain features of personal and social life. In the strongest versions of how 'cultural power' operates, advertising not only reinforces existing patterns of value but works to initiate new ones (for instance, around certain kinds of leisure product). I noted that one of the problems with seeing the 'selling power' of ads as illegitimately coercive is that of establishing the 'true judgements' people would make about their product needs if they were not the addressees of advertising. One of the problems with viewing the 'cultural power' of ads as an effective determinant of social value is that of situating the influence of ads within the context of other cultural influences, including those coming from other uses of media and from a range of formal and informal types of experiential setting (e.g. home, school, work, environment, leisure interest). It is the belief that advertising does indeed work in a 'dispersed' way to encourage certain values and beliefs, as well as in a 'concentrated' way to sell goods, that has generated so much controversy about advertising as a communicative practice. Although anxiety about 'selling power' remains a primary concern with consumer groups, it is forms of 'cultural power' which have, internationally, been at the centre of recent debate about advertising, particularly advertising on television.[12]

Arguments about Influence

The pursuit of arguments about advertising's cultural power has produced a vast literature of empirical research, textual analysis and commentary. At least as much has been written here as on the question of advertising's more limited (though still disputed) ability to sell products to consumers. Arguments both about the dangerous scale of such influence and, conversely, about its relative marginality, have had recourse to close analysis of advertising forms themselves. It is fair to say, however, that within the tradition of cultural critique, attention to advertising's images and words has played a greater role than either direct examination of the industry itself or, indeed, investigation of those who are deemed to be vulnerable before its powers – the television-watching and product-buying public. The shortage of work of this latter kind, on advertising audiences, is perhaps largely a result of the way in which the critical tradition in mass media research has only recently emerged from a phase where focus on textual forms was the dominant approach. In this phase, to some extent a consequence of the considerable influence exerted by structuralist and other linguistic paradigms on the human sciences, texts were regarded as bearers of ideological (and therefore mostly 'hidden') meanings which were open to relatively secure analysis through the concepts and methods of semiotics.[13] The re-evaluation of semiotics as a research tool now suggests problems with the 'scientific' levels of analysis which some of its advocates once propounded, as well as more general problems of social explanation.[14] Meanwhile, the more general and substantive question of 'ideological reproduction' (the various deployment of meanings in the maintenance of power relationships) has undergone revision too, making it much more an open question as to just how, and in what ways, the practical consciousness of media audiences is affected by what they see, hear and read. It is interesting to note here just how *frequently* the example of advertising was used within media studies employing semiotic analysis and theories of ideological reproduction. It is not hard to see why this should be. Constructed out of some of the most innovative devices of cultural technology for imaging and symbolising self and society, and constructed precisely to reproduce and develop a central function of the capitalist social system, commodity consumption for profit, advertising often exerted a strong (and strongly political) pull on the analysis of mass communication. This resulted in many questions about it being asked repeatedly and some questions about it hardly being asked at all.

In trying to engage with these issues as they affect television commercials, I have chosen to make extended reference to two contrasting pieces of analysis which avoid the limitations of structuralist formalism (notably, too much theoretical presumption and too little analytical inquisitiveness). In keeping with the main concerns of this book, both of them are interested in commercials as forms of public communication.

The Case Against – Advertising as Pornography

A strongly polemical criticism of contemporary television advertising form has been put forward by the American literary critic, Wayne C. Booth. His account (Booth, 1982) is part of a more general, pessimistic reflection on the way in which video culture has imposed new 'patterns of desire' on to social relationships. Booth's perspective on advertising emphasises its sociality – its routine, expressive presence in everyday life. Given this pervasiveness, his anxieties turn on the way in which adverts employ what he identifies as a 'pornographic structure'.

> Most traditional narrative has relied on imitating the seemingly natural form: 'roused appetite-fulfilled appetite'. But one prominent subgroup of narrative has always rivalled this pattern, the kind that rouses appetites and refuses to gratify them *within the form.*
>
> (Booth, 1982, p. 52)

By using the term 'pornographic', Booth is not referring to any particular erotic properties of advertising, though such properties are, of course, a major element of its desire system. He is talking of the general relationship between desire, fulfilment and narrative form. If narratives rouse appetites not gratified within the form, how *are* these appetites gratified? With pornography, it is by sexual activity of some kind. With advertising, Booth argues, by setting in train a requirement for possession:

> . . .unlike even the the shoddiest TV drama or talk show, the commercial is obviously and blatantly organised to leave itself uncompleted, to make us desire something that by definition the present moment cannot supply. . .If I imagine anything, it is only the steps I must take to go down town and get my hands on that new possession.
>
> (Booth, 1982, p. 53)

So, unlike the narrative forms of 'art' (traditional and modern), advertising does not offer any imaginative satisfaction; instead it points outside itself to something which it has been its express purpose to create a desire for. Insofar as its representations of social life have become part of the normative expression of the culture (and, I shall suggest later, we may need to be more careful than Booth in making assumptions about this), advertising is seen to be involved in the quiet, steady, instrumental rearticulation of social and affective relations. This general proposition is illustrated by Booth by reference to an AT&T (telephone company) advert shown on American television and designed to promote an increase in long-distance calling. He is particularly interested in the way a kind of vicarious experience of long-distance calling is constructed by the advertisers as a model (albeit a humourous one) for a 'new' mode of phone use. In the ad, a sequence of scenes shows varied social contexts in which being in touch by telephone brings pleasure. These include a proud father watching his daughter tap-dancing in her new shoes, at the same time holding the phone down to pick up the sound for the benefit of the person at the end of the line; a roughed-up rodeo rider phoning news of his competition success to relatives; a young women in muddy riding clothes phoning news of the race she has just won; an army recruit with freshly shaven head making one of his first calls home. Booth's reading of this series of cheery scenes picks up on the kind of desire being promoted:

> . . .It is essentially still a cluster of sentimental moments associating the telephone with the viewer's desire for love and victory and laughter. The makers rightly assume that we all desire these things, and if we can be made to desire them even more, and then to associate the desire with the next telephone call, as fulfillment, we will make more long distance calls.
>
> (Booth, 1982, p. 54)

The argument here is one about what I discussed earlier as the 'value transfer' mechanism. As it stands, it is an argument purely about *intentions*, but like many such arguments in the critical tradition, it starts to become an argument about *achieved influence*. Booth is quickly able to claim of such representations, without any further evidence, that 'it takes no very deep analysis to show that they are among the primary forces shaping modern American character' (Booth, 1982, p. 55).

I am suggesting, then, that Booth's case displays a characteristic shift from a formal analysis (one informed, of course, by Booth's own social and ethical criteria) to a social analysis in which a recognised cultural propensity in the advert is assumed to achieve its 'effect' upon the viewer. I want to discuss the general validity of Booth's position in more detail later, but as well as offering a negative account of the advert's representations, Booth goes on to identify precisely what his reasons are for disapproving of its mode of representation. In moving to this level of focused evaluation, he goes beyond many other form-based advertising critiques, where there is not felt to be any requirement to offer specific points of objection once a general negative judgement has been made.

Booth identifies eight different properties of the ad which make the kind of imaginative experience it offers distinctive and depressing in their cultural implications. Briefly, these are:

1. Its visual intensity deflects attention from words. It is, in this sense, an 'anti-literacy' device.
2. It promotes passivity through its redundancy and repetition.
3. It does not permit ambiguity and works with taken-for-granted moral values.
4. It forbids reflection; the movement through the sequence quickly replaces one sensation with another.
5. It links the deepest human emotions with material acquisition.
6. It depends on stereotypes, since 'raw types' are the only sort of representations that can be comprehended at such speed.
7. It portrays the goal of life as victory. There are no 'losers' or 'victims' in its world.
8. Unlike in literature and other narrative art forms, there is no 'author' to the ad who is, him or herself, caught up authentically in its communication. The ad is a piece of trickery, a communication constructed out of bad faith.

In outlining the above objections, I have drawn extensively on Booth's own words, though I have also paraphrased some of his comments in the interests of brevity. What impresses me about this list is the way in which it brings together many of the complaints about advertising (particularly the television commercial) voiced by other commentators in the critical tradition with an unusual degree of explicitness and clarity. This is partly because Booth's self-declared position is that of an ethical critic of advertising rather than a political critic of it. He does not have a pre-established theoretical position within which to fit his critique. Though, as we shall see, this has the disadvantage of giving many of his points a random and rather loosely speculative character, it also carries with it the advantage of requiring him to express his complaints in an accessible manner rather than depending on general theoretical propositions assumed to be beyond dispute.

What are we to make of this mixed list of grievances and how do they relate to the general thesis about the 'pornographic structure' of advertising form? First of all, I think it is interesting how much the force of the critique seems to depend on the commercial somehow setting itself up as requiring the same level of serious attention as a form of narrative entertainment which had been chosen *as entertainment* by the viewer. In other words, behind Booth's criticism there seems to lie a belief that ads are *displacing* other forms of popular culture, including other forms of narrative. Only if this were the case would the particular significatory character of ads (e.g. visual intensity, use of types, fast cutting) be thought by itself to be bringing about a general shift in cultural sensibility. It may well be that recent cultural shifts, particularly in the area of video, magazines and popular journalism, have shown promotional and advertising styles being applied to a wider range of cultural production, but this is far from being conclusive evidence that advertising is *the* dominant representational form. So the implication, carried by at least some of Booth's remarks, that advertising is establishing itself as the primary form of contemporary public expression, must be contested. We might think that it is as sensible to

expect ambiguity, depth, cognitive challenge, moral exploration and reflec-
tiveness from a television commercial as from a handbill that comes
through the letterbox or a holiday brochure. In fact, it would be wrong to
be dismissive of Booth's general attempts to connect advertising to the
general system of cultural values and to read its fictions in terms of the
organisation of real relationships. But to explore that connection properly,
Booth needs to consider more carefully those 'reading frames' within which
adverts are habitually interpreted by audiences in everyday life. Whatever
general lessons are learnt from adverts, it must be through the mediation
of popular dispositions towards them. These dispositions guide the *kinds*
of attention ads get. Only if it is assumed that the effect of advertising is
primarily through the *unconscious* can this factor be seen as irrelevant. It
then becomes incumbent upon the analyst to provide a satisfactory account
of precisely how such an effect is sustained and made manifest in
behaviour.

If Booth's criticism falls short in its address to what happens 'in front' of
ads, in terms of the kinds of routine interpretation they receive from their
intended audiences, it could also be more explicit about what lies 'behind'
them, in terms of the economic and marketing contexts in which ads are
components of public communication. Again, this weakness is reflected in
much of the critical literature. To see the representations of advertising as
broadly symptomatic of an 'over-commercialised' society does not take us
very far into an inquiry as to *how* or *why* advertising works as it does.

Booth's most general point, about the 'pornographic' character of advertising, is limited, then, by the failure to consider the modalities and consequences of actual viewing. Nevertheless, the relentless deployment around
advertised commodities of various kinds of cultural 'goodness' (health,
love, family, friends, sun, sex, leisure) remains a feature of advertising
depiction open to an ethical criticism independently of any particular
theory about 'effects' (although, finally, it is hard to press the ethical case
very far without assuming *some* degree of negative influence).

However, pursuing the analogy with pornography may be deceptive
insofar as, in this cultural form, the *intentions of the user* seem to outweigh
the *intentions of the producer*. The producers of pornography clearly intend
their representations to incite sexual appetite, ending in sexual release of
some kind. Booth is right that a pornographic narrative does not set out to
satisfy the reader imaginatively but pushes the reader towards a desire
satisfied by other means. How far is this true of advertising? Certainly,
advertisers seek to create desire for products in audiences. But do
audiences routinely 'use' adverts to inflame their desire for products, a
desire subsequently fulfilled by purchase? The point is one about differences in the social relations of textual use involved. This makes assumptions about short-term effects much more questionable in the case of
advertising, where motivated 'use' is harder to imagine and where the
advert may have to seek to 'infect' the viewer with desire against routine
levels of casual disattention. Compare this with the fetishistic scrutiny
conventionally afforded to pornographic depiction. In fact, the contrast
goes further than this. For, far from initiating a desire only to be fulfilled
outside of the text, ads may in some cases do precisely the opposite of what

Booth suggests – provide a stimulation to fantasy (of product ownership, of heightened status, of activity and location) *which substitutes for product purchase.*

All these reservations leave space, of course, for particular criticisms of the social imagery employed by advertising, about *what* it shows. However Booth has no great interest in pursuing the argument at this level, being concerned almost exclusively with the cultural consequences of general form. This is put most strikingly towards the end of his essay:

> . . .the effects of the medium in shaping the primary experience of the viewer, and thus the quality of the self during the viewing, are radically resistant to any elevation of quality in program content: as viewer, I become *how* I view, more than *what* I view.
>
> (Booth, 1982, p. 56)

Whilst an emphasis on the social contingency of form and mode of watching is a helpful corrective to social scientific studies which still place 'content' as their exclusive area of concern, it seems to me that Booth here moves out well beyond any kind of evidence or argument. Even if 'how' factors were to hold sway regardless of 'what' factors, it would still remain the case that, for most viewers, the 'how' varies considerably across their viewing experience, as different kinds of generic format require different kinds of relationship to on-screen activity. The greater this variation, the less hold over consciousness and sensibility exerted by any one generic form. And Booth could hardly bring to his defence here those more recent arguments about a new homogenisation of the television experience occurring as a result of 'channel zapping' and the 'restless viewer', for these arguments would point towards precisely those levels of *dis*attention which make the case for influence harder to sustain.[15]

Booth, then, raises a number of questions about the social relations of advertising form but, despite the useful explicitness and clarity of his objections, he falls well short of clinching his case about the cultural debasement which adverts cause. This is not by any means simply a matter of the lack of empirical proof (to hold out for 'clear proof' in the cultural sciences can be a way of denying the plausibility and cogency of cultural *argument*), but a matter of inconsistencies and of lack of caution in moving from one stage of the case to another. I shall return to Booth's claims again at the end of this section, but I now want to consider a piece of research which contrasts interestingly with them. It, too, has a focus on the advertising aesthetic and the social relations this entails.

The Case For – Advertising as Art

Defences of advertising from within the academic community are rare, though scepticism about some of the methods which have been used to find advertising guilty are a little more common. However, there has undoubtedly been a change of climate in the attitude of media research towards advertising. I suggested at the start of this chapter that this must be related, among other things, to the steady extension of commercial culture internationally and to the increasing implausibility of alternative systems to versions of the market economy. In a much cited and quite recent article,

Mica and Orson Nava (1990) explore television commercials from the point of view of both the advertising agencies themselves and an important section of the viewing public – young people. Their arguments are very much part of a revised perspective on advertising. The Navas' account has two main themes running through it. First of all, that advertising now draws so widely on different cultural forms and is so productive of aesthetic innovation itself that it can legimately be seen as a form of contemporary art. Secondly, that there is evidence to show that viewers, particularly the young, are thoroughly discriminating in their 'reading' of ads, knowing the techniques employed to produce certain kinds of effect and responding critically to the way in which ads work as cultural and as 'technical' products.

The second proposition carries with it two important implications, which the Navas are keen to develop. It suggests that television commercials have become relatively independent of their function as devices for selling, insofar as they are often enthusiastically received by people who have no interest whatsover in buying the product (and perhaps, in many cases, lack the means to buy it). Furthermore, it puts a large question mark alongside the 'selling power' and (less directly) the 'cultural power' of advertising, since the degree to which viewers are to be regarded as sceptical, discriminating and literate about advertising must be also the degree to which they are resistant to any manipulative intent it has upon them. Once again, an appeal can be made to the idea of *subconscious processes*, and this is not to be dismissed. But, as I suggested earlier, placing emphasis on this level of communicative process then creates special requirements both of evidence and of argument.

I want briefly to look at the strength of the Navas' points. As with the Booth essay, it seems to me that they connect with a much wider range of commentary and debate. What about the contention that advertising is properly to be regarded as 'art'? This idea takes us directly back to Booth's argument for, of course, it was precisely his fear that advertising was assuming the status of an 'official' popular art, displacing other more authentic and richer modes of expression. There are two related criteria to be considered here – whether or not the particular aesthetic character of ads is such as to warrant this categorisation, and whether or not ads are perceived and related to by people in the kinds of way people perceive and relate to forms of art (including popular art). Of course, the category of 'art' is so notoriously open to shifting definition that it might seem entirely inconsequential as to whether ads are declared to be art or not. But if we look at the range of cultural expression available to the typical thirty second to one minute commercial, allowing for all the complexities of sound–image combination and 'post-modern' bravura which can be brought to bear on its construction, it is very difficult to make a comparison with, say, the expressive possibilities of popular song, of cinema, of television popular drama and of fiction (again, including popular titles here). These forms all have the space to explore motivation, develop character, portray relationships and ask questions about experience. Ads generally cannot do this (Booth *criticises* them as a result, but he should perhaps be holding back his criticism until he has recognised them for the kind of communications they *are*). When the

Navas claim that 'advertising is no more homogeneous as a creative form than music, painting, film or drama' (Nava and Nava, 1990, p. 20) it does seem as if the case is being pushed to the very limit and then beyond.

In pressing this claim for increased esteem, the Navas also feel it necessary to protect advertising from the 'taint' of its commercial origins. In order to do this, they quite correctly point to the fact that many, if not most, other forms of cultural expression have a commercial character – books have to sell, plays have to attract audiences, people have to want to buy certain paintings etc. However, to move on from this to note that the ad 'is no more or less inherently implicated in the economic organisation of life than any other cultural form' (Nava and Nava, 1990, p. 21) is once again to overstate the case. For whilst it is true that other expressive forms have varying degrees of commodity status (a book of poems from a small press less than a hit album) it would be very hard indeed to find another form which was so grounded in the requirement to sell. This remains the case, *even if* the argument about ads increasingly displaying an independent aesthetic identity and value is accepted.

What about the current conventions of audience use? Do these suggest an 'art worthiness' in ads? The Navas are able to show that young people collect on video, and replay, favourite commercials, delighting in their detail. But they are not able to demonstrate that the investment of significance in these is of the same kind and/or degree that is put into songs, films, written fictions, television programmes etc. Ads are seen as 'clever' and frequently as 'entertaining' but do these discursive characteristics require their reclassification as art?

My view, then, is that the claim for advertising as art is a misguided one. All arguments about what is and what is not art have a futile character but what is unacceptable about the Navas claim (which might otherwise be conceded with a resigned 'if you like, why not') is that in pursuing the case for esteem it misdescribes advertising in relation to other cultural forms. Its cultural analysis is faulty.

However, the more important point made by the Navas concerns the 'sophistication' of viewer interpretation and the implications this has for the two kinds of ad power outlined earlier. Here, their attention to the actual viewing practices of groups of viewers is wholly welcome. But the fact that lots of people are entertained by ads for things they don't buy does not tell us about the way they interact with ads for things they do buy. It would have been interesting to have heard more from the young people interviewed about their response to the ads for the jeans, soft drinks, computer games, leisure goods etc. which are within their buying range. To the purchase of these goods, they could be expected to give precisely the kind of consideration in which the 'value transfer' effects of advertising might play *some* role in brand choice. It seems clear, for instance, that the marketing of certain items in this area – Levi 501 jeans would be a notable case – is highly responsive to strong product identity created through advertising. If the emphasis on 'indoctrination' can be overplayed in analysis, so too can the emphasis on 'cynicism' if it is meant to suggest an almost complete unresponsiveness to the promotional power of advertising communication.

Moreover, the fact that young people are critically appreciative and sceptical about advertising's messages, whilst it directly questions the degree of 'selling power' which ads can deploy, only indirectly engages with the operation of 'cultural power'. It is perfectly possible for someone to be technically knowledgeable and appreciative about adverts whose content serves to reinforce within them a whole range of social prejudices. To the extent that their 'awareness' is of a kind which prompts them reflexively to monitor the *social values* which adverts trade on, this is unlikely. But an appreciation of the fun of ads, and of their creative/technical qualities, is not the same thing at all as a critical sense of the political and social assumptions upon which they are based and to which they speak.

At the end of their essay, the Navas claim that their aim is not to 'exonerate' advertising from its role in the 'formation and perpetuation' of consumer society. A negative, if vague, concluding note is thereby sounded. But a positive one is sounded too, equally vague, to the effect that the critical viewing of ads may work to 'subvert and fragment' existing power systems. The authors admit that their own argumentative route has been such as to 'bypass. . .debates' at the more general level of social theory. This is unfortunate. Equally unfortunate is the way in which, as I have suggested, their arguments *do* carry implications of a more general character that are not recognised.[16] For the Navas bring to arguments about advertising a number of fresh and important observations both about the relations of television commercials to a wider range of aesthetic practice and about the kinds of critical viewing commercials receive within youth culture (we can contrast Booth here). Their observation that commercials are becoming more ingenious, eclectic and inventive partly, if not largely, as a result of an increased sophistication among the audience, and that this, together with other factors, is giving them more independence as a cultural form, needs further inquiry. However, only when the larger debates about 'consumer society' are not bypassed but fully engaged with can development of this point properly occur.

Television Advertising: A 'Revised' Aesthetics and a 'Revised' Debate[17]

Advertising has been with us for a long time, and even television advertising now has a history (in many countries, one well worthy of further scholarly attention). As some of the comments made above suggest, however, there is an emerging view that both the advertising and its relation to other aspects of culture and social life are now undergoing considerable revision. Advertising is being seen to be more complex and diversified as a phenomenon at the same time as it has clearly become more extensive. In a comprehensive survey of recent trends in promotionalism which I referred to in Chapter 2, Andrew Wernick (1990) has pointed to the way in which advertising activities of one kind or another constitute a chain of interdependent promotional images and terms binding politics to sport to television programmes to toys to entertainment 'celebrities' and so on. This 'chaining' of promotional discourses – a phenomenon which has to be viewed as a radical departure from the idea of self-contained promotional acts, each with its own separate 'influence '– Wernick describes as constituting a 'vortex of publicity'. His own assessment views this as pathological. Insofar as it is an assessment grounded in his sense of the pervasiveness of promotional forms, the negative judgement is convincing. However, insofar as it concerns questions about the kind of impact these forms are currently having on contemporary consciousness, then once again, the pessimism is not adequately supported by evidence of actually sustained cultural damage. Nor is there sufficient real argument supporting the claim.

In a way which recalls Booth, the entire case about the cultural effectiveness of advertising tends to go by default. A textual reading indicates the kinds of cultural value informing most ads (to a large extent, the observations made here are unexceptionable) and then this whole set of symbolised values is made over into audience consciousness. I have suggested that the formalism of this kind of approach is not acceptable as a grounding for *sociological* propositions about advertising's consequences. It has become just too familiar a move to proceed directly from a detailed analysis of signification to a comprehensive judgement of cultural effect. Even if, finally, the evidence of empirical research both on advertising practice and on audience interpretation does not seem to require much modification of these judgements (which I doubt), it is still a requirement for cultural analysts to address extra-textual factors and data. Wernick usefully draws our attention to recent changes in promotional form but we are presented with little to convince us why we should agree with his assessment of their cultural significance.

But if a revised perspective on the study of advertising is suggested by the continuing untenability of many critical ideas about 'cultural badness', it is also required by changes in the nature of advertising itself. The Navas' point about the level of autonomy which ads now enjoy warrants further exploration but so, too, does their suggestion that advertising (in many countries recently hit by recession and a subsequent cutback in corporate 'adspend') is not at all confident about how effective it is or about what directions might best sustain it as an industry.

In Britain, one sign of this uncertainty has perhaps been the shift towards the kind of aesthetic density which the Navas point to as part of their argument about ads as art. Here, cross-cultural allusions, the 'recycling' and 'periodising' of earlier styles, the cultivation of indirectness, enigma and irony, seem to suggest a giving up on the *referentiality* of conventional 'value transfer' as ads compete for audience attention and some level of memorability in the increasingly busy audio-visual space within which everyday life is lived. In this space, novelty and cleverness are at a high premium, driven by the rapid rate at which ideas become used up and require renewal in response to changes in style and taste elswhere. The way in which ads are forced by this relentless opportunism into being nervously parasitic upon other forms, as well as an influence themselves, needs more attention then it gets.[18]

Another indication of a certain instability in the industry has been the emergence in Britain of a self-consciously 'socially responsible' advertising, particularly associated with the newer agencies in London. In this approach, conventional stereotypes are either undercut or replaced by emphatically non-stereotypical representations. For instance, in one recent television commercial for a photographic firm, images of mentally disabled people were used to bring attention to the way in which photography can be a force for social understanding and social empathy. Of course, this particular approach can only work effectively with certain products and a cynical view might see it as just another way of riding shifts in general public concern in order to benefit the product (just another device of 'value transfer'). However, it is at a considerable remove from those banal projections of power, success and family joy which Booth took as the focus for his critique. Whilst it seems clear that most advertising is by its very nature committed to the maximisation of private profit and therefore fits awkwardly with any attempt to promote public values which are not instrumental to that end, this does preclude shifts in advertising discourse which align it more closely, if only partially, with non-commodified values and forms of social relationship. However, in the context of recent international shifts and tendencies (see Mattelart, 1991) any general optimism might seem misplaced.

Television advertising will remain an important focus for media analysis. Its iconography, narrative formats, use of character types and shifting pattern of themes and values will continue to be of technical interest in respect of developments in media discourse and of cultural interest insofar as they are indicative of broader aesthetic, ethical and social factors. But this indicative quality cannot be read either as directly expressive (advertising reflecting the culturally normative) or as directly constitutive (advertising shaping the culturally normative). As Michael Schudson has pointed out in his splendidly sceptical study of advertising power, 'the consumer culture is sustained most of all not by manufactured images but by the goods themselves as they are used and valued in social groups' (Schudson, 1993, p. 248). Unfortunately, far too much work in media analysis has been reluctant to move much beyond the clues (rich and suggestive though these are) provided by the advertising text. This has not helped to refine our sense of either the 'selling power' or the 'cultural power' of advertising and it has led to a situation in which the professional journals of the advertising industry frequently contain more valuable indications on these matters than the academic literature. A perspective is needed which seeks critical dialogue with the professional discourses themselves as well as with consumers.

Moreover, as a result of the analytic focus on the role of advertising as ideological reproduction, the industrial power of advertising, its massive underpinning of public communication systems in many countries, has tended to be marginalised as an issue in academic teaching and research. The two are related, of course, in that it is advertisers' belief that 'messages' about desirable life style in relation to commodity use are actually getting across which justifies their huge contribution to the budgets of the media industries. However, it seems to me that the more pressing requirement in many countries is to develop a public policy on media funding which guards against the overextension of advertising into the central system of public information. This, not primarily because of the bad effects of the ads themselves, but because of the kind of skew introduced into the routine management of such systems as a result of excessive corporate control. The experiences of old 'Eastern Europe' will be instructive here, as they shift from one kind of explicit control to a less obvious and less direct set of imperatives. To give an example of the kind of initiative which needs more attention, some kind of levy on advertising, which required advertisers to fund short periods of network airtime (together with associated production costs) for public use as 'access slots' might be attempted, despite the problems of administering this adequately.

The scale and reach of the television commercial in modern societies certainly provides everyday life with a steady, continuous stream of messages about 'good things' and about how these are tied to possession. They image and imagine a personal and social life lived almost exclusively as a happy consumer. With very few exceptions, they do this without any reference whatsoever to disease, poverty, unemployment or the global conditions which lie beyond the glow of the high street shop window. In registering this, we must certainly reckon with their impact on contemporary consciousness. But we must also reckon with the ways in which contemporary consciousness has 'learned to live' with advertising, not altogether in ways of its own devising but by no means altogether in the ways advertising projects for its own consumption either.

6

'INFLUENCE' AND INTERPRETATION

In other chapters, I have variously explored questions about the influence of television. I have also discussed the interpretation of television by viewers and how this works so as to make any 'transmission' of meanings a good deal more complicated than a straight linear flow. This was a particularly important strand of the previous chapter and not suprisingly, since advertisements, as self-declared attempts to influence, raise these matters in a direct and explicit way. Here, I want to look at what is broadly involved in conceptualising and researching media 'influence' and viewer interpretation. That the two are interconnected is clear. The core of this interconnection is the production of meaning. Most, if not all, the kinds of influence imputed to television require that, at some point, meanings (often ones seen in some way to be 'bad') are generated in viewers heads. Interpretation is the perceptual, linguistic and cognitive activity by which viewers' produce meaning from television's visual and aural significations.

It might be useful to start this chapter with an outline of those general ideas about the contingency of meaning which have informed much recent audience research, though not yet enough research into television influence. I will look at a number of ideas concerning 'influence' and at one area in which the study of influence processes has been particularly intensive and controversial – depictions of violence.

This will provide a substantial basis for a more detailed treatment of 'interpretation', for it is my intention to use each term both to question, and then to develop, the other.

The Contingency of Meaning

Inquiry following the approach of 'reception studies', now an internationally prominent strand of audience research, departs from previous work on media audiences insofar as it works with a proposition about the 'contingent' nature of meaning production. Put at its simplest, this proposition states that meanings are not inherent properties of televised texts, they are instead the product of viewer interpretation working upon significations. It therefore follows that there is nothing 'in' texts which acts of comprehension can be usefully seen to extract from them; instead, there is an interactive process within which meaning is consequent upon interpretative action.[1]

This is seen to be true of the most simple as well as the most complex texts. So the statement 'would you please shut that window' requires its meaning to be produced by reference to the hearer's competence in construing spoken English, while a non-representational image in an art gallery requires its meaning to be produced by reference to the onlookers' competence in 'reading' fine art and their familiarity with the particular formal ideas put to work in the picture. If the statement is made to a hearer who has no English, it will deliver no clear meaning at all. If the art work is seen by someone without a background in fine art appreciation, there is a good chance that it, too, will be seen as 'meaningless'. And whilst in the first instance, the hearer might immediately see that the problem lies with their own lack of knowledge of English, in the second instance the problem might be attributed to the non-communicative character of the artwork itself (thus, perhaps, producing a hostile disposition towards it as obscure and maybe 'fraudulent').

Such a view of how meaning is produced immediately has implications for ideas about the stability of textual meaning and about the variations which occur in interpretations of all kinds of television. It is no longer remotely suprising if people show considerable differences in the meanings they attribute to televised output if these meanings are in some measure the product of their own activity. The way is open, then, to discover more about the social relations of this activity – how social factors contribute to the interpretative frameworks upon which people draw, and thereby figure as factors in the constitution of meaning. It is worth pointing out here that what we refer to when we talk of the 'meaning' of a newspaper article or television programme is often quite a complex layering of different kinds of meaning. My two examples, above, of simple statement and artwork suggest this. As a result, a related complexity is introduced into ideas of meaning's contingency but for now I will ignore the full scale of this, returning to it later in the chapter. What I will note here, however, is the very important difference between the primary meaning accorded to signifiers (say, as words with a certain English meaning or as pictures of certain things) and the broader significance which may be attributed to them in specific contexts of use. It is an aspect of the expressive discourses of the arts, including the popular arts, to encourage readers and viewers routinely to expect such broader significance and therefore to carry out interpretation with this in mind (so that a statement banal in its obviousness in conversation can be invested with a considerable depth of meaning if appearing as a line in a play or, even better, in a poem). Of course, broader secondary significance, mostly of a less intensive kind, is a feature of everyday communication too.

Where does such a view leave the idea of 'influence'? How is it possible for a text to bring about any change in a reader or viewer if its meanings are a product of reading and viewing activity? Certainly, any idea of influence as linear transmission, the direct reproduction (by manipulation, implantation etc.) in the viewer of certain attitudes, is radically put into question by a theory of meaning as contingent on interpretation. For a start, the very fact of *variation* works against the idea of any uniform influence, while the emphasis on 'activity' works against that characterisation of viewers and readers as essentially passive which has been a feature of theories of 'heavy influence' (including theories about ideology).[2]

But within such a theory it is still possible to conceptualise how changes might be brought about as a result of a viewer's interaction with a programme. Texts (books, films, television programmes etc.) arrange signs within a certain order of combination and articulation which cues readers, listeners and viewers not only into the 'stock' production of old or familiar meanings, but into the production of new or at least unfamiliar meanings too. The more we emphasise the broader, significance-attaching processes rather than the primary ones (see above) the more this generative feature becomes apparent. Again, it might be best to proceed by example. Let us take the case of someone who finds a television play to have 'opened up' for them a whole new world around, say, what it is like to be disabled. (We could say of such a case that the programme had 'influenced' them but it might be better to leave this term until it, too, can be looked at more closely.) What of the nature of the communicative process at work here? It would seem likely that a particular mix of acting, scripting, direction and so on had 'cued' the reader into new imaginative behaviour, new alignments of sympathy and new areas of knowledge (for instance, about what being disabled actually meant in terms of daily, physical routine). At all points, the play depended on the reader using their linguistic and cultural knowledge to produce meanings from what they saw and heard, but this does not mean at all that there was no 'invention' or 'creativity' or 'suprise' or 'shock' at work. Nor does it mean that this was somehow the achievement of the viewer instead of the television team. The viewer produces the meanings, but does so in relation to the significatory work which has been undertaken by those who made the play. This productive relationship is a direct one for each viewer but it is also one which, given the differences in what viewers bring to the production, is open to variation (we would not expect everyone to agree in their interpretation of the play). Only if we remain committed to the old idea of meaning lying 'within' texts (admittedly, a convenient and innocent enough fiction for many everday purposes) will we find the terms of this interaction difficult to work with, appearing to thwart, for instance, any notion of authorial responsibility.

With this provisional sense of what is at stake in talking about 'meaning' and 'interpretation', I now want to explore what lies behind the use of the term 'influence' – without a doubt one of the most frequently used terms in the history of media research and one around which countless studies have been organised.

Television and 'Influence'

What is involved in thinking about television as exerting influence, what kind of relationship between screened material and viewer might be seen as an influential one and how might the level and direction of any influence detected be measured? My general approach to these questions will be theoretical rather than methodological, although I realise that many debates on the topic have turned on questions of method, perhaps more often than questions of theory. It has become a much remarked characteristic of 'influence' research that, taken as a whole, it has been resoundingly *inconclusive*.[3] The frequent implication placed on this within the academic community has been that, until harder evidence is forthcoming, it is best to remain sceptical. While there is some ground for taking such a brisk view, closer attention to public *assumptions* about television's 'influence' and to the various theories about influence which have been advanced in academic study, reveal a more complicated pattern to the inconclusiveness.

If we look at those ideas about television influence which figure in public discussion of, for instance, portrayals of violence or political coverage, it is quite clear that television is widely *assumed* to exert a considerable influence on public attitude formation and behaviour. Such assumptions are too implicit to count as theories and the kind of 'evidence' upon which they are based is not the product of systematic collection, but they are *instrumental* ideas nevertheless (a good deal more so than academic theories), because they inform policy and action in a number of areas of public life. Before assessing academic attempts to define and research influence, it is worth asking quite what is indicated by the term in this kind of lay context.

I think popular notions of influence assume that television has the power to change people's attitudes and also in certain cases directly to 'trigger' certain kinds of behaviour (for instance, stimulating violent action or action which is imitative of that seen on television). Television's capacity to do this is often (if a little unclearly) linked to its reportorial 'realism' or (and the difference is important) its 'explicitness'. That is to say, firstly, that the capacity of news and documentary output to offer plausible visual evidence of what is happening in the political and social world is seen to be potentially open to forms of manipulation in which 'false impressions' of a kind injurious to public truth and democratic process are produced. This is an anxiety which has been expressed in different ways since the start of television services. It is clearly there in the Lang and Lang study discussed in Chapter 1 and I have also discussed it briefly in relation both to news and to documentary output. Secondly, the sheer vividness and memorability of the television image is regarded as having the power to, as it were, 'sieze hold of the mind' in a potentially pathological way. This view is held with particular strength in relation to images of sexual explicitness (where it connects with the whole debate about the social consequences of pornography) and images of violence. Here, it is not so much that a modification of conscious opinion is achieved (although this can be argued too) but that a certain kind of disposition is 'implanted' in the viewer, setting up drives which may seek fulfilment in action.

I believe that propositions such as these, partially and sometimes rather vaguely held as they may be, are to be widely found among the contemporary television audience and therefore that it is not at all suprising that 'panics' and 'campaigns' about particular kinds of output receive widespread public support. Often, such support sees the more sceptical, questioning views of academics as of little consequence in addressing the 'influence' issue, as a dithering in the face of the facts.

Before examining what conceptualisations of influence have been employed in academic debate, however, I want to stay at the level of lay understanding and tease out further aspects of the way in which notions of television power figure in public life. I hope to show that these notions bear on academic argument too.

Take the example of the television weather forecast, in many countries a nationally networked item of output. Could we consider this to be implicated in processes of 'influence', an example itself of 'influential television'? It certainly has the 'effect' of modifying people's behaviour, causing the cancellation of certain events and the initiation of others as well as, more routinely, acting as a guide to the planning of the day and of what to wear.

The television weather forecast as an example of influence seems odd, even silly. Discussion about influence usually has something a good deal more 'interesting' to concern itself with than this. Why, then, does it fail to meet our criteria for being the object of a 'proper' argument about influence. I think the answers here are illuminating.

First of all, it might be claimed that the weather forecast is not a 'viewpoint' advanced, explicitly or otherwise, in an attempt at *persuasion*. It simply offers a predictive account based on the available knowledge at the time as processed by scientific procedures. The assumption here is that 'influence' relates only to the generation of attitudes and opinions and to change induced in these. To move from not knowing at all about what tomorrow's weather will be like to having some predicted indications is not to undergo a change in attitude.

Secondly, taking a different tack, it might be objected that the weather forecast is merely 'relaying' the knowledge obtained by a meteorological institution, even if this institution is owned by the television company. In this view, there is no significant media discourse at work in the forecast itself which could exert an 'influence'. Any influence is achieved as a result of *content*, and the content of a weather forecast is largely independent of its form of delivery. The assumption here is that only when a consequence follows from television-generated factors can the medium itself be regarded as influential.

Thirdly, it could be argued that there is no reason to feel ashamed, distressed or in any other way unhappy about acting in certain ways as a consequence of watching a weather forecast. It is a perfectly *rational* thing to do. Though weather forecasts are sometimes completely wrong and often not entirely right, they offer justifiable, logical grounds for taking action. The assumption here is that television influence can only occur when action is generated on other than reasonable grounds. Among other things, this brings influence closer to ideas about a subconscious level of response.

Finally, deploying a related objection, one could claim that the weather report is essentially a helpful type of communicative event, even allowing for its occasional inaccuracies. The assumption here is that 'influence', wherever and whenever detected, is a *bad* thing. The more influence we find, the more worried we should become.

I am aware that this does not exhaust the range of possible objections. For instance, it might be said that the forecast is heavily *predictive*, though it would then have to be admitted that many other forms conventionally seen as potentially 'influential' are predictive too (for instance, party political broadcasts). It might also be claimed that weather reports only exert a short-duration effect, being replaced daily if not more often. This is an important point, but it does not deny the relevance of my example. Instead, it indicates the need to make more explicit our assumptions about the durational aspect of influence processes. This would involve attention to matters of repetition (such as one finds, for instance, in arguments about advertising and 'video nasty' viewing).

If *all* the objections I have chosen to highlight were to be put, then clearly not only the weather forecast but a number of kinds of output more familiar within arguments about influence might have to be excluded. For instance, it is generally assumed in public discourse that certain kinds of television (types of children's programme for example) can exert a good influence.[4] It is also often believed that people can be influenced by programmes in ways which were not intended (hence the often convoluted arguments about how certain programmes are fine for some audiences but not for others who will 'misread' them with unfortunate consequences). As a set of objections which point in different directions and are activated by different presumptions and prejudices, however, these hypothetical responses indicate some of the contours of 'television influence' as an idea in public culture.

Against them, I might want to argue that the weather forecast is indeed an example of media influence, even if this means a radical revision of conventional criteria in order for it to be recognised as such. In pursuing this end, I could claim that the *knowledge environment* of a very large number of people has been changed by the predictions offered in the broadcast. This change counts as 'influence' even though it operates for the most part as a rational, non-opinionated, largely 'relayed' set of messages designed very much to serve a public good. The fact that every night this non-sinister event exerts its influence and the fact that the most manifest example of this is to be found in the mundane business of what people choose to wear and how, within the constraints of the day, they organise their outdoor activities, should not remove at all from its status in this respect.

If my case is conceded, along with the broadened criteria of what might reasonably be considered 'influence', then one of the things that follows is that there is a lot of influence around, some of it not at all bad and some of it not very 'strong' when judged against academic and public convention. This seems to me to be a good way to view things. It usefully displaces the idea of the key question being 'influence or no influence?' (a question which betrays its origins in behaviouristic social science). Instead, the key questions become 'what kind of influence, how exerted, in what direction, how strongly?' These are certainly hard questions, posing their own problems of definition but, as a concept, 'influence' loses some of the drama which has been been associated with it; it becomes less evaluatively charged.

It might now be interesting to see how my weather report example compares with those areas of television output which have received the most attention from academic researchers investigating influence. These areas I take to be advertising, politics and violence.

Advertising

In the last chapter, I looked at arguments concerning advertising. It was clear that many criticisms of this area of output stress its character as *strategic, persuasive communication* and its capacity to form *attitudes* both in a limited way, towards the product being marketed, and in a more general way, towards aspects of contemporary cultural and social life. This emphasis on intentions and attitudes clearly distinguishes the 'influence' issue here from that in my example, although one of the things which advertising also undoubtedly does is routinely to change the public knowledge environment about product availability and product performance.

Politics

A variety of theories have been employed in researching the consequences of the more directly political kinds of television item. An extreme example would be the ideas about 'brainwashing' and 'indoctrination' which, as I noted earlier, have frequently been aired in public debate (particularly in the United States) and which were given some support in the more behaviouristic social science studies, especially those issuing from psychology.[5] Currently, however, what is increasingly the dominant approach in researching this area is one we can call 'cognitive–interpretative'.[6] It emphasises the kinds of knowledge produced by political accounts on television and the way the classificatory system and substantive propositions of these accounts interact with viewers' own understandings and judgements. This is much closer to the weather report example; changes in the knowledge environment are precisely what are at stake. Of course, political accounts are taken to be much more open to differences of evaluative interpretation, *both by journalists and by viewers*, than are weather reports, so here there is a more developed sense of the possible significance of variation and the kind of motivations, causes and consequences it may carry. But if we wished to follow my earlier suggestions, we could well suppose that the political output of television, across its various forms, is routinely influential in changing the public knowledge environment about policies, about politicians and about the political system as a whole. This view would fit in with the routine way in which politicians themselves behave towards the media. I have noted, though, that in my usage the term 'influence' does not carry anywhere near the charged meaning which it does in other usages. To get to a controversial level with my usage, it has to be argued not that there is influence, but that it is of a certain (undesirable?) strength, too much in one direction (for the maintenance of a democratic public sphere) and perhaps exerted too extensively through appeals to the non-rational (thereby placing emotions as superior to thought in political decision making). If I wanted to go on to make convincing arguments about these matters, it would clearly involve me in questions about evidence and the methods for its collection and interpretation.

Violence

Taken as a subfield of inquiry, research on violence has been informed by ideas of influence which differ quite strongly from those in my weather report example. A dominant strand of investigation has worked with the idea of the direct behavioural consequences which, for some viewers, follow from the watching of certain types of violent material. Although notions of 'arousal' and the 'triggering' of emotions have been applied to inquiries into advertising and into television's political accounts, the investigation of violence has placed far more stress on them, often in the process bypassing altogether a phase of meaning production in which sense is made by viewers from what they see and hear. Research perspectives using cognitive hypotheses can be found, such as those which argue for the 'densensitising' effect of violent viewing or for an increasing fear of violence among those who regularly watch such material, but 'trigger' theories have often dominated the debate.[7] Even the converse of the usual thesis about an increased tendency towards violence, the argument that viewing violent acts works cathartically to *decrease* the chances of the viewer engaging in violent behaviour, usually depends on a version of the 'trigger' idea. This situation is partly a consequence of the fact that violence is often regarded as an intense, emotionally driven behaviour, performed in an abnormal state of mind. Researchers have frequently bypassed the phase of meaning production in their accounts because they have felt that, here, the influence process itself is one which bypasses the 'informational' level or anything to do with 'knowledge'. In a popular, public version of the relationship between violent texts and violent behaviour, an appeal to some kind of 'basic instinct' is often imagined to occur. Indeed, here it seems not so much that something is 'implanted' as that something is 'released' by the screened material. This gives an altogether different inflection to the process of influence from that in the examples discussed above. Another important factor, which I shall bring out in more detail below, is that concern about the influence of violent depictions is often focused on television *fiction*. This does not mark out an unproblematically clear division in relation to advertising and politics of course (advertising is a kind of fiction, whilst much drama is strong in political implications) but it poses questions about the relationship between form and influence in a specific way.

Having established some preliminary ideas about 'influence' and the problems of investigating it, I want to look in more detail at some of the issues involved in researching 'television violence'. I do this not only because I have already given some consideration to political output and to advertising elsewhere, but because study of television's depictions of violence and their probable or actual influence upon viewers raises several conceptual questions which any consideration of television as 'public communication' needs to ponder. This is especially so since, in many courses on media, the 'violence' issue has not received as much attention as the debates surrounding advertising and political output. This may be partly due to the way in which the issue can seem to be in a state of permanent play-off between the less accessible kind of quantitative inquiry and the more dogmatic kind of moralism.

In keeping with discussion elswhere in this book, I shall relate my examination of this area to questions about the forms through which violence is depicted. I am aware that a substantial body of research exists which does not attend much if at all to matters of form. I am also aware of the dangers of formalism. But I cannot see much progress being made unless a concern with the precise nature of what appears on the screen becomes more fully integrated with the sociological character of inquiries.

The 'Violence Issue': Values and Meanings

The researcher intending to look at the ways in which portrayals of violence on television might have consequences for viewers' attitudes and behaviour is faced immediately with the oddness and paradox which surrounds the *cultural* character of violence in many societies. Violence is generally seen to transgress the codes of public morality, to be in breach both of secular ethical codes and religious teaching. Given this, most societies have then to legitimise 'official violence' for a variety of purposes, including most obviously military ones. Western societies have tended to do this by the use of a 'regrettable but necessary' clause in relation to such breaches of the basical ethical code. So, for instance, the killing which a soldier may have to perform in defence of his country's interests is still a bad thing. But his is not a bad act, since it receives justification in the context of the wider good it serves. Naturally, there is some awkwardness and deviousness surrounding such routine justifications, which allow plenty of opportunity for the exercising of hypocrisy and are frequently the focus of critical challenge. But the basic fact of this co-existence, in many societies, of criminal and non-criminal violence is something which I think has implications for the discussion of television portrayals.

Even more important than this 'inconsistency', though, there is the fact that a form of activity which is generally regarded as 'bad' in real life is a key component of popular entertainment when presented in fictions. We can contrast this situation to that of sexual activity, where precisely the opposite kind of relationship obtains. Though sexual acts are a central and normal part of human relationships, the explicit depiction of these is in many countries deemed offensive and deviant. I would not want to pursue this further here, since there are a number of complicating factors which quickly emerge (for instance, the guilt still associated with sexual expression in many cultures and the intensely private meanings attached to sexuality) but I think the contrast is nevertheless an interesting one.

How can we explain a situation where something which is deplored in reality, at almost whatever level it is carried out (a slap on the face; a murder) becomes entertaining, the source of pleasure, when regarded as an element of fiction (and a staple element in, for instance, the thriller, the Western, war stories and 'cop show' television)? Clearly, violence is often regarded as an essential part of 'good narrative', providing both *action*, the possibilities for different forms of *plot resolution* and also a means of intensifying aspects of *characterisation*. Its widespread occurrence, in different forms and degrees, as an aspect of everyday life, gives portrayal of it something of a 'socially reflective' character, although we have to differentiate between depictions in which the aim is to produce feelings related to those which might accompany the witnessing of violence in real life (revulsion, condemnation, sympathy for the victim etc.) and depictions in which the aim is to produce feelings of a distinctively *aesthetic* kind (excitement, pleasure, fulfilment etc.). There is, of course, a long history of drama and fiction which 'moves' between these two modes or exists somewhere between them (revenge stories are a good example) as well as a history of condemnatory depiction and one of almost exclusively entertaining portrayal. Nor must we forget the historical continuity of situations in which *real* violence is seen as pleasurable, often-cited examples being the atrocities committed in Roman amphitheatres and (perhaps more ambiguously) the British and European tradition of large public attendance at executions. Recent instances of this general kind more often involve *mediated* real violence, as in the debate about the kind of spectator pleasure provided by the extensive use on television of target video footage during the 1992 Gulf War.

I am not qualified, nor do I have the space, to pursue an inquiry into the particular psychodynamics by which pleasure is got from that which is socially proscribed, but in the discussion which follows I shall try to keep in view the rather discomforting duality which the *cultural meaning* of violence has.

There is a final aspect of the matter which might be given a mention here. This is the well-documented fact that the disturbance or aversion which a fictional portrayal of violence can cause among viewers is not directly related to the seriousness of the violence as it would be judged in reality. So, for instance, a murder can be far less disturbing than a beating-up. Such a situation points even more strongly to the way in which 'television violence' is very much a matter of depictive form rather than the straight 'relaying' of types of action.

One of the few researchers to engage fully with these complexities of fictional violence is David Docherty, in a clear and useful monograph for the Broadcasting Standards Council (Docherty, 1990). Docherty has an extensive background in the empirical study of television 'influence' but in this monograph he connects with a wider, anthropological, debate about the meaning of mediated violence in society. In doing so, he makes extensive use of the ideas of Clifford Geertz (as found in Geertz, 1973), an anthropologist whose detailed study of cockfighting in Bali has become a classic essay in cultural analysis, attracting both widespread citation and a developing literature of critical commentary. Geertz attempts to 'read' the cockfight as a socio-symbolic event, so that the question of how its violence relates to other factors in Balinese society can be explored. This relationship is perceived by him to be of an indirect and curious kind since, whilst the cockfight involves 'aroused masculinity and destructive power. . . hatred, cruelty, violence and death', the Balinese themselves are 'shy to the point of obsessiveness of open conflict. . .cautious, subdued, controlled' (cited in Docherty, 1990, p. 8). To carry out his interpretative exploration, Geertz uses the idea of 'deep play'. 'Deep play' indicates a kind of recreation, of entertainment, in which wider social values are deeply implicated though not made explicit or consciously registered.

Docherty applies this idea to television fiction, suggesting that we can differentiate between 'deep' and 'shallow' play as follows:

> Deep play may occur when British viewers feel that a fiction is an indictment of British life, or if a drama contains violence which viewers can see on our streets. Such entertainments may trigger anxious concern about the possible effects of the images or resentment at the inaccurate depiction of British society. However, if the same acts of violence are portrayed in a cartoon, in a Western, in a Hollywood Gangster film, or in a Hammer Horror film, this may constitute shallow play which leaves most people untroubled. Culturally, and socially, there is little or nothing at stake in shallow play.
>
> (Docherty, 1990, p. 10)

By such a division, Docherty hopes to make more sense of how 'violence on television' is related to 'violence in society'. However, whilst his address to the question of *how* televised violence engages the imagination of viewers and his reading of how anthropology has tackled this issue are admirable, his application of 'play' terminology has the effect of confusing more than it clarifies. This is in large part due to the way in which his argument falls foul of ideas about the social relations of 'realism'.

Docherty sees fictional violence as 'troubling' to viewers to the extent that it occurs within contexts that reflect directly on contemporary Britain; its values and laws. So, for instance, a play about football hooliganism would be likely to promote 'deep play' involvement precisely because of its realism of theme and therefore its pertinence to the everyday lives of audience members. But then to go on to observe that the more obviously generic forms of fictional entertainment engage viewers only as 'shallow play', and to note that 'culturally, and socially, there is little or nothing at stake in shallow play' is to miss connecting with the most recurrent focus of public anxiety and the most promising area for the application of anthropological ideas about violence and culture. Moreover, such a limiting usage of the 'deep play' notion seems out of line with Geertz's own approach. For 'what is at stake' culturally and socially in the watching of violent fictions, *principally for entertainment*, may be far more 'deep' and socially consequential than what is involved in being disturbed by images of violence within 'serious', socially realist drama. And in public debate about violent media content it is most often this former kind of depiction (be it in the new genres of action cinema, in 'video nasties' or in television popular drama) which is cited as potentially a 'bad influence'.

By placing his emphasis on realistically themed material, Docherty directs the whole exploration down too narrow a route. This forecloses considerably on the range of questions which he is able to ask about the links between the aesthetics of violent depiction and ideas of influence. For instance, once the scope of the inquiry is framed in such terms, it is not suprising that a number of respondents turn out to be at least as much disturbed by the implications about social values and social practices (e.g. police procedures) carried in the fiction than by any act of violence itself. Furthermore, within this range of realist dramatic portrayal, the question of whether a particular depiction of violence was 'justified' or not in relation to character, narrative or theme is a relevant question to ask. But it is a nonsensical question to ask of the newer forms of violent fictional entertainment, in whose generic terms the violence does not require to be justified by reference to other aesthetic criteria *at all* – it is there as a staple feature of audience appeal and, to a large degree, other features are built around it. To use a cliché of public debate, it is therefore always 'gratuitous'.

Although it risks too sharp a division between aesthetic modes, I think it is useful to differentiate between two broad kinds of fictional depiction here. One I would call 'turn-off' violence, and I would see the function of such depictions as most frequently conforming to thematically realist representation, in relation to which the audience is expected to respond by drawing on the system of ethics it uses in assessing reality. The other I would call 'turn-on' violence, and by this I mean the various ways in which violence is designed to promote pleasure in the viewer and to do so (necessarily) by appeal to interpretative criteria other than those provided by ethical norms. By using the term 'turn-on', I may seem to be suggesting that violence found to be entertaining always has the effect of promoting a disposition towards violence in viewers. I do not want to suggest this, since it is almost certainly untrue, but simply to note how this kind of depiction produces a positive response, characteristically taking the form of pleasurable excitement.

The Aesthetics of Entertaining Violence

In exploring the forms of 'turn-on' violence, the wider generic conventions within whose terms specific portrayals are constructed will be important in determining viewer expectations. To take the case of film, a gun battle in a 1950s' Western (a genre which, like the war film, sometimes mixes 'turn-on' and 'turn-off' modes) is not likely to follow anything like the same conventions as a gun battle in a 1980s' gangster movie, let alone a more recent high-action blockbuster in the manner of, say, *Die Hard* (1988). In the history of popular cinema, there are moments when degree and kind of violence become important in shifting generic 'rules' and expectations or in (temporarily) breaking the generic system altogether. Kubrick's *A*

Clockwork Orange (1971) provides an interesting case here, one in which not only the level of the violence but also its placing on the 'turn-on/turn-off' scale becomes extremely controversial. The 'Spaghetti Westerns' of the 1960s and 1970s (for example, Leone's A Fistful of Dollars, 1964) put a radically new level of explicitness into the ritual violence of the frontier, whilst nevertheless seeking to continue in the broad tradition of pleasurable excitement and at the same time to add a level of self-consciousness bordering on parody. The 'second wave' Vietnam movies of the 1980s (for example, Stone's Platoon, 1986) attempted a revised approach to the brutality-of-war theme, using visualisations generally attempting a strong 'turn-off' effect, though not always succeeding in persuading critics of their purity of purpose on this score. Very recently, a debate in Britain about new levels of extremity in filmic portrayal followed the London opening of the American-made Reservoir Dogs (1993) and the Belgian-made Man Bites Dog (1993).

Television fiction, in most countries more restricted than cinema by public codes and by networking anxieties concerning 'violent material', nevertheless shows an equivalent if less sensational history of controversy and generic shift. For instance, in Britain the development from the police series Dixon of Dock Green (BBC from 1955 – showing a policeman on the beat, occasionally having to respond to violent crime) through Z Cars (BBC from 1962 – showing squad car teams more frequently handling such incidents) to The Sweeney (Thames Television from 1975 – showing a detective duo routinely involved in car chases and gun battles) was a shift in the amount of violence shown, the seriousness of it and also in its mode of depiction. It was generally seen as a development towards the use of 'turn-on' violence in police series, following the American precedent.

In assessing conventions of depiction and the broader shifts of generic code with which they are often associated, the idea of 'realism' is relevant, as are those terms which indicate the various possibilities for 'non-realist' depiction. However, unlike its use by Docherty, 'realism' here does not indicate the thematic realism of narrative or characterisation so much as a real-seemingness in the portrayal of the violence itself. It is thus partially synonymous with 'explicitness', referring to the degree of graphic detail in which the simulation of physical injury and the suffering of pain is organised for the camera. The contrast is, of course, with the long tradition of stylised depiction, in which portrayals of violent acts (often with technical limitations serving to reinforce codes of taste) were free of virtually all the physical messiness which would accompany such acts in real life. So shot people simply fell to the ground, beatings-up were a matter of a few kicks and groans after which rapid recovery could usually be assumed, and serious bodily injuries (whether sustained by accident or design) were often indicated by metonymical, 'partial' images (a flashing saw blade, a dropping cargo hook) and by cutaway and time elapse (the scream, the crumpled body, the rush down the hospital corridor). At the far end of the spectrum of stylisation lies the often-cited instance of the cartoon, in which injury takes on an almost entirely non-realist character, becoming a matter of comic mishap.

But the coding of 'turn-on' violence does not work solely by a sustained explicitness of physical representation (explicitness can be a feature of 'turn-off' violence too, though this far less frequently employs the marked duration of 'turn-on' depictions). It is also conventionally accompanied by elements of an *excitement aesthetic*, of which the most prominent are music and rhythm of editing. These frequently combine to set the explicit depiction within a cultural framework which cues and stimulates pleasure, displacing and marginalising any potential which the image and sounds have for negative resonance. Aesthetics of excitement relate closely to the *pace and scale of action* in a depiction and to *suspense*. So fast-moving events using a broad spatial setting (car chases, battle sequences, gun duels) have conventionally been used as a vehicle for entertaining violence [the success of Spielberg's *Indiana Jones* movies (first title 1984) was in large part the result of mixing traditional and innovative recipes to this end and, in a different mode altogether, the success of many violent video games seems partly to be grounded in a related appeal]. Sequences of sustained anticipation, developing viewer tensions in respect of 'what will happen next', also provide a classic framing for viewing violence pleasurably. Here, once again, the rhythm of editing and music are likely to provide a local 'guide' to viewing, reinforcing the expectations derived from basic generic knowledge. It is perhaps in those cases where depicted violence of an explicit kind is both low in action values and in suspense values that the kind of pleasure being obtained by a viewer becomes more directly open to a pathological interpretation. So, for instance, it is not suprising that protracted scenes of torture or rape have been a central point of concern in recent controversies about both cinema and television fiction (as in the debate about *Man Bites Dog*).

Imagination, Fantasy, 'Influence'

Clearly, when we talk of violent depictions having to be transformed into meanings for the viewer before they can even be considered as potentially influential, we are not suggesting that such depictions are meaningful in the same way as, for instance, news broadcasts are. They do not have any direct propositional sense at all (and therefore do not raise questions about comprehension except in respect of a basic clarity of dramatic projection). Perceived as representations of certain *types* of act, however, they are accorded a significance. This significance we can usefully see as being achieved in relation to two axes of variation. Following a suggestive and influential terminology first employed by the linguist Roman Jakobson (1960), these can be called the *referential* and the *poetic*. Referentially, the depictions are interpreted in relation to the acts they depict and the kinds of cognitive and affective responses which are socially appropriate for responding to such acts. Poetically, they are read within the terms of the generic rules informing the kind of fiction being watched. In certain kinds of violent portrayal (cartoons provide, once again, a useful if extreme example) the referential axis is barely operative at all for most viewers (although the situation in which young children are upset even by cartoon 'injury' indicates that it cannot be discounted altogether). In other kinds of portrayal, the force of realism may temporarily suspend the poetic axis for some viewers, making them quite literally sick or causing them to stop viewing. Within current conventions, this might be more likely to occur with portrayals of what I have called the 'turn-off' type, though it may occur as a personal reaction to violence projected primarily for entertainment too.

Allowing for the rather simplistic character of this binary scheme, the idea of violent depiction exerting a bad influence on viewers through a process of interpretation rather than through any direct behavioural stimulus would seem to require a particular combination of the referential and the poetic. Within the terms of this combination, the poetic axis provides part of the pleasure taken (in the imaging of the violence itself, together with accompanying music and sound effects) but another part is provided by a referential reading (deriving from the nature of the event being depicted). It is this latter source of satisfaction which would then be seen as indicative of a dangerous psychic traffic between the levels of 'fiction' and of 'reality'. The taking of a *referentialised* pleasure in screened violence would, no doubt and understandably, suggest to many commentators the potential for desensitisation to real violence or, worse, the encouragement of a predisposition towards it.

One response to this view of things would be to argue for the primacy of the aesthetic and its transformative workings in violent entertainment, and to see the referential as a secondary factor of response at best. Of course, such a position would do little to counter the claims of those who see 'influence' in this area as largely a matter of subconscious mechanisms and who might, therefore, reject the very idea of separating out a referential plane of response. But it would also fit oddly with the formal character of much recent violent entertainment, which frequently possesses a high degree of local, incidental 'realism' in its graphic depiction of physical hurt. It is hard to see such a realism working other than to feed into interpretation and response an element of referentiality. The level and duration of this local realism, the amount of screen time it cumulatively occupies in certain kinds of fiction and the degree to which this tends to break the narrative up into a series of violent episodes, also works against any suggestion that the violence itself is somehow subordinate to considerations of story and character.

The theory that the enjoying of violence 'encoded' as pleasure has implications for dispositions towards violence in real life poses questions about the kind of *imaginative* relationship which viewers have with what is on the screen. This can be seen as a relationship in which pleasure is primarily got through *observation* or one in which *vicarious participation* is involved. The latter situation might generally be judged the more harmful, as it involves fantasies about violent agency. It is a common assumption that to encourage people to imagine themselves as performing violent acts and furthermore to do so by graphically explicit depictions of violence is to risk weakening the ethical and social constraints on their real behaviour.

Against this, there is the argument that to extrapolate at *all* from fantasy life into real dispositions and behaviour has absolutely no warrant in theory or findings. This position has been most frequently articulated in relation to pornography, where it has been used in opposition to the idea that 'pornography is the theory, rape is the practice', an idea which pithily encapsulates the view that fantasies *do* have real consequences. Arguments about the 'influence' of explictly violent depiction and of explicitly sexual depiction have many points of similarity, but here a difference has to be noted which puts into question any neat separation of fantasy and real life.[8] For the purpose of pornographic texts is certainly, in most cases, to stimulate sexual desire and to provide a stronger motivation for some form of sexual activity. In many societies, this particular use of representations as a stimulant to action is openly accepted, in many others it is intertwined with various levels of hypocrisy and reticence. That there is, internationally, a debate about the forms of sexual representation used in pornography does not alter the fact of widespread recognition of its *routine*, functional character. Insofar as it is perceived to enhance masturbatory pleasure or sex between consenting partners, this functional character has often been viewed as culturally uncontroversial.

Arguments about the influence of violent material work with a totally different perspective on function. Here, *any* significant element of 'real' dispositional change occurring as a result of fantasy involvement would be seen as immediately and radically controversial.

In claiming that the dynamics of fantasy and of real dispositions and actions are in significant relationship with one another it is not, of course, necessary to see the relationship as one in which elements in fantasy are simply *reproduced* in reality. To go back to the example of the Balinese cockfight, it was one of the possibilities explored by Geertz that the relationship could involve an *inversion*, so that enjoyment of violence at the level of 'play' was in fact complementary with a peaceful and harmonious way of life in reality.[9] Far from seeming hypocritical, or a sinister, 'deep' psycho-cultural essence giving the lie to apparent social convention, this relationship *could* be regarded as a non-pathological aspect of the cultural system, 'regulating' it in its maintenance of ethical norms. However, to establish such a view with anything like adequate cogency in respect of television and violence would require a general account of the culture's relation to violence and a good deal more data about the scale and character of 'violent viewing' itself. This data would not only have to indicate the social profile of the phenomenon across different modes of depiction and contexts of viewing, but also examine examples of the meaning and use made of violent depictions by different viewers (whereupon, among other things, a strong gender variation might be expected to appear).

Influence and Meaning for the Viewer

We have seen that the question of the influence of depictions of violence, like the question of the influence of pornography, centrally involves *meaning*, and therefore interpretative activity. Unlike the kind of interpretative activity which is routinely required in watching a news programme, however, the meanings generated by depictions of fictional violence *directly* connect with the primary emotions, 'playing' with fears and desires. This is not to say that the representations of news programmes do not sometimes have the capacity to engage emotions in a comparable manner. But the news is an informational genre; its images of violence are communicatively organised in terms of descriptions and propositions about their character as representations of specific events and acts. And as I discussed in Chapter 3, the visualisations of the news lack both the continuity and the scopic mobility of the fictional image.

What kind of assessment of the potential 'influence' of violent entertainment would be made if the criteria which I used earlier in this chapter to discuss the weather forecast were applied? All that was needed to identify influence here was a change in the knowledge environment of the viewer. Does this happen with fictional images of violence? Whilst viewers may gain new knowledge about violence from such images, and use this knowledge to guide their real world behaviour, the situation is less secure than in the weather forecast example. There, viewers were quite clearly put in possession of relatively discrete items of information not available to the vast majority of them before. In a very large number of cases, this information was incorporated (albeit for a short period) into life decisions. The *changes* brought about by attention to dramatic images, though they may be far more profound, are less open to immediate specification. They are also far less detectable as 'short-term' consequences.[10]

I have looked at some of the factors involved in thinking about television 'influence'. I have suggested that a definition of this can be used which has the effect of moving debate away from the question of whether there is influence or not to questions of kind and degree. These questions require attention to be paid to the 'social contingency of meaning', to the interaction between communicative form and taken meanings. Whilst in some cases there might be extensive commonality in the interpretation of screened material, in others there will be widespread differences. These will include differences in what the material is taken to *mean* by viewers. The implications which such differences have for research on the consequences of media representation are far more fundamental than those which follow from those variables of *response* which have long been noted in the psychological and sociological literature on influence.[11] This kind of variable (for instance, whether or not a particular news item is deemed to be 'fair') is usually plotted as a differentiation of uptake in relation to a relatively stable 'message'. As I noted at the start of this chapter, recognition of the 'contingency of meaning' requires that such assumptions about stability be rejected.

I want to finish my exploration of the influence/interpretation question by focusing again on the ways in which interpretation is constitutive of television meaning. For generalisations about this need to be given more refinement if they are to guide empirical research, and there is some evidence both of reluctance to do this and of a confusion of ideas when it has been undertaken.

The Variables of Interpretation

While television meanings (and therefore any kind of influence which they might be thought to have) are 'contingent' upon interpretative activity, the character of this contingency varies according to the different 'levels' at which text–viewer interaction occurs. For the purposes of exploring the general nature of the influence/interpretation relationship, it is useful to differentiate between three such levels.[12] These are the level of comprehension, the level of implication and association and the level of response. This splitting of 'meaning' into layers is, of course, a product of analysis rather than a discovery of pre-existing difference, and like all analytical schemes its divisions have the effect of drawing attention to some things while obscuring others. In particular, a sense of continuity and simultaneity is replaced by an exaggerated sense of separateness and sequence which has then to be 'repaired' by extensive qualification. Nevertheless, social analysis, by definition, requires a halting and an unweaving of process and this is particularly true of research on 'meaning', a term quite notorious in its capaciousness. Various literary critics, philosophers and social scientists have found it necessary somehow to 'break meaning down' into constituent dimensions or levels in order to get clarity into their account of meaning-making acts and my simple typology is just one more version of this.

Comprehension

At this level (sometimes labelled the 'literal' or 'denotative') viewers transform what they see and hear on the screen (itself subject to variations of selective perception) into a basic 'sense' of what is being shown, what is being said, what is actually going on. In the case of speech, this primary sense-making activity exercises the viewer's linguistic competence (a competence both about usages and contexts of use); in the case of visuals, they are required to construe the basic pictorial organisation on the screen including, perhaps, the shifts of space and time through which continuity of action is maintained. Failure to comprehend, say, the opening remarks to camera of a game-show host would be an unusual problem to find in someone with a native speaker's knowledge of English, but failure to comprehend sections of a documentary or sections of a certain kind of dramatic production might be more common and, indeed, are often instanced in audience research inquiries. Here, we would need to distinguish between *direct* and *indirect* forms of address. In the former case, an explicit, determinate communication is produced. Turning signs into understood meaning may be a relatively straightforward task. In the latter, for instance in drama, interpretative *schema* (subsets of rules for recognising and linking what is seen and heard) may have to be employed in order to figure out 'what is happening' in certain scenes. The more that the direct modes of televisual discourse employ specialist vocabularies (for example, those of literary criticism or of physics or economics) the more likely it is that the general viewer's comprehension will falter. Similarly, the more that indirect modes move from established generic conventions of language and image use towards more innovative and 'difficult' forms and devices, the more there may be a comprehension problem here too. This parallels those differentiations of comprehension which occur in relation to other forms of cultural expression, for instance newspapers, literature, film and painting.

Implication and Association

'Above' the primary meanings attached to word sequences and image sequences, there is the implicatory and associational meaning which they generate in specific contexts of use. In Barthes' classic account of mediated meaning (see, for instance, Barthes, 1977) these were seen as constituting a plane of 'connotation'. As well as being an important dimension of the speech forms of television, implication and association provide the means by which the visualisations of television achieve a broader symbolic signification than is carried merely by *what* they depict. To varying degrees, the generic conventions of television deploy implicatory and associative signifiers as a routine part of programme making. They are more densely to be found in advertising than in news, for instance, but their use is functional for a wide range of communicative aims. At the end of a news item on industrial decline, a held close-up of a rusty lock on a factory gate signals much more than its immediate, denotative information – a rusty lock. Similarly, a distant shot of a nuclear power station's cooling tower framed, in near shot, by the barbed wire of a security fence, may well signal more than the fact of the existence and proximity of these objects along the angle of filming.

It might be suggested that the construing of meaning here [in the case of the rusty lock, 'the neglect and abandonment of manufacturing', in the case of the cooling tower/barbed wire composition, 'the high security (high risk) factors intrinsic to the nuclear industry'] is simply a continuation of comprehension and does not warrant separation as another 'level'.

While there is something to be said for taking this position (and thus expanding the notion of 'comprehension'), I would want to point out the increased degree of *interpretative hazard* which enters into the meaning-making process here. For quite what a particular scene was 'implying' is sometimes the source not only of interpretative variation but of complaint and argument. This has been a frequent aspect of complaints against adverts considered 'offensive' in non-explicit ways and has also occurred regularly in discussion of news and documentary material, as we have seen earlier in the book.

Moreover, if we look at my attempt to gloss the evaluative associations which might be generated from the two examples, we can see how *indeterminate* they are. That is to say, even if it proves in practice that a large proportion of the audience produce implications and associations of this kind from the shots, these will by definition remain implicit in source and therefore enjoy a considerable degree of *deniability*. Such deniability can quickly move from an assertion about intentions ('we didn't mean that') to an assertion either about presence ('such a meaning is not there') or about contingency as deviance ('you read that into it'). Matters which start out being about improper implication can quickly become matters about unwarranted *inferral*. I noted at the start of this chapter that to regard contingency as a *condition* of all meaning making did not require communicators to be absolved of responsibility for communicated meaning.

Clearly, however, such a responsibility is harder (though not impossible) to ground at the level of implication and association than it is at a primary level, for the reasons just discussed.[13] This, together with the fact that implicatory and associative meaning is so central to the symbolic work of texts, including television programmes, suffusing them with evaluations, makes this level at once so politically important and so contentious.

Response

The two levels which I have discussed above are essentially levels of meaning attributed, in everyday viewing, to the text itself. That is to say, it is a viewing convention to objectify meaning as completely a textual property, even though this is strictly a falsification of the processes involved. 'Response' is a level of interpretation which stays, as it were, 'on the viewers' side' of the interaction, involving the viewers' own conscious assessment of what they have seen and heard as this attains significance within their own established knowledge and dispositions, perhaps exerting modifying pressure on these. Obviously, responses to television programmes will vary considerably, both those to journalistic accounts and those to fiction and entertainment. This variation is interesting, but although it is related to them, it is not the same thing as the variations at the two levels which I have previously discussed. It has *always* been recognised that programmes elicit a varied response – how could it be claimed otherwise? – but variation in attributed textual meaning has provided a relatively recent focus of analytic attention. Whereas the former is an unsuprising consequence of variations (both group and individual) in human disposition and taste, the latter points to problematic aspects of textuality itself. I have noted elsewhere how use of the term 'reading' in television studies (as in 'different readings were made of the programme') has tended to refer primarily to the level of response while appearing to say something of a more fundamental kind about the processes of meaning production (Corner, 1991b). This has been especially true of work on television drama, a genre which generally lacks modes of direct address and explicit propositional content. Here, separation between the 'levels' of meaning (always, as I have indicated, awkward to sustain) is particularly prone to blurring.

Interpretative Dynamics: Phases-in-Process

My division of interpretation into three levels inevitably suggests not only an undue firmness of separation between parts of the interpretative process but also a linear sequencing in which the viewer works 'upwards' through to response. Though it is impossible to have a response to a television item without having first attributed some meaning to it, there are problems if the process is seen as remorselessly one directional. For responses involve the use of evaluative schema which are applied 'downwards' in basic interpretative work too, such that the processes of comprehension, and certainly those of inferral and association, are modified accordingly. And though I have worked above with a convenient analytic fiction in which the process is at least *started* from the bottom, in practice it never is. The understanding of the very first image and voiced-over word of a particular television programme will often be informed by an evaluative predisposition originating in anticipation, in foreknowledge of the kind of programme it is and what it is about. Despite this, it is my view that research into television interpretation and its bearing upon influence needs to 'model' the interpretative process in a differentiated and phased way if progress is to be made.

But, if this 'model' is provisionally allowed, there is yet another set of basic questions which need to be posed. These are questions about how the meaning-making process relates to the scale of programme element to which attention is being given. One might sensibly talk about the meaning which the opening shot of a commercial carried for viewers. One might also, less sensibly, talk about the meaning of a full-length documentary (less sensibly because 'meanings' seems immediately to be a more useful way of talking here, and because engaging with interpretation at 'whole programme' level is likely to slip the focus on to questions of response to the exclusion of the other, more fundamental, questions). Following the inquiries of psychologists into text processing, television research needs to think more carefully about how meanings are incrementally produced across the duration of a particular item or programme as sequence follows sequence, interview follows voice-over or (in drama) scene follows scene.[14] What I have seen to be three levels of interpretative activity will be concurrently operating throughout the viewing experience. Shifts and developments in them will occur in direct relationship to the organisation of programme elements as these are cumulatively apprehended by the viewer. Such interactivity seems to me to be the nodal point of television as communication, albeit that inquiry into it requires extensive contextualisation before the significance of what is going on can usefully be drawn out. Not to ask questions about precisely *how* meanings are produced from texts in the act of viewing is to give up on the very idea of television as cultural process.

Influence and Interpretation in Television Research

'Influence' has been a key word in the history of television research. A lot of argument has been conducted around it, much of it concerned with whether this or that aspect of television does or does not exert an influence. The restricted intellectual character of this debate, and of many of the procedures used to provide evidence either way, has been such as to cause some scholars to abandon the term altogether. Of course, to claim that television 'doesn't have *any* influence' is a silly, evidence-begging statement, unless the definition of influence here is such a strongly behavioural one as to exceed in its criteria all current usage. On the other hand, using my example of the weather forecast, it seemed quite easy to demonstrate the ways in which routine television output *was* influential, by changing the 'knowledge environment' of viewers and providing them with information upon which many of them clearly acted. But this might not seem a terribly exciting discovery to those professionally committed to researching influence. For them, influence most often means a persuasive effect exerted in a non-rational way against the interests of the viewer and perhaps against those of the public as a whole too. This is influence as self-evident threat both to individual integrity and democracy. My suggestion is that this is far too grandiose and overblown a use of the word and that, whilst it is important to research the persuasive and suggestive power of television and to raise questions about appeal to the unconscious in so doing, making 'influence' synonymous with such a potential is not useful. An updated version of this long-standing error appeared in the late 1970s and early 1980s, when the term 'ideology' was used by several researchers and critics in such a way as to indicate that it was *the* key mode of media influence. Research on ideological influence usually had the intellectual subtlety to recognise the complexities of textual form and the perceptual and cognitive character of viewing but it, too, became exclusively concerned with the most radical kinds of consequence which programmes could have for viewers.[15]

Against both the strongly behavioural tendencies of classic 'influence' research and the assumptions about omnipotent textuality made by many researchers into ideological effects, the newer emphasis on interpretation has been placed as a corrective. A very wide range of work has been done which documents the way in which viewers vary considerably in the interpretations they make of what they watch. To note that all the 'effects' that a programme can have on a viewer invariably have to work through meaning of some kind, and that meaning is a product of interpretation does not require that the whole idea of the media exerting effects (including persuasive, non-rational and 'bad' effects) be abandoned. It is true that the ideas of 'influence' and 'effect', quite apart from the conceptual impoverishment they have received within certain bodies of theory, have a tendency to suggest simplistic cause and effect relationships unsuited to researching the complex combinations of social factors which bear upon the viewing of television. But, as other chapters have suggested, the notion of television having the potential power to form and to change people in certain ways needs to continue to inform research. Not to see this as still a pressing question, if a much more various and subtle one than was previously thought, is to disengage academic study from its political, social and cultural responsibilities. The almost continuous, low-level, public debate about television and society will continue to operate with assumptions about such power. So will many of those people who work within the television industry, despite their disclaimers.

Given the points I made above, it follows that the programme forms of television's generic system, and the moves of mode within each form, engage the viewer in meaning making in different ways. The direct exposition of news and of current affairs represents the world differently from the visualisations of filmed reports. The extended accounts of documentary, variously organised around narrative and the indirectness of the onlooking relationship are generally very distinct from realist drama, even where the two forms overlap substantially in theme and in visual language. Some of the newer kinds of dramatic entertainment connect with the primary cultural pleasures of spectacle and action in a manner which corresponds closely to the appeal of contemporary popular cinema. A whole range of other entertainment formats, while not having any direct exposition to offer or actuality for the viewer to witness, nevertheless provide address, performance and display of a kind which engages, and in part helps variously to constitute, the audience's sociality.

Faced with this variety, any attempted general theory of television influence or of interpretation will only be able to go so far with its analysis of process. To trace those 'contingencies of meaning' out of which both are constructed requires more local and intensive inquiries into the relationships possible between the variables of television representation and those of modern social consciousness.

7

QUESTIONS OF 'QUALITY'

Since the late 1940s, when television first emerged as a cultural force within the United States, the medium has been the focus of debate about 'quality'.[1] The terms of this debate have connections with some of the themes already discussed, particularly with the relation of the medium to democratic political process and with conceptualisations of it as a source of social influence. The direction of national media policy, in respect of the degree of public organisation and regulation and the scale and character of commercial involvement, has also been a major factor, particularly at points where major shifts in funding have either occurred or been mooted. Nevertheless, the relationship between television and ideas of 'quality' has sufficient continuity as a topic, and as a source of recurrent cultural anxiety, to deserve separate consideration in any exploration of television's public character. In this chapter, I propose to look at some of the main features of the 'quality' question and to note the way in which they appear in current writing about television and in argument about policy.

One aspect which I am particularly keen to investigate further is the way in which television 'quality' is regarded as an *aesthetic* matter, having to do with television's function as an agency of popular art, and the way in which it is seen, more broadly, as having to do with the general quality of life in society. That these two ways of viewing 'quality' are related (often within a notion of 'culture') is immediately clear, but the form of the relationship itself, the dominance given either to the more aesthetic or to the more social dimension, warrants analysis.

In examining the issue of quality I want to refer both to British and American examples, but it is worth noting at the outset a quite radical difference in the place occupied by television in the two cultures and a consequent difference in the way in which it is written about by cultural critics. In the United States, the emphatically commercial character of much television and the particular forms of popular programming which are the result have produced something of a tradition of generalised polemic against the medium. 'Classic' works in this idiom would include Jerry Mander's *Four Arguments for the Elimination of Television* (1978) and Neil Postman's *Amusing Ourselves to Death* (1986). A more conventionally academic account which nevertheless shares something of the same tone and scale is Joshua Meyrowitz's *No Sense of Place* (1985). In this vein of commentary a great deal of concern is usually shown about the erosion of traditional cultural ties and values, the decline of common rationality and the coarsening of feeling which television has brought with it. Particular attention is often paid to the vulnerability of children. In Britain, while a strong and comprehensive critique of commercialised mass culture was a feature of literary criticism at Cambridge in the 1930s, this was a pre-televisual judgement. Even Richard Hoggart's *The Uses of Literacy* (1957), the most important and most influential attempt to assess shifts in postwar British popular culture, has virtually no references to television. Its preoccupation with print-based forms is grounded in an analysis started before television became the primary medium of popular entertainment. Partly because of the 'public service' principles and practices of British television, principles which were extended in the mid-1950s to the operation of channels run for commercial profit, British cultural critics have generally been much more selective and focused in their commentary. Early work which engages directly with the question of television and cultural quality, such as Stuart Hall and Paddy Whannel's *The Popular Arts* (1964) and Raymond Williams's *Communications* (1962), certainly criticises broadcasters for their lack of commitment to the idea of a truly 'public' television and for the inadequacy of their view of the audience, as well as for the socially distortive consequences of certain kinds of output. However, this work also finds much to celebrate at the level of individual programmes, both 'serious' and 'light'. Moreover, there is always a strong sense of cultural potential put forward.

This national difference in the broad cultural character of the medium, one reflected in the kind of relations obtaining between those who work in television and 'intellectual society', puts into different contexts the recent shifts (on both sides of the Atlantic) towards a more sympathetic approach to the study of popular programmes, an approach typified in closer engagement with 'fan culture'.[2] Whilst in the United States, this type of work appears strongly and, to some, suspiciously redemptive when compared with the dominant tendency towards cultural pessimism, in Britain it often seems no more than a deeper, more positive inflection of an established critical–appreciative disposition.

I want to look first at the different *kinds* of argument which are used in making general judgements about television as a cultural agency. I then want to look at some aspects of the cultural debate which surrounded the arrival of commercial television in Britain. This should provide a useful basis upon which to give more sustained attention to the way in which broader cultural anxieties relate to specific questions of television form and content.

Television as 'Bad Culture': A Typology of Arguments

We can usefully identify five lines of argument about the bad cultural consequences of television:

1. Television as a time waster. This argument concentrates on the amount of time spent watching television instead of doing other things. The appeal of television as a way of easily filling time is seen variously to work against the taking up of more active, creative pastimes (including reading), the pursuit of social and community life outside the home and full engagement in family conversation and family recreation. A reduction in personal and social development is judged to be the result.

2. Television as cultural invader. This is an argument often used by critics in the smaller Western countries, in the new 'Eastern' Europe and in the Third World. The claim here is that the heavily American origin of much imported material carries with it a system of values alien to the native culture but often seductively attractive to the young. This system of values, highly materialistic and carrying with it a distinctive set of aspirations and anxieties, is seen to be weakening the hold of more indigenous cultural norms, causing problems of cohesion and identity.

3. Taste debasement. A more widespread version of 2. The argument is that a regular diet of low standard television entertainment (and perhaps 'infotainment') is having the effect of lowering the taste of many viewers, encouraging them to 'settle for less' and, indeed, to develop a preference for the safe, the undemanding, the formulaic etc. A classic expression of the general process at work here is given by John Stuart Mill:

   > Men lose their high aspirations, as they lose their intellectual tastes, because they have no time or opportunity for indulging them; and they addict themselves to inferior pleasures not because they deliberately prefer them but because they are either the only ones to which they have access or the only ones which they are any longer capable of enjoying.
   >
   > (Mill, 1861, p. 261)

   Applied to television, arguments of this kind often use the idea of there being an appeal to the 'lowest common denominator' as a consequence of the need to maximise audiences. This denominator, the argument goes, then becomes gradually installed as the cultural norm.

4. Attitudinal influence. In other chapters, I have explored what is principally at issue here. Either generally or in relation to specific forms of output (e.g. political journalism, depictions of violence, advertising) it is claimed that television exerts an influence upon the attitudes and behaviours of viewers. This influence is seen to be sufficiently widespread and strong enough to have a general effect upon social values and action.

5. Cognitive impairment. This takes the 'influence' argument in a particular direction, arguing not so much for any specific effect of form/content but for a general effect upon perceptual and cognitive processing skills. Usually advanced by reference to pyschological data or psychological hypotheses, this argument sees cultural deterioration as a consequence of reduced mental capacities. It is, understandably, a claim most often made in relation to children and attainment levels in the classroom.

All of these positions, either independently or in various combination with each other, have been advanced in recent debates. Some of them have a considerable history. They clearly pose the matter of television form and television content in different ways. For instance, the 'time wasting' charge, though it involves a prior judgement about the general worth of television programming, is aimed at the medium as a whole. 'Influence' arguments are usually much more specific about types of programming and even about the devices by which bad influence is produced. 'Taste' clearly involves what is primarily an aesthetic judgement but it is one which is often linked to cognitive criteria too (about the kind of social knowledge which popular television typically produces). In varying degrees, the arguments have a tendency to 'essentialise' television around particular characteristics or particular types of programme (I discussed in Chapter 1 the way in which essentialism has become a problem in academic research). This is not suprising since too strong a sense of differentiation, of the *heterogeneity* of television, would detract from the force of the argument. Indeed, it is quite frequently a part of many such arguments that the *homogeneity* of television is bringing about an homogeneity in culture generally, an homogeneity of (in one way or another) reduced quality.

In this chapter I am more concerned with sketching out the ways in which the issue of television and quality has been debated than with engaging directly with every claim. To do this would in many cases require the adducing of evidence or counter-evidence which I simply do not have or which would require much space to document. However, certain aspects of the issue, certain 'moves' in the general debate, are so salient as to require closer analysis. A few of these can be seen in controversies surrounding British television in its formative period.

Television, Commerce and Cultural Quality: The 1950s

Until 1955, British television was a single channel service produced by the BBC. Although it was the subject of regular, if mostly minor, controversy about 'taste' (for instance, in relation to material contained in children's programmes, scenes of dramatised violence, portrayal of figures of authority, 'bad language' etc.), it had followed BBC radio in becoming a part of the British cultural establishment as well as an increasingly popular recreational medium.[3] As its popularity grew, the question of scheduling, and the balance achieved between different kinds of programming, became more subject to dispute. This had already been an issue in radio, 'solved' finally by giving the three national radio channels separate cultural identities and thereby introducing a degree of cultural segregation.[4] Television continued very broadly to follow the ideals of the BBC's founder, John Reith, that broadcasting should be an instrument of national cultural improvement and that it should therefore have a scheduling policy in which the 'serious arts' were strongly represented. Perhaps Reith's most controversial formulation of this educative policy was in his early comments about listeners' 'needs' and 'wants':

> It is occasionally indicated to us that we are apparently setting out to give the public what they need – and not what they want, but few know what they want and very few what they need.
>
> (Reith, 1924, p. 34)

The attempted enhancement of the quality of life of audience members by the programming of material of an initially unfamiliar and perhaps 'difficult' kind was always likely to run foul of the relations between cultural taste and social class. Its character as an exercise in the expansion of opportunity, in enablement, was offset not only by the difficulty of avoiding condescension but of avoiding a sense of taste *imposition* ('compulsory uplift' as it was termed by one of Reith's opponents).[5] Reith's use of the language of 'wants' and 'needs' did little to ease suspicion on this score, though quotation of his comments usually fails to include his remark, a sentence later, that 'In any case, it is better to over-estimate the mentality of the public, than to under-estimate it'. This, though it does not reduce the controversiality of the earlier comment, gives the observation as a whole a rather more complex character.

Television in the 1950s, whilst still 'Reithian' in tendency, operated a programme policy at some distance from these early, briskly patrician formulations. Without becoming essentialistic, it is possible to argue that television's sheer visuality and the kind of relationships with the world and with people which it projects makes it difficult to retain the level of mediating cultural control possible in radio. Nevertheless, despite this point and despite the range of popular entertainments which it broadcast, BBC television was becoming steadily more vulnerable in its commitment to certain ideas of cultural quality. With the contrast provided by shifts elsewhere in popular culture, its own 'taste' profile was increasingly visible as a particular pattern of preferences, linked to those of the educated upper middle classes of the south of England. Though not initially a major topic of public concern, such partiality was beginning to be seen as undemocratic.

The rifts and tensions of the 1950s' version of 'television culture', a culture committed to the upkeep and extension of certain standards of taste and yet also a site of popular energies, enthusiasms and pleasures, came to a head in the debate about the introduction of commercial television.

The Conservative government elected in 1951 had quite quickly indicated its intentions to break the monopoly of the BBC and set up a commercial (later to be dubbed 'Independent') network which would be financed from advertising. For the next three years, there was a running debate in Britain about television and national culture, conducted in Parliament, in the press and by the intervention of a wide range of public figures and bodies.[6] For a while, the proposed shift in the economics of the medium generated a debate about its cultural character comparable to the debates about the media and 'mass culture' which had been conducted in such pessimistic terms by critics in the United States.[7] America was, of course, the main point of reference for those who wished to draw attention to the disaster which could befall British culture as a result of commercial television.

Opponents of commercial television drew variously on all five of the positions I identified earlier, though perhaps the charge of cultural debasement was the one most frequently put. 'Trivialisation' of many areas of output was seen to be an inevitable consequence of the need to attract and keep large audiences. In a pamphlet written to warn of the imminent dangers, the Labour M.P. Christopher Mayhew observed:

> It is true that the more enjoyable a programme is, the larger the audience it tends to attract. But keenness of enjoyment is by no means the only thing that attracts large audiences. Sensationalism and horror do it too. Can they be rightly classed as 'enjoyment'? We do not 'enjoy' street accidents, but they draw us into crowds. And for creating large audiences pride of place must go not the enjoyability of a programme but to the universality of its appeal. This may seem a subtle distinction, but it is immensely important. To get a maximum audience a TV programme must appeal to everyone at once, even if this means appealing keenly to no-one...It must play down to the lowest common factor in us all, treating us as units in a mass, without personality, without individuality. This is why so many commercial programmes are so utterly without character of any kind. Long experience shows that the perfect formula for a commercial broadcast is variety plus sex plus crime.
>
> (Mayhew, 1953, p. 7)

It is worth quoting this view at length because it clearly connects together a number of ideas about the relationship between 'commerce' and the 'popular' as well as being premised on an idea about the *cultural vulnerability* of the viewer when exposed to 'low quality' material (a view which I have touched on in other chapters). This is by no means an essentialistic dismissal of television, however. The possibility of television as a positive cultural force is an important part of the argument.

It is interesting to compare Mayhew's account with that of Sir Robert Fraser, the first Director-General of the Independent Television Authority, speaking on the question of television quality a few years later:

> Every person of common sense knows that people of superior mental constitution are bound to find much of television intellectually beneath them. If such innately fortunate people cannot realise this gently and considerately and with good manners, if in their hearts they despise popular pleasures and interests, then of course they will be angrily dissatisfied with television. But it is not really television with which they are dissatisfied. It is with people.
>
> (Sir Robert Fraser, Speech to Manchester Luncheon Club, 17 May, 1960).

Unlike many defenders of the commercial network, who tended towards a resolute populism in which any concern for 'quality' was immediately seen as a sign of closet elitism, Fraser (admittedly, with some irony) recognises a 'cultural gap' and allows the idea of taste superiority. He does not, however, allow the likelihood of any 'bad influence' resulting from the indulgence of popular taste, nor does he seem to believe that television is bringing about any taste decline. Whereas Mayhew's view is implicitly premised on a desired commonality of 'standards', Fraser recognises a hierarchy of taste difference in relation to intellectual level and sees this as a matter for tolerance from the intellectually more 'developed'. (It is interesting that the difference is seen to be a matter of 'innate fortune' rather than of 'class privilege'; registering the socio-economic factors behind taste difference would be a *much* more awkward argument to make for someone in Fraser's position).

The question of *taste formation* is clearly at the heart of many of these arguments about quality. This is essentially a question about whether television works to shape and change popular taste or whether it is primarily a form of cultural response to it. Although it may be a matter more of emphasis than exclusive claim, whether television output is seen to be formative of popular taste or to be formed by it continues to be a crucial variable in argument. The extensive and polemical use of the phrase 'giving people what they want' is testimony to this. And such a 'giving' can, of course, then be seen as a matter of democratic choice, a choice as essential in the cultural as in the more directly political realm. In arguing his case for the introduction of commercial television, the conservative M.P. Selwyn Lloyd made this a key point:

> If people are to be trusted with the franchise, surely they should be able to decide for themselves whether they want to be educated or entertained in the evening.
>
> (HMSO, 1951, p. 205)

Once again, the terms used here are essentially strategic ones, skirting the question of whether all entertainments are to be available on consumer demand (the Conservative party is not notable for its opposition to censorship). However, the difficulty of combining an idea of television as taste forming for the individual with an idea of democratic cultural choice *informed by* individual taste is further illustrated. That the BBC inclined to an emphasis on the first of these is not suprising given that their 'improvement' policy could only have had theoretical coherence if this were the case.

The bill breaking the BBC monopoly finally went through Parliament with a slender majority in July 1954. Some of the heat had been taken out of the debate by the decision to regulate the operation of the new channel through a public body, the Independent Television Authority, which would oversee matters of programme quality and require companies to observe a 'proper' balance in their schedules.[8] Nevertheless, national discussion of the question of 'commerce', 'culture' and the role of television did not end there. Five years later, an official Committee on Broadcasting published the findings of its review [the Pilkington Report (HMSO 1962)] and these included substantial commentary on the decline which, it was claimed, had now occurred since the introduction of commercial services.

One of the members of the Pilkington Committee was the academic and cultural critic Richard Hoggart, whose *Uses of Literacy* (1957) had become something of a key text on the drift towards a more commercialised and Americanised popular culture in Britain. His influence on the Committee's verdict was judged to be considerable and a comparison of its language with that of his own writings on culture seems to confirm this. Using criteria drawn from literature and from traditional popular forms, the committee noted something of a 'quality crisis' in current television output, with a particular emphasis on the products of the independent channel. One resoundingly general observation was that 'much that is seen on television is regarded as of very little value' (HMSO, 1962, p. 33). This remark was grounded in the 'written submissions and spoken opinion' which the Committee had consulted in the course of its enquiries, but questions about its representativeness of national viewing opinion were quickly raised. As a verdict, it seemed conveniently close to the one which the Committee had come to itself.

The rhetorical force of its critical commentary makes the Report an original contribution to the debate about television and culture rather than merely a rerun of previous negative opinion. So, too, does its relative explicitness on matters of qualitative judgement. Of course, unlike the debate which had taken place prior to the introduction of the commercial channel, the focus here was on actual rather than *imagined* programmes. Working with a strong thesis about debasement and influence, the Committee noted that:

> Programmes which exemplified emotional tawdriness and mental timidity helped to cheapen both emotional and intellectual values. Plays or serials might not deal with real human problems, but present a candy-floss world.
>
> (HMSO, 1962, p. 35)

A key defect was seen to be 'triviality', defined as follows:

> A trivial presentation may consist in a failure to take full and disciplined advantage of the artistic and technical facilities which are relevant to a particular subject, or in a reliance on 'gimmicks' so as to give a spurious interest to a programme at the cost of its imaginative integrity, or in too great a dependence on hackneyed devices for creating suspense or raising a laugh or evoking tears.
>
> (HMSO, 1962, p. 34)

In speculating on the reasons for the apparent triumph of triviality on the new channel, the Committee remarked:

> In all, one had to infer either that those who provided these programmes *mistakenly* assumed that popular taste was uniformly and irremediably low, and popular culture irresponsible; or worse, that they did not care about them.
>
> (HMSO, 1962, p. 33)

In the context of my earlier remarks about taste formation, this comment is both interesting and questionable. How could the Committee be sure that popular taste had been *mistakenly* interpreted by the programme makers? Especially if (as other evidence would suggest) many programmes of the kind receiving the most disapproving judgement of the Committee (such as game shows, quiz shows, popular series drama and celebrity talk shows) were regularly achieving high audience figures. This attempt to blame the programmes without disparaging the cultural taste of the audience itself certainly fits neatly with the idea that most of the criticisms made by the Committee were a reflection of those made by ordinary viewers. But a

representative claim of this kind is a hazardous exercise in passing judgement on a major public service. Its attribution of a 'mistake' to broadcasters in their quest for audiences seems to be just one more indicator of the
problems which *public* assessment of television quality posed for those who
were personally unhappy with what television (especially of the 'new'
kind) offered.

Two years earlier, in an influential essay on divisions within British
culture, Raymond Williams had got himself into a rather similar position
of awkwardness ('Culture is Ordinary', Williams, 1958). As part of a call
for radical changes in the organisation of the media, he had noted the
'observable badness of so much widely distributed popular culture' (p. 12)
but had firmly rejected the idea that one could move from this to a verdict
about the 'quality of living of its consumers' (p. 12). Drawing on his own
experience of working class family life, he commented on the 'natural
fineness of feeling' and the 'quick discrimination' (p. 12) which were to be
found there. He expressed it as a paradox, 'a rather suprising fact', that
'people whose quality of personal living is high are apparently satisfied by
a low quality of printed feeling and opinion' (p. 13). Such a way of addressing the problem is far more open and self-aware than the Committee's
(which veers towards tactical ambivalence) but it still leaves Williams with
the difficulty of calling for an improvement in the 'quality' of a media
system which seems to him to be having little discernible effect upon the
'quality' of its viewers' lives. The Committee, by contrast, appear to believe
strongly in the bad cultural influence that television can have. Their
problem is in squaring this with their idea of a critical viewing public,
indignant at the low quality fare which it is currently being offered as a
result of an underestimation of its taste. Later in this chapter, I shall
examine more recent manifestations of this kind of conceptual wobble
around 'quality'.

As a final point on the Pilkington Committee's observations, it is worth
noting their remark, in winding up their reflections on 'triviality', that: 'Our
own conclusion is that triviality is a natural vice of television' (HMSO, 1962,
p. 35). This does not mean that they saw matters as completely irremedia-
ble. Their own recommendations disprove such a view. But it frames their
criticism of television with an estimation of its general cultural status which
other commentators genuinely wanted to hold back from ascribing and
others, still, felt it imprudent to make explicit.

The Pilkington Report received a hostile reception from the press, which
presented its findings on quality as elitist and moralising.[9] The M.P. and
columnist Woodrow Wyatt, writing in *The Sunday Pictorial*, gives a sense of
the response at its sharpest in an answer to his own question 'who is disssat-
isfied?' – 'a tiny handful of pretentious prigs who look down their noses at
simple pleasures'. Although many of its recommendations for institutional
change were not implemented and much of its cultural commentary was
travestied in the manner that Wyatt's remarks suggest, the Committee's
comments had significance for the way in which the issue of television and
cultural quality was addressed in subsequent public debate. This was
particularly true for those working in the universities and the schools, where
a more extended questioning of the character and direction of British culture

in the 'television generation' was beginning to take place. Although flawed by a failure fully to address the complexity of the issues of taste formation and taste difference which it raised, the Report's boldness of cultural judgement provided a datum for many critiques which followed. Some of these, issuing from the developing area of media studies, would replace its ethical approach to the medium's aesthetics with a more directly political perspective on the media and the 'popular'.[10]

Television, Imagination and Sensibility

The above account of public judgements on television's cultural value in the context of changes in policy and funding takes us some way from matters of communicative form but then, as I hope to have demonstrated, returns us to them again. In this section, I want to focus on formal questions, for it is clear that low estimations of television (as 'trivial', 'superficial', 'formulaic' for instance) often turn as much on television's particular modality of communication as on types of content. Although at a number of places elsewhere in this book I have given detailed attention to the organisation of images and sounds in particular genres of television, I want to review some of those features here in relation to the idea of quality and aesthetic value.

Before doing this, there are two preliminary observations I want to make. First of all, as television is still frequently a broadcast medium, going out to a socially heterogeneous audience, the questions of 'quality' it raises are different from those posed in, for instance, book publishing or in the theatre and the film industry. In these latter cases, questions of value are focused on specific cultural products (books, films and plays) which are related to readerships and audiences by direct purchase, hire or attendance. Television services embrace a whole range of cultural products and their relationship to audiences is most often at the level of the general service being offered (whether this is paid for by licence fee, subscription or advertising).

The *commodity* character of television is thus different from that in other areas of cultural production (i.e. viewers do not usually pay for a specific programme). As the forms of subscription 'narrowcasting' become more prevalent culturally, the character of the evaluation of the medium may change, but at the moment it is generally at a 'taste range' rather than any one narrow 'taste' grouping that much television is aimed. This has the effect that, with few exceptions, television has not developed a specialist, minority 'high culture' mode. We can compare this situation to that in cinema, where there has been for some time an established and flourishing 'art cinema', particularly in parts of Europe. We can also compare it with the rapidly developing area of video art, where the connections with both the modes of exhibition and the modes of appreciation of conventional fine art are clear. Of course, television's very heterogeneity as a medium, quite apart from its typical institutional requirement to attract popular audiences, makes it difficult for it to achieve high cultural status in the way that, for instance, a certain kind of cinema has done by producing fictions drawing adaptively on the modernist aesthetics of literature and fine art.

Insofar as art is defined by the criteria of established high cultural practice, television (particularly network television) would always seem therefore to have a tendency towards the 'low'. It literally cannot afford to sustain a 'high' aesthetic for very long (although the first years of Channel Four in Britain are interesting here) since the limits which this imposes on its possible audience, and therefore on its revenue, are unacceptable.[11] It is *ephemeral* (always an un-art-like thing to be) insofar as much of it is produced quite rapidly for a single 'performance'. Because it is often radically *heterogeneous* in the forms it allows and contains (though this, of course, has not always been the verdict of its critics), so it becomes harder to describe the criteria for excellence within it. It is interesting, here, how the particular hybrid realisms of drama-documentary (see Chapter 4) came to be seen for a period as *quintessential* television. Another regular critical choice for this description is 'live' television. Both modes significantly emphasise the *transparency* effect over the discursive/symbolic, over artefactual features.

All these factors have combined not only to make the attribution of cultural value to television problematic and negatively inclined, they have made the business of 'television criticism' an oddly unspecific affair, in which the ability to write humorously is regarded as a better qualification than an interest in offering the kind of detailed, serious 'appreciations' which an arts pages' critic is paid to produce.[12] In the circumstances, one can see the difficulty. Television criticism is written for 'everybody', the literary pages, the gallery reviews and the theatre notices are for specialist interest groups, however large these may be.

My second point is much briefer. It is to note how central *fiction* is to judgement of the general quality of television. In the light of my comments above about television as art this is not suprising. For it is the 'literary test' which television is most often required to pass by those writing about it in the serious newspapers. If the single play or television film is highlighted then, in British television at least, the critical appreciation can confidently proceed in terms not too removed from those used in assessments of the theatre and the cinema. If, however, popular series drama is selected, then the evaluation is usually something of a foregone conclusion. Professional critics are not part of the intended audience for the popular fictional television of soap operas and sitcoms (although in their columns they occasionally recruit themselves to it with varying degrees of conviction). The gap between their assessment of 'good fiction' and that of the popular audience is a frequent factor in the continuing discussion about 'quality', policy and funding, a discussion to which I shall return in the last section of this chapter.

Given that the 'art' status of television is troubled by those general features which it has as a medium and as a kind of service (the channel, the station), what is it about its particular discourses and the forms of engagement which they encourage (the nature of 'watching television') which affect its evaluation?

Perhaps the first factor requiring attention here is the relative lack of *symbolic density* of most of the genres of television when these are compared with literary, theatrical or filmic modes. Elsewhere I have talked about the way in which generic shifts have increased the 'density' of various kinds of programme (this would be particularly true in documentary and, differently, in commercials). I have warned against the dangers of essentialism but, across its diverse forms, television often uses dispersed rather than intensive strategies of depiction, needing a certain level of redundancy and repetition in order to take account of its often non-intensive contexts and relations of viewing. Again, a significant comparison can be made with the art discourse of literature, in which description and evaluation, objective and subjective rendering of the world, are merged in the various modes of authorial voice and the strong guidance which these exercise upon the reader's perceptions. Like film (but with less scope for asserting a strong directorial presence), television primarily has to work through a dramatic 'showing'. But this is then quite often futher restricted in its symbolic yield by the very worldliness and 'ordinariness' of the medium and a large amount of its content.

Secondly, there is the degree of dependence upon the pre-televisual in many of the most successful formats. In Chapter 1 I discussed the distinction Stuart Hall drew between 'medium' and 'channel' functions. Recent high-rating shows on international television, like the spectacular sports/game show *Gladiators* (derived from an American format), continue the practice of 'relayed' entertainment. Whilst there are certainly exceptions to this (for instance, in the newer type of game show based on the hectic, non-realism of the videogame), it further contributes to the 'dispersal' of the television aesthetic, a dispersal not only across the varieties of genre and depictive form but also across the kinds of thing depicted. Television's extensive range of non-fiction formats 'leak' it into the world and the world into it in a way which means that it frequently cannot maintain clear enough borders and edges to offer its products as *defined artefacts*.

Thirdly, this blurring of edges is promoted by television's high level of *sociability*, which I have referred to in other chapters as it manifests itself in particular modes of address. This sociability is part of television's communicative repertoire for being a *relaxant*, a mode of temporary transportation from the cares of the occupational and domestic day. Much has recently been written on the centrality of television to the routines and rhythms of everyday life and on its normative, reassuring, ready availability.[13] It is precisely the 'friendliness' of television, projected by the direct address of its presenters, show hosts, continuity announcers etc., which works against its attainment of the 'special' and often causes critics to see as pretentious any attempted moves in this direction. A large part of the 'friendliness' stems, of course, from the need to keep viewers watching, to strike up an affective bond not only between viewer and programme but also between viewer and channel flow. It remains to be seen how the modality of television's social address will change in the context of multi-channel availability and the habit of frequent channel 'grazing'.

Fourthly, and again partly as a consequence of the emphasis on relaying 'events' (whether constructed for television or not), there is the *literalness* of television. Although there has always been work which has broken away from the pull which this exerts, television has generally constructed its depictions from varieties of realism and naturalism, thereby emphasising its reality connections in a way which, certainly in its early years, proved useful in establishing it as formally separate from cinema and with a distinctive 'destiny' as a medium.

Despite the growth of the non-literal in recent television fiction (the BBC's 1992 *Vampyr: A Soap Opera*, blending serious operatic form and 'soap' narrative is a good example, as is Peter Greenaways' 1990 interpretation of The Inferno for Channel Four – *A Television Dante*), its imaginative reach is still more confined by the conventional modes of realisation than that, say, of radio (which has always had its joke about 'better pictures') and of contemporary written fiction. There are signs, though, that image/sound combinations in television are in a phase of transformation. I have commented earlier in this book on how a certain 'post-modernisation' of style has occurred (a de-referentialising of images, a destabilising of form via pastiche, a mixing of apparently incompatible modes, a shift to the subjective/expressive use of colour, extensive use of irony etc.), even in prime time programming. However, the gravitational pull of the literal is likely to remain a factor in the cultural profile of television for some time yet.

Fifth, and finally, there is the *rhythm* of much television, a rhythm which has become increasingly organised in terms of the delivery of regular and frequent moments of intensity ('little peaks' in the viewing experience). This shift, a response to intensified multi-channel competition, has occurred both in fictional and non-fictional forms, including event-based entertainments. Although strategic attention to the placing of 'high points' has always been a feature of television production, particularly in the more directly competitive climate of the United States, the new emphasis has started to make 'regularity of strike' a first principle. Along with this has gone the development of a more exclamatory style of presentation and commentary. In certain genres (for instance, youth programmes and kinds of adult game show) the shift towards a more 'post-modern' aesthetic has had the effect of making this more easily achievable than in older conventions. But one consequence of the development is a further fragmentation of programme form, often occurring at a level beyond the final *containment* even of those progammes which are conceived of in terms of a fragmentation effect (again, the frenetic pace and rapid 'switching' across programme elements of children's television and pop music shows have provided a model here). Whatever the initial success of such an approach in countering boredom, and indeed in creating new expectations and norms for entertainment, the 'new rules of duration' seem likely to exert limits on the continuity and sustained address which mainstream television can achieve.

Put down as a list like this, the characteristics of television might seem to add up quite incontrovertibly to 'low' cultural quality. But to work exclusively within the terms set by other, older cultural forms is to miss recognising the positive, dynamic forms of depiction and engagement and the sheer potential which television's expansive, dispersed and highly socialised modes of representation have generated. It has been a feature of the best critical commentary on television that these qualities, so widely represented in ordinary viewing experience, have been registered even where forms of depictive inadequacy provide the main focus of critical attention. Raymond Williams, always exercised by the ways in which television reproduced cultural inequalities, was nevertheless keen to note just how socially isolated and complacent much contemporary high culture was when compared with the best work in television (O'Connor, 1989, *passim*).

I want to bring together some of the historical and formal themes I have raised by looking at the most recent debates about quality in British television, those developing around the ITV franchise allocations of 1991 and around the future of the BBC.

'Quality' and Policy in the 1990s

Debate about 'quality' was, as I have shown, a long-running feature of television's developing presence in British public life. It came to a head again in the early 1990s. The focus was another imminent shift in policy. The Thatcher governments of the 1980s had embraced the idea of 'privatisation' in almost every sphere of public life and broadcasting was not exempt. Both the Independent system and the BBC were under pressure to show themselves as more cost-efficient and more responsive to 'consumer' requirements. Within the terms of the Conservative's view of social order, such an emphasis on consumer-led demand was potentially in contradiction with a cultural conservativism, anxious about relinquishing 'controls' on broadcasting culture (particularly in respect of output involving depictions of a sexual or strongly violent character). A strand of moral authoritarianism fitted ill with neo-liberal economics and this tension showed itself in a number of ways and at a number of levels. The setting up of a body to monitor 'standards' in broadcasting (the Broadcasting Standards Council) at precisely the same time that the move to deregulation reached its peak was one indication. It also came through very clearly in the debate about 'quality' which preceded allocation of the regional ITV franchises by a newly formed body, the Independent Television Commission, in 1991. The principal allocative means for this was to be a 'sealed bid' auction, with the franchise for each regional area going to the highest bidder. However, it was also required of bidders that they cross a 'quality threshold' in order to be considered as proper contenders. Although this 'quality clause' started off as a relatively quiet piece of secondary legislation, it soon became the subject of intensive speculation and debate. Finally, on the day of allocation, it proved a decisive and controversial factor in several of the awards, certain big bidders being judged to have 'failed' at the quality hurdle.

With colleagues, I have written elsewhere on the questions of funding and policy raised by this recent chapter in broadcasting history, the implications of which are still unfolding (Corner *et al.*, 1993). Here, I want to focus on the way in which different criteria of quality emerged in the run-up to the bidding, criteria which had continuity with older debates but which also introduced fresh inflections and new elements.

It might be useful to quote the 'gloss' on quality offered by the ITC itself in its guidelines for bidders:

The ITC considers that the categorization of programmes as of high quality is a matter which cannot be reduced to a single formula. There may be programmes which have a special one-off character or programmes of marked creative originality, or programmes, from any category, of exceptionally high production standards, or any combination of these factors. Programmes of high quality may not be regarded as mainly or exclusively of minority appeal, and it is important that programmes of wide audience appeal should also be of high quality. High quality cannot be guaranteed by any particular combination of talent and resources, although both are normally crucial elements. Moreover, those who seek to achieve high quality in one of the ways mentioned above may not always succeed even in their own terms. It would be wrong to penalise them for making the attempt.

(ITC, 1991, p. 31)

This is certainly a long way from the vulnerable explicitness of the Pilkington Report's judgements, and it is not suprising that a quasi-theological debate about precisely what it meant quickly got under way. The level of abstraction to which 'quality' was lifted in the 1990s debate is an indicator both of its awkward controversiality as a notion (a factor already amply documented) and yet its apparent indispensibility to any debate about change in British television. In a phrasing which must be read as strategicially defensive, the Government had publicly outlined its initial plans for broadcasting with a paper subtitled 'Competition, Choice and Quality' (HMSO, 1988). This suggested that the three principles were to be inextricably bound together within the new scheme of things, well knowing that it was precisely fears about their mutual incompatibility which were causing alarm both inside and outside broadcasting circles.

Why should a notion (*some* notion) of 'quality' be found indispensable to arguments on *both* sides of the issue; by those supporting regulation and by those resolutely opposed to it? Because, I think, the strongly 'public' history of British broadcasting and the growing usage of the term 'quality' to signify managerial efficiency in public and private sectors made it difficult for advocates of change to adopt an open position of populist consumerism ('lots of people seem to like it so what's all this about quality?').

Certainly (and predictably) many defenders of the *status quo* interpreted 'quality' very much in terms of established literary judgement. This inevitably put an emphasis on the aesthetics of television fiction, approved of insofar as they were compatible with the conventions of literary 'seriousness'. The frequent citation by heavyweight cultural critics of two successful series in particular – *Brideshead Revisited* (1981) and *Jewel in the Crown* (1983), both from the Independent company Granada – reached the point of suggesting that nothing worthwhile had appeared on television for a decade apart from these two book adaptations and that any departure from the broad formula they represented would be lamentable. This 'closing down' of television quality around the more obviously respectable literary instances was bound to fall into the trap of seeming far too taste partial to be cogent in public debate. Especially as it quite often went along with a vigorous rubbishing of some of the most popular programmes in the schedules.

Rupert Murdoch, owner among other things of *Sky* satellite operations, and therefore by no means disinterested in the outcome of the debate, noticed these tones of class partiality and connected them back to entrenched 'taste' interests in the broadcasting institutions themselves:

> Much of what passes for quality on British television really is no more than a reflection of the values of a narrow elite which controls it and which has always thought its tastes are synonymous with quality – a view, incidentally, that is natural to all governing classes.
>
> (Murdoch, 1989, p. 5)

This position interprets the deregulatory dynamic of the Government as anti-elitist radicalism, a strange property indeed for British Conservative policy, and, again, very much a product of Murdoch's 'strategic reading'. However, this is a reading which shrewdly picks up on the significance of those taste/class correlations which surround British discussion of cultural value.

A more novel feature of the debate, albeit a secondary one, was the introduction of the idea of 'quality demographics', an idea which had received development and discussion in the United States.[14] This way of addressing the quality issue identified distinctive and sometimes quite small 'taste cultures' in the larger potential audience, some of whom had socio-economic profiles making them of considerable interest to advertisers. It then followed up this recognition by recommending the production of programmes designed to attract specific kinds of 'quality viewer', thereby delivering them to potential advertisers, as well as catching a more general following too. In what is essentially a version of 'life style' marketing, detailed awareness of consumer taste informs the design of the product, which is then marketed with a firmly projected 'quality look' in order to brand itself as culturally conspicuous and different. Of course, although the dynamics of the process are essentially grounded in consumption, the aesthetics drawn into play in creating desirable programmes might well have strongly conventional, 'high cultural' elements (e.g. allusive humour, character 'depth', self-reflexivity, theming around 'social issues'). This way of linking programme aesthetics to 'non-mass' audiences was only properly applicable in a media system where diverse availability (through cable and/or satellite) allowed narrowcast choices to be made. However, it had become a factor in the discussion about Channel Four's success in appealing to specific minority audiences, of whom some were highly desirable to advertisers. This success had occurred in a context where fragmentation of the old, 'mass' audience was widely predicted for a number of reasons, increased channel availability being clearly one of these. Given funding and policy changes currently under way or planned, including decisions about the future of the BBC (whose charter is up for renewal in 1996), the 'quality demographic' approach may well have yet to exert its full effect upon issues of quality and taste in British television.

With such a foregrounding of 'quality' as a new, all-purpose principle, both as 'that which has to be defended against change' and as 'that which change will achieve', it is not suprising that a few other blurrings occurred. One of them was the distinction between programme and schedule. Criteria for the one were certainly not going to be same as for the other. A schedule could be defended in terms of balance, variety, appeal to different groups etc. (clearly, very much virtues of public broadcasting) while a programme needed recourse to *formal* criteria of one sort or another. We can see above how the ITC wrestled with some of the ensuing problems in its own formulation, finally getting dangerously close to metaphysics.

Another blurring was that between journalism and non-fiction forms. Criteria for broadcast journalism are not taste related *in the same way* as drama and entertainment are. The varieties of journalism may have appeal to different social class groupings and it would be foolish to suppose that education and occupation play no part in the pattern of this difference. But, as I explored in Chapter 4, the case for an accessible and independent television news service is usually made by reference to broad principles of democracy and citizenship and by a recognition of the vital role that television plays in public information. That there are continuing debates about how best to carry out this function and about the scheduling and length of news bulletins does not mean that the issue is best handled by being fused with other aspects of the argument about quality. Nor is it useful for questions surrounding broadcast journalism to be given an emphasis which then excludes consideration of broader aesthetic issues. Both occurred.

In contrast to the strategic high abstraction of many of the exchanges, there were also some attempts to see 'quality' in *craft* terms; quality was 'good production values' (direction, lighting, camerawork, sound, set design, acting and so on). This was certainly relatively uncontentious – it's hard to find an open commitment to *bad* production – but it failed to engage at the level where the real tensions and conflicts were being played out. As I have shown, this was at the level of cultural standards and cultural choices, the level where questions of elitism and the 'popular', of exploitation and 'market liberation' intersected around what was, and what was not, going to be found on the small screen.

The academic contribution to the debate was slow to start. Charlotte Brunsdon's call for television researchers to address themselves afresh to the 'quality' issue (Brunsdon, 1990) was deservedly much cited, though its very originality was an indication of how little attention questions of value had received in academic work. However, the relative inability of academics to contribute was also a function of the extent to which the language of television studies had become inaccessible to those working in the medium, let alone the public at large. Despite this, some academic work tried to pitch its analysis at a level where the broader debate could be influenced.[15] The sheer difficulty of articulating a clear response should not be underestimated. It was one thing to suggest that researchers and teachers turn their attention to the analysis of 'quality', it was quite another to expect them to champion particular aesthetic standards. Cultural criticism had become a good deal more circumspect about judgements of value since the days of the Pilkington Report!

In this discussion, I have looked at both historical and contemporary instances of policy debate as well as at the character of television itself. I want to conclude by looking at the likely future of television aesthetics and

at the future of debates about their cultural role, whether these are related
to ideas about 'art' or are seen more generally as matters of social representation and social expression.

As the number of channels available to British viewers increases, quite
radical changes in the cultural character of television can be expected.
Somewhat artificially, we can divide these into changes in *production
aesthetics* and in *consumption aesthetics*.

Since the movement is one towards a more direct and strong
'consumerist' element in television, it might be best to start at this end. With
multi-channel systems, the frequency of channel switching becomes an
important factor in the viewing experience. The older, 'longitudinal' model
of viewing in which limited choice meant sustained periods of same-
channel viewing is being replaced by a 'latitudinal' model involving little
channel continuity at all. Research on viewing patterns during the transitional period will be interesting in the kinds of movement and rehabitu-
alisation it shows. Although much relatively superficial commentary has
been offered on the pleasures of channel 'grazing', 'surfing' or 'zapping',
it is hard to predict how the new patterns of viewing will settle down once
the period of multi-channel novelty is over. It seems very likely, however,
that for a very wide range of viewers, *tolerance periods* will decrease. That
is to say, the amount of time a viewer is prepared to spend being under-
satisfied by what they are watching will shorten. In addition, the threshold of 'satisfaction' may be raised, in relation to selective critera such as
intensity, development, visual interest etc. (clearly, partly subjective and
generically specific criteria). One effect, indicated earlier, will be to add
another, significant dimension to common viewing experience – that of the
'part-watched' item, perhaps right down to the level of the single action,
the single scene, even the single shot. I say 'add' because, despite apocalyptic predictions about post-modern sensibility, we are a long way from
the complete displacement of 'whole programme' viewing. Nor, of course,
is 'part-watching' by itself an entirely new phenomenon, but its nature and
scale may become so.

On the production side, one of the issues will be how programmes can
lower their vulnerability to being switched from. In my discussion above,
I commented on the increased frequency and intensity levels of 'high spots'
as one obvious recipe which will be followed within some genres. Yet not
all programmes will feel the need to develop a more emphatic 'stay tuned'
aesthetic as a response to the new circumstances. With channel *specialisa-
tion* another feature of multi-channel systems, certain genres will have more
of a 'narrowcast' warrant to innovate and expand and to develop sustained
formal integrity, assuming (though not *too* complacently) a certain habitual
commitment in their viewers.

What I am describing is perhaps a gradual, further dispersal of 'television' as an entity. This is both an aesthetic dispersal, as indicated, and a
slow dispersal (not at all the same thing as a disappearance) of its identity
as a public agency. Certainly, 'quality' issues would take on a new and
more individualistic tone at the end of such a process. But throughout this
book I have worked with a sense that, to use Raymond Williams's terms,
'residual', 'dominant' and 'emergent' versions of the *public* are all inscribed

deeply into current television and into its development and that, for some time yet, recognition of this will be an important element of study, analysis and argument.[16]

NOTES

Introduction

1. Fiske (1987) – a hugely influential textbook – employs semiotic analysis, though with more circumspection than several other writers. See Caughie (1984) for a discussion of different analytic approaches to television form. The essays in Allen (1992) offer the best recent review of approaches and methods in television studies, including semiotics.
2. I questioned aspects of the semiotic approach in Corner (1980). More recently, a strand of critique and revision has appeared in media analysis, although this is mostly offered 'in passing' and no sustained critical account of media semiotics has come to my notice at the time of writing.
3. Again, Fiske (1987) has been influential, though the issue has provoked such intensity of debate that no one particular version has become definitive. Hall (1977) provided a much-cited and relatively early discussion.
4. Schlesinger (1990) usefully identifies the problems for social inquiry which follow from media-centricity.
5. Ang (1985), Morley (1986) and Silverstone (1993) are attempts to trace the different dimensions of this aspect of television, which is now gathering around it a sizeable literature of research and debate.
6. Scannell (1989) is very useful here in respect both of definitions and historical exemplification. The more general issues involved will be referred to extensively in later chapters.
7. See the general analysis of Tulloch (1990) and the collected studies in Brandt (1993).

Chapter 1. Television as Public Communication

1. A useful recent gloss on the usage of this term in media analysis is found in Nichols (1991).

2. Feur (1983) discusses both 'liveness' and 'live effect' in contemporary television, relating these to 'immediacy'.
3. Paddy Scannell has explored this aspect of radio in a number of articles. See, particularly, Scannell (1989).
4. Williams (1974b) focuses on this and its cultural consequences.
5. See Corner (1992) for a brief critical survey of 'realism' as a term in media research.
6. An interesting survey of camcorder use, and a discussion of how attitudes to broadcast television might change as a result, is Vale (1990). Current British television has a number of camcorder-inspired programmes and this tendency is likely to get stronger.
7. Ellis (1982), discussed in detail later, puts particular emphasis on the 'domesticity' of the medium. Morley (1986) documents how home routines and activities relate to viewing by taking a sample of families and researching them through extended interview.
8. Murdock (1993) develops a general account of the relations between television and modernity, drawing extensively on the theoretical work of Anthony Giddens (see Giddens, 1990). The essays in Mellencamp (1990) are among the best recent explorations of how television form connects with the parameters and dynamics of modern experience. Carey (1989) presents a broad and brilliantly suggestive account of the interconnections between communications technology and the modernisation of space and time, drawing on North American history.
9. A history of this programme, together with an analysis of its aims, structure and success with both police and viewers, is presented in Schlesinger and Tumber (1993).
10. I am particularly grateful to the director of the item analysed below, Robert Del Maestro, for talking to me about his general perspective on *999* as drama-documentary and about the decisions he made during the shooting of the item.
11. The ways in which the new media are able to construct social groupings which transcend place and time has been the subject of much discussion. The phrase 'imagined community' (Benedict, 1983) has been widely employed. See also the discussion of community-at-a-distance in Willis *et al.* (1990).

Chapter 2. Medium and Political Order

1. A major study of the live broadcasting of civic and political events on contemporary television is Dayan and Katz (1992). Their approach is essentially symbolic anthropology, sharing some features with the Langs' research design and similarly under-evidenced in relation to ordinary viewing experience.
2. A wide range of references is possible for citations on this topic from Habermas, whose translation into English has considerably lagged behind his extensive publication in German. Habermas (1989) is probably one of the most important translated writings in respect of this chapter's concerns.
3. Among the most useful are those in Garnham (1990), Thompson (1991), Curran (1991) and Peter (1993). The literature is vast and growing, though increasingly inclined to hair-splitting.
4. For some indication of the recent work in this area see the articles in *Media, Culture and Society*, 15.3. 1993, a special issue on 'Public Relations and Media Strategies'.
5. A detailed analysis of presentational strategy in U.S. politics is given in Jamieson (1992). This includes television advertising and press relations' planning. The use of extensive opinion polling by the media, to the point where

this becomes both a factor in strategic personalization and changes the basis for electoral decision making, also receives critical comment here. See Franklin (1994) for a British study of political marketing.

6. Thompson (1991) reviews the literature on this aspect of media.
7. For an analysis of the organisation and character of Gulf War coverage see Mowlana *et al.* (1993).
8. The questions about democratic organisation, democratic principles and the media raised by Keane (1991) have provided a focus for another round of argument on these and related points.
9. The 'live audience discussion' format is the focus of Livingstone and Lunt (1993). Their study is both political and psychological as well as concerned with television form. Livingstone (1994) directly engages with the relationship between specific programmes and general changes in the nature of, and opportunities for, public debate.
10. I am aware that a more historical account of politics, as well as of television, is needed in the study of political television. In the interests of clarity of main theme, my discussion has tended to underplay this factor, as it has also underplayed factors of national difference.

Chapter 3. 'See it Happen'

1. I take this title from Cox (1983), though it is a phrase which has been widely used in news programme promotion, both in America and Britain.
2. Mowlana *et al.* (1993) give many aspects of war coverage detailed attention, including 'dependency' among the television audience.
3. Roshco (1975) is among the best accounts of news as a general category of public knowledge. Cohen and Young (1973) brings together many studies which critically assess the nature of news as a media commodity.
4. Not suprisingly, 'selectivity' is the focus for a number of news studies. For British television, Schlesinger (1978) is a classic account, based on observation of newsroom practice over a period of time.
5. There is a large literature on news form. Among the most useful studies are Brunsdon and Morley (1978), Hartley (1982) and Ericson *et al.* (1987).
6. The work collected in Mowlana *et al.* (1993) documents shifts and 'turns' in coverage.
7. Cox (1983) provides a useful background to these developments from the perspective of the first editor of ITN. He notes the early differences between BBC and ITN approaches. Chapter 2 in Schlesinger (1978) 'The Formation of BBC News', remains an excellent, concise account of key developments.
8. Among the important analyses of how those notions apply to journalism are those by Tuchman (1972), the Glasgow University Media Group (1976), Schlesinger (1978) and Philo (1990). Lichtenberg (1991) gives a provocative and clear account of some of the major theoretical issues surrounding 'objectivity'.
9. Of course, during election campaigns, this tendency is radically increased, especially where, as in Britain, no political advertising is permitted on television and therefore 'news share' counts (or is seen to count) for more.
10. In a short and shrewd critical essay on the presence of subjectivity in claims of 'bias', Tracey (1986) moves close to this sort of relativism. See also Cox (1976) for reflection on the impartiality/bias debate from a working journalist and news editor.
11. Full transcripts of the BBC and ITN broadcasts, of the Conservative Central Office's letter of complaint and of the BBC's response are published in *Index on*

Censorship, 16.3. 1987, pp. 7–31. In citing from the broadcast and noting aspects of the issue which attracted press attention, I have used *The Guardian* Friday 31 October, 1986, p. 6 and Thursday 6 November, 1986, p. 5. I have also drawn on material, including news replays, contained in editions of *Newsnight* (BBC2) on Thursday 30 October and Wednesday 5 November 1986.

12. Morrison (1992) researches this incident using audience group discussion. See also BBC (1991).
13. Again, Morrison (1992) documents this fully, through group discussion and a method of questioning using hypothetical as well as real circumstances.
14. During the miners' strike, one incident shows with particular clarity how this 'part-for-whole' process works to generate controversy around publicly circu-lated images. A television news bulletin, as part of a longer sequence of police/miner confrontation shot at a distance, included images of a police-man striking a fallen miner with a truncheon. Police 'defence' of this was that it was a regrettable but isolated incident, whereas the miners and their supporters claimed it was the *instancing* of a *general* fact about police behaviour.
15. The screening on BBC2 for several weeks of a brief (2 minute) daily account of some aspect of ordinary life in beseiged Sarajevo, transmitted on the same day as filmed, was one of the most interesting innovations in coverage of this conflict. Its immediacy and its juxtaposition of the ordinary with the extraordi-nary was both original and powerful, reorganising the terms of the viewers' relationship with 'news'.
16. *Tonight* is briefly placed in the context of early television developments in Corner (1991a).

Chapter 4. Civic Visions: Forms of Documentary

1. A good discussion of Grierson's ideas about the documentary genre, placed in their contemporary intellectual context, is contained in Aitkin (1990).
2. The opening sentence of 'First Principles of Documentary' (1933), in Hardy (1979).
3. See, for instance, Miles and Smith (1987) and Aitkin (1990). The latter includes an extensive bibliography. Hillier and Lovell (1972) is still a valuable, pioneer-ing study, with a good general account as well as perceptive commentary on individual films. In my own discussion of the 'documentary movement' I have drawn on the wide range of articles now available on formal and social aspects of the work, though a major study of the films is still awaited.
4. Unpublished BBC memo, 29 October, 'Television and the future of broadcast-ing'. I am indebted to Elaine Bell for this quotation. See her essay 'The Origin of British Television Documentary' in Corner (1991d, pp. 65–80).
5. Paddy Scannell is the major historian of British radio form. See his 'The Stuff of Radio' in Corner (1986, pp. 1–26).
6. For a more detailed study of the emergence of documentary as a television genre, see John Corner, 'Documentary Voices' in Corner (1991d, pp. 42–59).
7. Vaughan (1976) is illuminating on the origins of television work, whilst Goodwin *et al.* (1983) brings together a number of valuable items on drama-documentary forms.
8. In doing so, I draw on two extremely rich bodies of work on documentary. That of Dai Vaughan (see Vaughan, 1976, 1992) and that of Bill Nichols, whose theoretical study (1991) is a major text in documentary analysis, although it is concerned primarily with cinema.

9. Richard Collins discusses the question of 'intervention' in *vérité*, at both shooting and editing stages, in his article 'Seeing is Believing' in Corner (1986, pp. 125–138).

10. Early instances of presenting the documentary interview as a social encounter are discussed in Corner (1991c).

11. One widely shown film which adopts this approach is Connie Field's *The Life and Times of Rosie the Riveter* (1980), referred to elsewhere in this chapter.

12. This debate about drama-documentary 'naturalism' is well discussed in Goodwin *et al.* (1983) and in Paget (1990). Caughie (1980) explores the conventions of the 'new' documentary-drama, making the distinction between it and dramatised documentary.

13. Elaine Bell's work on 'Origins' (see note 4) discusses how early drama-doc was often a response to technical limitations. Nowadays, it is often a response to the limitations on access to certain kinds of institution and event.

14. For a study of how viewers variously attribute intentions to documentary material where such material presents itself as 'neutral', see Richardson and Corner (1986).

15. An assessment of the form of this series by a writer who was also a pioneer documentary director is given in Swallow (1966).

16. Nichols (1983) discusses this film in some detail, as an innovative mixture of interview and archive materials.

17. The range of independent cinema work in the U.S.A is clear from the critical commentary of Nichols (1991).

Chapter 5. Adworlds

1. Packard (1957) is the classic text on psycho-social risk. Dyer (1982), with a strongly negative assessment of cultural consequences, has been an influential textbook in British media studies. Booth (1982) develops an American anti-advertising case, discussed later, whilst more recently Haineault and Roy (1993) criticises the effect of advertising on the unconscious, drawing on the French experience.

2. Mattelart (1991) reviews developments in Western Europe and then globally. Schudson (1992) examines the implications in Eastern Europe whilst being primarily concerned with the United States.

3. Agencies themselves have commissioned research into the changing conditions of reception, including video recorder use.

4. Williams (1970) is scathing about the manner in which this was institutionalised in Britain.

5. Such links in French culture are analysed in Guyot (1992).

6. A musicological and social analysis of the function of music in advertising is developed in Klempe (1993).

7. Lee (1993) reviews the arguments about how current advertising culture is linked to economic and cultural shifts in Western societies.

8. A similar point is made by John Thompson (1990). In teaching advertising together to first-year, first-term undergraduates we were confronted with an interesting range of assumptions about how advertisements work and about their 'effects'.

9. Davidson (1991) draws on his own agency experience to discuss 'branding' strategies, including methods of 'value addition'.

10. Dyer (1982) suggests both possibilities, in line with a large critical literature in the United States and Britain.

11. This is described fully in a 'case study' contained in Broadbent (1984, pp. 141–154).
12. The forms of racism and sexism which advertising or particular advertisements might serve to promote is a frequent focus not only of academic but also of journalistic commentary.
13. Williamson (1978) is perhaps the most cited text here.
14. A sustained critique of the application of structuralism to advertisements is Francis (1986). Given its range of examples and its clarity, it deserves to be more widely known.
15. Mellencamp (ed.) (1990) engages with this phenomenon at various points. It is one which will clearly figure more prominently in future research.
16. McGuigan (1992, Chapter 3) has a strongly negative assessment of the Navas' case.
17. The most comprehensive and lucid account of the 'revised' view of advertising is Schudson (1992), cited briefly later. It is interesting that this concludes on a note of measured ambivalence rather than a positive assessment. Curran (1990) is an important essay on the more general tendency towards a 'revisionism' in media research.
18. These kinds of changes in the industry are discussed in Davidson (1991).

Chapter 6. 'Influence' and Interpretation

1. The now extensive literature on television interpretation includes the work of Morley (1980, 1986), Ang (1985), Jensen (1986), Dahlgren (1988) and Corner *et al.* (1990). General overviews include Moores (1993).
2. Morley (1992) discusses this aspect of interpretation in the context of a decade of audience studies.
3. McGuire (1988) gives a concise, polemical assessment along these lines.
4. The 'how can we say there is no bad media influence if we want to believe that there can be good' argument is often heard in various forms. Sometimes new media (television – bad) are played off against old (literature – good). The issue deserves more thorough attention than it usually gets, since it points to a quite fundamental cultural inconsistency in thinking about influence.
5. The popular appeal of the 'brainwash' idea as a direct, simple effect of 'propaganda' is well documented. McQuail (1992) reviews some of the assumptions involved and the kinds of research which have lent support to them.
6. See, for instance, Neuman *et al.* (1992). The signs are that this approach will remain the most significant one in new research.
7. Cumberpatch and Howitt (1989) discuss various elements of academic and popular attitudes to violence on television. See also Gerbner and Signorielli (1990) for an engagement with the links between viewing and fear of crime. Schlesinger *et al.* (1992) is an original and important study of viewer attitudes to violence and contains much that relates to my broad 'turn-on/turn-off' division.
8. For a recent collection of articles on the cultural influence of pornography see Gibson and Gibson (1993).
9. Geertz's own analysis here is not without its critics. Indeed, his study has been the focus of considerable argument both as to its working assumptions and its methods. Crapanzanu (1992) is a good example of recent critique.
10. The question of over what period of time to research media influence has always posed a problem. Too long term an approach risks obscuring significant correlation under a wide range of contextual variables, too short term risks

working with a naively 'heavy' and monocausal idea of influence processes. As I noted earlier, the question of *frequency* of exposure to specific forms, as in repeat viewing of the same item or regular viewing of certain *kinds* of item, is a further relevant factor here.

11. See the review of these issues in Cumberpatch and Howitt (1989).

12. A version of this 'levels' approach to interpretation is contained in Corner (1991b). What follows involves some revision and (hopefully) improved clarity.

13. Not impossible because the argument can still turn on the 'probability' that an item, image or phrase will carry a certain association for many if not all viewers, or for a particular, relevant group of viewers. This matter of 'probability', and the size of the group for whom a particular interpretation is judged as a likely one, is more vulnerable than the establishing of common denotations, but 'associations' can still be argued for in relation to empirical evidence (e.g. forms of joke, concurrent media usage).

14. I have found the articles in Bradac (ed.) (1989) useful in indicating the scope of this area of inquiry.

15. The critique and revision of the very notion of 'ideology' is a prominent aspect of current social science and humanities thinking. The new context for use of the term in research is helpfully discussed in Barrett (1991).

Chapter 7. Questions of 'Quality'

1. The nature of this concern in the early days of U.S. television, particularly insofar as it involved the use of theatrical and cinematic criteria, is well brought out in Boddy (1991).

2. See, for instance, the attitudes to taste differences and popular pleasures developed in the essays on 'fandom' in Lewis (1992).

3. A concise account of the formative period of television in Britain is to be found in Corner (1991a).

4. Briggs (1985) provides the best comprehensive history of key developments in BBC radio and television services.

5. A comment by Selwyn Lloyd M.P., a Conservative critic of the BBC monopoly. See HMSO (1951, p. 205).

6. The best overview of this debate is that in Wilson (1961). A version more favourable to the commercial lobby is put forward by Sendall (1982).

7. Rosenberg and White (1957) is a good example of discussion on what was already an established theme in the United States.

8. The details of the final stages of the debate and the institutionalisation of commercial television are reviewed in Sendall (1982) and Briggs (1985).

9. Hall and Whannel (1964) quote extensively from press responses to the Report (pp. 428–430).

10. The Stencilled Papers series produced from the early 1970s by the Centre for Contemporary Cultural Studies, University of Birmingham, were initially the most influential publications here. Hoggart was the founder of the Centre, so there is a degree of continuity with the earlier, moral, critique.

11. See Harvey (1989) on the particular combination of funding system and programming policy involved here.

12. Poole (1984) examines the development of television criticism in the press and notes its weaknesses and lack of integrity alongside other arts specialisms.

13. As I write, Moores (1993) is the most recent, comprehensive treatment of this topic.

14. Feur (1985) increased awareness of the relations between television quality and 'niche marketing' on both side of the Atlantic. However, part of Feur's argument concerns the requirement to attract a substantial, broad audience, who will nevertheless view certain types of programming as 'alternative' and 'cult'.

15. The British Film Institute pursued a policy of interventionism, which included publishing discussion of a kind accessible outside the sphere of media research. Mulgan (ed.) (1990) focused on 'quality' questions from a range of perspectives and positions.

16. These terms are used by Williams in a number of his later works to indicate the co-existence of different cultural formations within the process of cultural change. They are given explicit definition in Williams (1977).

REFERENCES

AITKIN, I. (1990) *Film and Reform*. London: Routledge.

ALLEN, R. (ed.) (1992) *Channels of Discourse Re-assembled*. London: Routledge.

ANDERSON, B. (1983) *Imagined Communities*. London: Verso.

ANG, I. (1985) *Watching 'Dallas': Soap Opera and the Melodramatic Imagination*. London: Methuen.

BBC (1991) *Annual Research Report*, Ch. 6, 'The Baghdad Broadcasting Corporation?: How television dealt with the Gulf War.' London: John Libbey.

BARRETT, M. (1991) *The Politics of Truth*. Cambridge: Polity.

BARTHES, R. (1977) 'The rhetoric of the image.' In *Image–Music–Text*. London: Fontana.

BENNETT, T. *et al.* (eds) (1981) *Popular television and film*. London: British Film Institute.

BERGER, A. (ed.) (1988) *Media USA*. (Part 9, 'Media Effects') London: Longman.

BLACK, PETER (1972) *The mirror in the corner*. London: Hutchinson.

BODDY, W. (1991) *Fifties television: the industry and its critics*. Illinois: University of Illinois Press.

BOOTH, W.C. (1982) 'The Company We Keep', *Daedalus*. III.4 1982.

BOURDIEU, P. (1984) *Distinction*. (tr. Richard Nice) London: Routledge.

BRADAC, J. (ed.) (1989) *Message effects in communication science*. London: Sage.

BRANDT. G. (ed.) (1993) *British television drama*. Cambridge: Cambridge University Press.

BRIGGS, A. (1985) *The BBC: the first fifty years*. Oxford: Oxford University Press.

BROADBENT, S. (1984) *The Leo Burnett Book of advertising*. London: Business Books Ltd.

BRUNSDON, C. (1990) 'Quality in Television', *Screen*. Vol.31, No.1. 1990.

BRUNSDON, C. and MORLEY, D. (1978) *Everyday television: 'Nationwide'*. London: British Film Institute.

BRUNT, R. and JORDIN, M. (1988) 'Constituting the Television Audience: A Problem of Method' in P. Drummond and R. Paterson (eds) *Television and its audience*. London: British Film Institute. 231–249.

CAREY, J. (1989) *Communication as culture*. London: Unwin Hyman.

CAUGHIE, J. (1980) 'Progressive Television and Documentary Drama', *Screen* 21.3.

CAUGHIE, J. (1984) Television Criticism: A Discourse in Search of an Object. *Screen* **25**, 4–5: 109–120.

COHEN, S. and YOUNG, J. (eds) (1973): *The manufacture of news: deviance, social problems and the mass media*. London: Constable.

CONRAD, P. (1982) *Television: the medium and its manners*. London: Routledge.

CORNER, J. (1980) 'Codes and Cultural Analysis', *Media, Culture and Society* 2 January 1980, 73–86.

CORNER, J. (ed.) (1986) *Documentary and the mass media*. London: Edward Arnold.

CORNER, J. (1991a) 'Television and British Society in the 1950s'. In Corner, J. (Ed.) *Popular television in Britain*, pp. 1–21. London: British Film Institute.

CORNER, J. (1991b) 'Meaning, Genre and Context: The Problematics of "Public Knowledge" in the New Audience Research' in J. Curran and M. Gurevitch (eds) *Mass media and society*. London: Edward Arnold.

CORNER, J. (1991c) 'The Interview as Social Encounter' in Paddy Scannell (ed.) *Broadcast talk*. London: Sage.

CORNER, J. (ed.) (1991d) *Popular television in Britain: studies in cultural history*. London: British Film Institute.

CORNER, J. (1992) 'Presumption as Theory: "Realism" in Television Studies' in *Screen*. 33 January 97–102.

CORNER, J. (1993) 'Debating Culture: Quality and Inequality' *Media, Culture and Society*. 16.1, 141–148.

CORNER, J. and SCHLESINGER, P. (eds) 'Public Relations and Media Strategies', theme issue of *Media, Culture and Society*. 15.6.

CORNER, J., RICHARDSON, K. and FENTON, N. (1990) *Nuclear reactions: form and response in public issue television*. London: John Libbey.

CORNER, J., HARVEY, S., and LURY, K. (1993) 'British Television and the "Quality" Issue' in *Media information Australia*. **68**, 78–55. An expanded version of this article is to be published in S. Hood (ed.) *Behind the Screens*. London: Lawrence and Wishart (forthcoming).

COTTLE, S. (1993) *Television news, urban conflict and the inner city*. Leicester: Leicester University Press.

COX, G. (1976) 'Impartiality is Not Enough' *The Listener*, 20 May, 626–628.

COX, G. (1983) *See it happen: the making of ITN*. London: Bodley Head.

CRAPANZANU, V. (1992) *Hermes' dilemma and Hamlet's desire*. Cambridge, Mass.: Harvard University Press. 61–69.

CROSLAND, C.A.R. (1962) 'The Mass Media' in *Encounter*. November.

CUMBERPATCH G. and HOWITT, D. (1989) *A measure of uncertainty: the effects of the mass media*. London: John Libbey.

CURRAN, J. (1990) 'The New Revisionism in Mass Communication Research: A Reappraisal', *European Journal of Communication* **5**, 135–164.

CURRAN, J. (1991) 'Rethinking the Media as a Public Sphere' in P. Dahlgren and C. Sparks (eds) *Communication and citizenship*. London: Routledge.

DAHLGREN, P. (1988) 'What's the Meaning of This?: Viewers' Plural Sense-Making of TV News' *Media, Culture and Society*. 10.3, 285–301.

DAHLGREN, P. (1991) 'Introduction' to P. Dahlgren and C. Sparks (1991): *Communication and citizenship*. London: Routledge, pp. 1–24.

DAVIDSON, M. (1991) *The consumerist manifesto*. London: Routledge.

DAVIS, H. and WALTON, P. (1983) 'Death of a Premier: control and closure in international news' H. Davis and P. Walton (eds) Language, image, media. Oxford: Blackwell

DAYAN, D. and KATZ, E. (1987) 'Performing Media Events' in J. Curran, A. Smith and P. Wingate (eds) *Impacts and influences*. London: Methuen.

DAYAN, D. and KATZ, E. (1992) *Media events: the live broadcasting of history.* Cambridge, Mass.: Harvard University Press.

DOCHERTY, D. (1990) *Violence in TV fiction.* London: Broadcasting Standards Council Annual Review.

DYER, G. (1982) *Advertising as communication.* London: Methuen.

DYER, R. (1992) *Only entertainment.* London: Routledge.

ELLIS, J. (1982) *Visible fictions.* London: Routledge.

ERICSON, R., BARANEK, P. and CHAN, J. (1987) *Vizualizing deviance.* Milton Keynes: Open University Press.

FERGUSON, M. (ed.) (1990) *Public communication: the new imperatives.* London: Sage.

FEUR, J (1983) 'The Concept of "Live Television": Ontology vs Ideology' in E.A. Kaplan (ed.) *Regarding television.* Los Angeles: American Film Institute/University Publications of America.

FEUR, J. (1985) *MTM: quality television.* London: British Film Institute.

FISKE, J. (1987) *Television culture.* London: Methuen.

FISKE, J. and HARTLEY, J. (1978) *Reading television.* London: Methuen.

FRANCIS, D. (1986) 'Advertising and Structuralism: The Myth of Formality'. *International Journal of Advertising,* 5 197–214.

FRANKLIN, B. (1994) *Packaging politics.* London: Edward Arnold.

GARNHAM, N. (1990) 'The Media and the Public Sphere' in N. Garnham, *Capitalism and communication: global culture and the economics of information.* London: Sage, 104–14.

GEERTZ, C. (1973) *The interpretation of cultures.* New York: Basic Books.

GERBNER, G. (1976) 'Where we are and where we should be going'. Address to Annual Conference of the International Association of Mass Communication Researchers, University of Leicester, August.

GERBNER, G. and SIGNORIELLI, N. (1990) *Violence profile 1967 through 1988–89.* Washington: Corporation for Public Broadcasting.

GIBSON, C. and GIBSON, R. (1993) *Dirty looks.* London: British Film Institute.

GIDDENS, A. (1990) *Modernity and self-identity.* Cambridge: Polity Press.

Glasgow University Media Group (1976) *Bad news.* London: Routledge.

Glasgow University Media Group (1980) *More bad news.* London: Routledge.

Glasgow University Media Group (1986) *War and peace news.* London: Routledge.

GOODWIN, A. *et al.* (eds) (1983) *Drama-documentary: B.F.I. Dossier 19.* London: British Film Institute.

GRIERSON, J. (1932–4) 'First Principles of Documentary' in Hardy, F. (ed.) 1979: *Grierson on documentary.*

GUYOT, J. (1992) *L'Ecran publicitaire.* Paris: Editions L'Harmattan.

HABERMAS, J. (1989) *The structural transformation of the public sphere.* Cambridge: Polity.

HALL, S. (1975) 'Television as a Medium and Its Relation to Culture'. Centre for Contemporary Cultural Studies, Stencilled Working Paper, July 1975.

HALL, S. (1977) 'Culture, the Media and the "Ideological Effect"' in J. Curran, M. Gurevitch and J. Woollacott (eds) *Mass communication and society.* London: Edward Arnold.

HALL, S. and WHANNEL, P. (1964) *The popular arts.* London: Hutchinson.

HALLORAN, J., ELLIOTT, P. and MURDOCK, G. (1970) *Demonstration and communication: a case study.* Harmondsworth: Penguin.

HAINEAULT, D.L. and ROY, J.-Y. (1993) *Unconscious for sale: advertising, psychoanalysis and the public.* Minneapolis: University of Minnesota Press.

HARDY, F. (ed.) (1979) *Grierson on documentary.* London: Faber.

HARTLEY, J. (1982) *Understanding news.* London: Routledge.

HARTLEY, J. (1992) *The politics of pictures.* London: Routledge.

HARVEY, S. (1989) 'Deregulation, Innovation and Channel Four' in *Screen* **30**, 60–78.

HEATH, S. (1990) 'Representing television' in Mellencamp P. (ed.) *Logics of Television*, pp. 267–302. British Film Institute, London.

HIGSON, A. (1986) 'Britain's Outstanding Contribution to Film' in Charles Barr (ed.) *All our yesterdays: 90 years of British cinema*. London: British Film Institute.

HILLIER, J. and LOVELL, A. (1972) *Studies in documentary*. London: Secker and Warburg.

HMSO (1951) *Report of the committee on broadcasting 1949*. (Cmnd 8116), 'Minority Report Submitted by Mr Selwyn Lloyd', pp. 201–210. London.

HMSO (1962) *Report of the committee on broadcasting 1960*. (Cmnd 1753). London: HMSO.

HMSO (1977) *Report on the committee on the future of broadcasting*. Cmnd. 6753. London.

HMSO (1988) *'Broadcasting in the '90's: competition, choice and quality'*. (Cmnd 517). London.

HOGGART, R. (1957) *The uses of literacy*. Chatto and Windus.

HOIJER, B. (1990) 'Studying Viewers' Reception of Television Programmes: Theoretical and Methodological Considerations', *European Journal of Communication*, **5**, 2–3, 29–56.

HORTON, D. and WOHL, R (1956) 'Mass Communication as Para-Social Interaction: Observations on Intimacy at a Distance.'in *Psychiatry*, **19**, 215–229. Reprinted in J. Corner and J. Hawthorn (eds) *Communication Studies*, 4th edn. London: Edward Arnold.

ITC (Independent Television Commission) (1991) *Invitation to apply for regional channel 3 licences*. London: ITC.

JAKOBSON, R. (1960) 'Closing Statement: Linguistics and Poetics' in T. Sebeok (ed.) *Style and language*. Cambridge, MA: M.I.T. Press.

JAMIESON, K.H. (1992) *Dirty politics: deception, distraction and democracy*. Oxford: Oxford University Press.

JENSEN, K. (1986) *Making sense of the news*. Aarhus: The University Press.

KEANE, J. (1991) *The media and democracy*. Cambridge: Polity Press.

KELLNER, D. (1990) *Television and the crisis of democracy*. Oxford: Westview.

KLEMPE, H. (1993) 'Music, Text and Image in Commercials for Coca-Cola' in J. Corner and J. Hawthorn (eds) (1993) *Communication Studies* (Fourth Edition). London: Edward Arnold.

LANG, K. and LANG, G (1953) 'The Unique Perspective of Television' in *American Sociological Review* 18. Reprinted in J. Corner and J. Hawthorn (eds) 1993: *Communication studies* (Fourth Edition), London: Edward Arnold.

LASSWELL, H. (1971) 'The Structure and Function of Communication in Society' in W. Schramm and D. Roberts (eds) *The process and effects of mass communication*. (Revised Edition) Urbana: University of Illinois Press. pp 84–99.

LEE, M. (1993) *Consumer culture reborn*. London: Routledge.

LEIBES, T. and KATZ, E. (1990) *The export of meaning*. Oxford: Oxford University Press.

LEISS, W., KLINE, S. and JHALLY, S. (1986) *Social communication in advertising*. London: Methuen.

LEVI-STRAUSS, C. (1970) *The raw and the cooked*. London: Cape.

LEWIS, J. (1985) 'Decoding Television News' in P. Drummond and R. Paterson (eds) *Television in transition*. London: British Film Institute.

LEWIS, L. (ed.) (1992) *The adoring audience: fan culture and popular media*. London: Routledge.

LICHTENBERG, J. (1991) 'In Defense of Objectivity' in J. Curran and M. Gurevitch (eds) *Mass media and society*. London: Arnold.

LIVINGSTONE, S. (1994) 'Watching Talk: Gender and Engagement in the Viewing of Audience Discussion Programmes', *Media, Culture and Society* 16.3.

LIVINGSTONE, S. and LUNT, P. (1993) *Talk on television.* London: Routledge.

MANDER, J. (1978) *Four arguments for the elimination of television.* Brighton: Harvester.

MARCUSE, H. (1972) *One dimensional man.* London: Paladin.

MATTELART, A. (1991) *Advertising international.* (tr. Michael Chanan), London: Routledge.

MAYHEW, C. (1953) *Dear viewer.* London: Lincolns Prager.

McGUIGAN, J. (1992) *Cultural populism.* London: Routledge.

McGUIRE, W. (1988) 'Who's Afraid of the Big Bad Media?' in Berger, A. (ed.) *Media USA.* London: Longman. 272–280.

McQUAIL, D. (1992) *Media performance.* London: Sage.

MELLANCAMP, P. (ed.) (1990) *Logics of television.* London: British Film Institute.

MEYROWITZ, J. (1985) *No sense of place: the impact of electronic media on social behaviour.* New York: Oxford University Press.

MILES, P. and SMITH M. (1987) Chapter 6 of *Cinema, literature and society.* London: Croom Helm.

MILL, J.S. (1861) 'Utilitarianism' Chapter 2. (Fontana Edition 1962: ed. Mary Warnock) p.261.

MOORES, S. (1993) *Interpreting audiences.* London: Sage.

MORLEY, D. (1980) *The 'Nationwide' audience.* London: British Film Institute.

MORLEY, D. (1981) 'The Nationwide Audience: A Critical Postscript' in *Screen Education.* **39**, 3–14.

MORLEY, D. (1986) *Family television.* London: Routledge/Comedia.

MORLEY, D. (1992) *Television audiences and cultural studies.* London: Routledge.

MORRISON, D. (1992) *Television and the gulf war.* London: John Libbey.

MOWLANA, H., GERBNER G. and SCHILLER, H. (eds) (1993) *Triumph of the image.* Oxford: Westview.

MULGAN, G. (ed.) (1990) *Questions of quality.* London: British Film Institute.

MURDOCH, R. (1989) MacTaggart Lecture delivered at the Edinburgh International Festival, 25 August.

MURDOCK, G. (1993) 'Communications and the Constitution of Modernity' in *Media, Culture and Society*, 15.4, 521–539.

NAVA, M. and NAVA, O. (1990) 'Discriminating or Duped? Young People as Consumers of Advertising/Art', *Magazine of Cultural Studies*, **1**, pp. 15–21.

NEUMAN, W.R., JUST, M. and CRIGLER, A. (1992) *Common knowledge.* Chicago: Chicago University Press.

NICHOLS, B. (1983) 'The Voice of Documentary', *Film Quarterly* 36.3. 17–30.

NICHOLS, B. (1991) *Representing reality.* Bloomington: Indiana University Press.

O'CONNOR, A. (ed.) (1989) *Raymond Williams on television.* London: Routledge.

PACKARD, V. (1957) *The hidden persuaders.* New York: D. McKay.

PAGET, D. (1990) *True stories? documentary drama on radio, screen and stage.* Manchester: Manchester University Press.

PATEMAN, T. (1983) 'How is Understanding an Advertisement Possible' in P. Walton and H. Davis (eds) *Language, image, media.* Oxford: Blackwell. pp. 187–204.

PETER, J.D. (1993) 'Distrust of Representation: Habermas on the Public Sphere' in *Media, Culture and Society*, 15 April, pp 541–571.

PHILO, G. (1990) *Seeing and believing.* London: Routledge.

POOLE, M. (1984) 'The cult of the generalist: British TV criticism 1936–83. *Screen* 25.2. 41–61.

POSTMAN, N. (1986) *Amusing ourselves to death.* London: Methuen.

REITH, J. (1924) *Broadcast over Britain.* London: Hodder and Stoughton.

RICHARDSON, K. and CORNER, J. (1986) 'Reading Reception: Transparency and Mediation in Viewers' Accounts of a TV Programme', *Media, Culture and Society* 8.4, 485–508.

ROSENBERG, B. and WHITE, D.M. (eds) (1957) *Mass culture*. Glencoe, IL: The Free Press.

ROSENTHAL, A. (ed.) (1988) *New challenges for documentary*. Berkeley: University of California Press.

ROSHCO, B. (1975) *Newsmaking*. Chicago: University of Chicago Press.

SCANNELL, P. (1989) 'Public Service Broadcasting and Modern Public Life' in *Media, Culture and Society*. 11.2 pp. 134–66.

SCANNELL, P. and CARDIFF, D. (1991) *The social history of British broadcasting volume one*. Oxford: Blackwell.

SCHLESINGER, P. (1978) *Putting reality together*. London: Constable.

SCHLESINGER, P. (1990) 'Rethinking the Sociology of Journalism' in M. Ferguson (ed.) *Public communication: the new imperatives*. London: Sage. 61–83.

SCHLESINGER, P. and TUMBER, H. (1993) 'Fighting the War Against Crime' in *The British Journal of Criminology*. 33.1. 19–32.

SCHLESINGER, P., MURDOCK, G. and ELLIOTT, P. (1983) *Televising 'terrorism': political violence in popular culture*. London: Comedia.

SCHLESINGER, P., DOBASH, R.E., DOBASH, R.P. and WEAVER, C. (1992) *Women viewing violence*. British Film Institute: London.

SCHRODER, K. (1992) 'Cultural Quality: Search for a Phantom?', in Schroder, K. and Skovmand, M. (eds) 1992: *Media cultures*. London: Routledge.

SCHUDSON, M. (1978) *Discovering news*. New York: Basic Books.

SCHUDSON, M. (1993) *Advertising: the uneasy persuasion*. (Second edition), London: Routledge.

SENDALL, B. (1982) *Independent television in Britain vol.1: origin and foundation 1946–62*. London: Macmillan.

SILVERSTONE, R. (1985) *Framing science: the making of a BBC documentary*. London: British Film Institute.

SILVERSTONE, R. (1993) 'Television, Ontological Security and the Transitional Object' in *Media, Culture and Society*. 15.4, 1993. 573–598.

SINCLAIR, J. (1988) *Images incorporated*. London: Croom Helm.

SMITH, A. (1978) *The politics of information*. London: Macmillan.

SUSSEX, E. (1976) *The rise and fall of British documentary*. Berkeley: University of California Press.

SWALLOW, N. (1966) *Factual television*. London: Focal Press.

SWINSON, A. (1955) *Writing for television*. London: Adam and Charles Black.

THE GUARDIAN. (1986a) 'Tories castigate BBC for "flawed editorial line" on Libya raid'. October 31. p.6.

THE GUARDIAN. (1986b) 'Unrepentant BBC rejects Tory charges "out of hand"'. November 6, p.5.

THOMPSON, J.O. (1990) 'Advertising's Rationality' in M. Alvarado and J. Thompson (eds) *The media reader*. London: British Film Institute. 208–212.

THOMPSON, J. (1991) *Ideology and modern culture*. Cambridge: Polity.

TRACEY, M. (1986) 'Less Than Meets the Eye' *The Listener*. 13 November, pp.7–8.

TUCHMAN, G. (1972) 'Objectivity as Strategic Ritual: An Examination of Newsmen's Notions of Objectivity' in *American Journal of Sociology*. **77(4)**, 660–70.

TULLOCH, J. (1990) *Television drama: agency, audience and myth*. London: Routledge.

VALE, L.J. (1990) 'Captured on Videotape: Camcorders and the Personalization of Television' in Dobrow, J. (ed.) *Social and cultural aspects of VCR use*. London: Erlbaum 195–209. Reprinted in Corner, J. and Hawthorn, J. (eds) (1993) *Communication Studies*. London: Arnold.

VAUGHAN, D. (1976) *Television documentary usage*. London: British Film Institute.

VAUGHAN, D. (1992) 'The Aesthetics of Ambiguity' in P. Crawford and D. Turton (eds) *Film as ethnography*. Manchester: Manchester University Press, pp. 99–115.

WERNICK, A. (1990) *Promotional culture*. London: Sage.

WHANNEL, G. (1992) *Fields in vision*. London: Routledge.

WILLIAMS, R. (1958) 'Culture is Ordinary', reprinted in Williams, R. 1989, *Resources of hope*. London: Verso.

WILLIAMS, R. (1962) *Communications*. Harmondsworth: Penguin.

WILLIAMS, R. (1970) 'ITV'S Domestic Romance', *The Listener*, 30 July. Reprinted in O'Connor, A. (ed.) (1989) *Raymond Williams on television*. London: Routledge. 109–112

WILLIAMS, R. (1974a) *Television, technology and cultural form*. London: Fontana.

WILLIAMS, R. (1974b) 'Drama in Dramatized Society' in O'Connor (ed.) 1989: 3–13.

WILLIAMS, R. (1977) *Marxism and literature*. London: Macmillan.

WILLIAMSON, J. (1978) *Decoding advertisements*. London: Marion Boyars.

WILLIS, P., JONES, S., CANAAN, J. and HURD, G. (1990) *Common culture*. Milton Keynes: Open University Press.

WILSON, H.H. (1961) *Pressure group: The campaign for commercial television*. London: Secker and Warburg.

WINSTON, B. (1988) 'Documentary – I Think We Are in Trouble' in Rosenthal, A. (ed.) *New challenges for documentary*. 21–33.

ZHEUTLIN, B. (1988) 'Documentary: A Symposium' in Rosenthal, A. (ed.) *New challenges for documentary*. 227–242.

INDEX